the *flavors* of ASIA

the *flavors* of ASIA

MAI PHAM

THE CULINARY INSTITUTE OF AMERICA

PHOTOGRAPHY BY BEN FINK

DK

LONDON, NEW YORK, MUNICH, MELBOURNE, AND DELHI

executive editor ANJA SCHMIDT

designer JESSICA PARK

managing art editor MICHELLE BAXTER

art director DIRK KAUFMAN

dtp coordinator KATHY FARIAS

executive managing editor SHARON LUCAS

senior production editor CLARE MCLEAN

photographer BEN FINK

food stylist SUSAN VAJARANANT

Published by DK Publishing, Inc., ·
375 Hudson Street, New York, New York 10014

09 10 10 9 8 7 6 5 4 3 2 1

© 2009 by DK Publishing, Inc.
Text © 2009 by The Culinary Institute of America

DK Books are available at special discounts for bulk purchases for sales promotions,
premiums, fund-raising, or educational use. For details contact DK Publishing
Special Markets, 375 Hudson Street, New York, New York 10014
or SpecialSales@dk.com.

A catalog record for this book is available from the Library of Congress.

ISBN 978-0-7566-4305-8
Color reproduction by Colourscan, Singapore
Printed and bound in Singapore by Tien Wah Press

Discover more at www.dk.com

contents

preface

RICHER THAN IMAGINED

Mid-afternoon in the grand teaching kitchens of The Culinary Institute of America at St Helena, CA. The three chefs in my delegation, all of them from the Sichuanese capital, Chengdu, are hard at work. A small crowd of American students watches pastry specialist Lan Guijun use a fearsomely large knife to cut noodles from sheets of pasta colored by spinach, carrot, and beetroot. Some of them are shaped like willow leaves; others are thin as hairs. Further up the room, the ceaselessly inventive Yu Bo is putting the finishing touches on a virtuoso display of Sichuanese hors d'oeuvres: Chinese chives wound into "silk bobbins," bamboo shoots cut into "fans," string beans tied into complicated knots. And, nearby, cooking master Xiao Jianming is preparing the ingredients for a classic "fish-fragrant sauce." This scene is just a tiny part of the extraordinary activity that goes into preparing for the CIA's Worlds of Flavor Conference.

In the past, Asian cuisines have had a limited profile in the West. Chinese cuisine, for example, was best known for a handful of dishes that weren't really Chinese at all, like chop suey and General Tso's chicken. Even enthusiasts were unlikely to encounter much that went beyond an Americanized version of Cantonese cuisine. But all that has changed in recent years by the region's unprecedented opening up to trade and travel.

In the case of China, Americans are increasingly traveling there for work and pleasure, and seeking out more authentic flavors after returning home. A new wave of highly educated Chinese immigrants are demanding smarter restaurants serving better dishes than the old Chinatown staples, and, in particular, dishes representative of Chinese regional cuisines. Meanwhile, the range of fresh ingredients and seasonings from Asia that are available to American cooks is growing all the time.

The CIA's Asian conference has brought together some amazing talent from many parts of China. Chefs have flown in from Beijing, Sichuan, Hunan, Hong Kong, Guangzhou (Canton), Shanghai, and Hangzhou, representing all the main culinary regions. They have cooked dishes that are not only geographically diverse but that represent strands of Chinese cuisine ranging from street food to Muslim cooking, *dim sum* to haute cuisine. And judging from the participants' comments, these presentations and tastings have opened their eyes to a culinary tradition that is richer than they imagined.

Some aspects of Asian foodways have a particularly contemporary appeal, like the diverse traditions of "small eats," and the thrilling layering of flavors found in cuisines like the Sichuanese. The Chinese appreciation of texture has much to teach adventurous Western chefs and diners. And the healthfulness and balance of the traditional Chinese diet— so different from that old stereotype of deep-fried foods and MSG—has a special resonance in an age of anxiety about modern Western eating habits.

The recipes in this book have been gathered from participating chefs and reflect the diversity of the foods they showcased. Some were part of demonstrations in the main conference hall; others were whipped up in smaller workshop sessions. Many were served in the World Marketplace, where conference participants were able to sample from a dizzying range of dishes from all over Asia.

On the last night of the 2007 conference, I gathered in the kitchens with all the Chinese chefs and anyone else who wanted to join in. We stood around a big table and made *jiaozi*, a kind of simple northern Chinese dumpling. Some of us rolled the

FUCHSIA DUNLOP
Author of *Sichuan Land of Plenty: A Treasury of Authentic Sichuan Cooking* and *Revolutionary Chinese Cookbook: Recipes from the Hunan Province*

dough into circles, others wrapped these around a minced pork stuffing. Someone brought a huge panful of water to a boil. Before long we were all tucking in with our chopsticks to bowlfuls of steaming hot dumplings, dipped in soy sauce, dark rice vinegar, and chile, and toasting each other with bottles of beer. A simple homestyle supper was just what we needed after three days of gastronomic stimulation. And the cheer and camaraderie in the kitchen on that last night was typical of the atmosphere of the whole event.—FUCHSIA DUNLOP

INSTANT REVELATION

As an Asian chef working in America, I am gratified with the growing interest in Asian foods among my chef colleagues, American diners, and home cooks. Even more exciting is the prominent placement being given to "hot" Asian flavors on the covers of leading magazines and other media. Yet I am still acutely aware of how little people really know of the real, authentic Asian cooking.

As I travel across the country, people often speak to me about their love or fear of curry. And yet to us Indians, there is no one dish that is called "curry." Rather it is the Hindi word for sauce, the name of one herb, the curry leaf, and the name of a spice blend created by the English. Indian cuisine is hard to define in one sentence or book. It is the cuisine of a billion plus people, speaking eighteen distinct languages, coming from almost every religion one can name and then some, and from strongly different geographic regions. How then could their food be placed into one category?

At my restaurants, as a consultant for Sodexo, a food-service giant, and as I teach across the country and speak to people all over the world, I have discovered first-hand, a hunger in the minds and palates for the authentic, varied, complex, simple, exotic, and comforting flavors of the Indian pantry.

The reactions that I see on the faces of diners eating Indian cuisine for the first time in one of my classes or restaurants is something I wish words could capture. In one smile or look, they give away what pages and pages strive to achieve after much careful study. The nutty magic of coconut in our simple but far from simplistic vegetable stir-fries from the southern parts of India; the aromatic sweet-and-spicy edge of the Gujarati curry; the heady, addictive comfort of the many varied beans and legumes prepared across the Indian landscape; and the masterful grilling done in the Tandoor oven that is unrivaled anywhere, provide instant revelation to anyone eating the authentic cuisine of the subcontinent. These discoveries may be

SUVIR SARAN
Chef/owner of Devi Restaurant and American Masala and author of *Indian Home Cooking* and *American Masala*

new to the diner but they reflect centuries of studied spicing and flavoring by a vast amalgam of peoples and cultures. India and its food guarantee even the most tired and dull among us to wake up and find new meaning in life and at the table.

These experiences compelled me to join the CIA as a co-chair of its recent "Rise of Asia" Worlds of Flavor conference. The talented culinary stars we managed to gather were a reflection of the many precious gems that Asia is known for. What gilded them and their creations was the rich history of their traditions. The smells, flavors, textures, colors, and overall kaleidoscopic culinary wizardry were awe-inspiring and humbling. The CIA had become the communal pot where the mother spoon of civilization, unbeknown to anyone, tempered the dishes with its own desire to live in the richness of diversity and plurality, of flavor complexity and culinary comfort.

Now, in the recipes shared within these pages, you will discover foods that shall bring you back into the kitchen sharing, speaking, exchanging ideas, and taking adventures to worlds near and far. I hope that as a result of this collection, you come to feel less that Asian cooking is exotic and difficult and instead discover that these flavors, from India and Southeast Asia to China and Japan, can easily be re-created and become your family's new classics and favorites.—SUVIR SARAN

introduction

The first time I bit into a piece of *bai makrut* or kaffir lime leaf, I was five years old. What was this dazzling new food in my mouth, this mélange of incredibly intoxicating flavors, this bright, perfumy, citrusy taste that was so unlike anything else? Though none of these adjectives were known to me at the time, the flavors jolted me. The leaves were floating in *kaeng kew wan*, an utterly delicious green curry that my Thai nanny had made. Although I was born and raised on my mother's fabulous Vietnamese cooking, I had never tasted anything like that before.

That was back in the mid-1960s when my family lived in Bangkok and when my passion and curiosity for food was first kindled. Fortunately, these days I don't have to be in Thailand to experience *makrut* because Asian ingredients are much more accessible than ever. *Pho*, the beloved noodle soup of my childhood, is eaten with great fervor around the world. Fish sauce—once a specialty ingredient found only at ethnic grocers—is now easily available at many supermarkets.

Immigration, changing demographics, and the quest by consumers for new flavors have all led to dramatic shifts in the American food scene. In past decades, French- and Italian-influenced foods have dominated the restaurant sector. Now chefs, food manufacturers, and retailers are reaching out to all corners of the world, rolling out new menus and products that showcase, in the case of Asia, flavors beyond Chinese and Japanese to include Vietnamese, Thai, Indian, and Korean, to name a few. As a result, home cooks are also constantly teased in every flavor direction.

On one level, this book mirrors that trend and sets out to unravel some of the mysteries of Asian cuisine. The recipes collected here are the outcome of "The Rise of Asia: Culinary Traditions of the East and Flavor Discovery in 21st Century America," the latest in a groundbreaking conference series created by Greg Drescher and his team at The Culinary Institute of America's Greystone campus in Napa Valley, California. One of the college's missions is to educate chefs and foodservice leaders about world cuisines, and the conference series provides a valuable forum toward that end. This book now takes that effort one step further by translating the knowledge gleaned from that event for you, the home cook.

I'm grateful to have had the opportunity to work with the CIA on this project, and with my conference co-chairs Fuchsia Dunlop and Suvir Saran in compiling the amazing recipes that our talented guest chefs and food experts so generously shared.

This book is by no means comprehensive. As a culinary region, Asia is much too vast and complex to be completely covered in a single title. But we do hope this will be your go-to reference for some of the very best foods of China, Japan, Korea, India, Vietnam, Thailand, and Singapore. We want to tease you with all the vibrant flavors, but also inspire confidence and encourage you to immerse yourself in the culinary wonders of Asia.

To help prepare you for the recipes, I've included a quick culinary snapshot of each country for you as a reference point as you set out to cook a particular cuisine. I've always believed that when one has even a glimpse into the culture that inspired a dish, then that recipe becomes more meaningful and delicious.

The power of sharing food is truly amazing. For me, each time I experience something utterly wonderful, I can't help but feel grateful and reflect back to a favorite poem that reminds us that food is not only an elemental need of mankind but a foundation upon which all great civilizations were built:

In the water there is fish
In the fields there is rice
The faces of the people shine bright

—stone inscription dated 1292, attributed to King Ramkhamhaeng the Great of Sukhothai, Thailand

I invite you to join me in savoring the Asian table and sharing in its transformative spirit.—MAI PHAM

MAP OF THE FLAVORS OF ASIA

The seven countries—India, China, Thailand, Vietnam, Singapore, Korea, and Japan—highlighted in their respective colors here are featured throughout the book, color-coded appropriately.

VIETNAM

Say Vietnam and depending on whom you're talking to, what comes to mind might be the Vietnam war, a popular travel destination, or a great Southeast Asian cuisine.

Bordering China to the north and Laos and Cambodia to the west and the South China Sea to the east, this elongated, S-shaped country hugs more than 1,400 miles of coastline. Much of the country is mountainous and the most fertile land lies in the South in the Mekong Delta and the North in the Red River Delta.

Vietnam's distinctive cuisine evolved in these two primary regions as well as in the central region around Hue, the former imperial capital and birthplace of royal cuisine. Perhaps more so than any other in Southeast Asia, Vietnam's cooking was shaped not only by geographic and climate factors but a succession of foreign occupations and wars. The Chinese ruled for a thousand years beginning in the second century B.C.; the French occupation lasted a hundred years from the mid-nineteenth century; and the Vietnam War ravaged the country from the early 1960s to 1975.

The Chinese millennial occupation had a profound influence. The introduction of rice cultivation led to a wide variety of rice flour–based foods such as noodles, rice papers, and cakes. Soy sauce, ginger, and tofu became an important part of the local diet. But at the stove, Vietnamese cooks create flavors quite differently from their Chinese rulers. Lime juice, aromatic herbs, and the ubiquitous *nuoc mam*, or fish sauce, are used extensively to create flavors that are refreshing, bright, and savory. A typical meal often consists of a large table salad, a generous mound of lettuce leaves and aromatic herbs, which diners use for wrapping small pieces of grilled meat or seafood at the table and eat out of hand along with a dipping sauce. Fish is typically pan-seared and served with a spicy, limey Ginger-Lime Dipping Sauce (page 229) or simmered as in Catfish in a Clay Pot (page 164). Thanks to the French legacy, foods such as baguettes, butter, yogurt, coffee, and pâtés as well as dishes such as bifsteak and ragout have blended into the local cooking, giving the cuisine that East-West character that many find intriguing and appealing.

JAPAN

As with many other countries in Asia, Japan has historical links to China, but, in its case, the connection is less obvious. Unlike other Asian cooking styles where ingredients and spices are blended to create a certain spectrum of flavors, the Japanese prize singular dimensions and strive to showcase individual flavors and textures of each main ingredient.

The Japanese table is very much an extension of the Japanese belief in which restraint, purity, modesty, harmony, and balance should not only dictate life but also the way one cooks and enjoys food. Food is prepared with utmost care, from the delicate manner of handling seafood to the ritual of cooking and serving perfect rice (page 195). Fish, soybean products, seaweeds, vegetables, and rice are pillars of the cuisine. Since a large amount of fish is consumed raw, quality and freshness are key.

Seasonality is a central theme. In the summer, menus may feature chilled tofu and *somen* or soba noodles, the latter sometimes presented in a lacquer box and eaten with a light *shoyu*-based broth. In the autumn, mushrooms and chestnuts are simmered and enjoyed with rice and in the winter, hearty one-pot *nabemono* dishes are served. Cooking preparations are simple, from serving fish raw in sushi and sashimi to simmering and grilling. *Shoyu*, miso, and the Japanese horseradish wasabi are used extensively but in a manner that no one flavor overwhelms the dish.

Presentation is also paramount. Food is artfully arranged and dishes are chosen based on seasonality, balance, and aesthetics. Sauces are typically light as in a glaze, and batter-fried foods are airy and crisp as in a well-prepared tempura. A dashi broth made from kombu and bonito flakes is cooked over a gentle fire (never boiling) to preserve their ocean flavor and nutrients.

Whether you're attracted to the more elaborate, small-dish *kaseiki* cuisine, or to foods popularized by restaurants, the Japanese kitchen offers great inspiration for those seeking healthy dining as well as foods that many believe help balance mind and body.

KOREA

One way to understand Korean food is to look at *mit banchan*, a ubiquitous family of vegetable sides of which kimchi (page 110) is the most important and considered the soul of Korean cuisine. Made from fermented cabbage, chiles, and garlic, kimchi is eaten with rice and used as a seasoning in stir-fries, noodles, stews, soups, and pancakes.

With kimchi as the backbone of flavor, the Koreans enjoy a variety of food, seafood being the most abundant. A peninsula that juts into the ocean with Japan to the east and Manchuria and China to the northwest, the country faces harsh climates and its rugged mountain-covered interior equals limited agricultural land and products. As a result, the Korean appetite slants heavily toward hearty, warming soups and stews that have been robustly seasoned with chiles and garlic or cooked at the table and eaten with *gochujang*, or fermented red chili paste. Rice accompanies most meals including lovely versions cooked with sweet potato and gingko nuts (page 196).

Due to its proximity and historical ties to the cattle-grazing culture of Mongolia, beef plays an important role, more so than in other parts of Asia. Some of the world's best barbecues come from here, including *bulgogi* and *galbi*, the latter made with thinly sliced short ribs, grilled, then eaten with lettuce wraps, rice, and *gochujang*. If you're new to this cuisine, definitely try the barbecues and serve them with *jap chae*, a stir-fry of sweet potato noodles and vegetables and, of course, some kimchi. If you don't have time to make it from scratch, don't worry, it's easily available at Asian markets and supermarkets.

SINGAPORE

If you love Asian food but can only visit one country, make it Singapore. A tiny island off the southern tip of the Thai-Malaysian peninsula, it's at once a slick, skyscraper-filled metropolis and yet one of the most dynamic food capitals in Asia because of centuries of cultural exchanges with the Chinese, Indians, and Indonesians. Walk into any of the hawker's centers—the many open-air or enclosed food courts throughout the island—and you'll be greeted with mind-boggling

kiosks and carts where vendors flip and stir local favorites, from Chinese noodles to Hainan chicken (page 199) to Singapore Roti Prata (page 209) to Malaysian curries. But the renditions here are often quite different from how they might have been prepared in their home countries.

Char kwey tew, a mild Chinese dish, in its new home became wok-fried noodles but made with chiles, cockles, and *kecap manis*, an Indonesian black soy sauce. Laska, an iconic dish of Nonya cuisine—a style of cooking that evolved when immigrant Chinese men married local Malay women—takes a Chinese noodle soup classic and transforms it into an entirely different dish with noodles bathed in luscious coconut milk with chiles, spices, and *balachan*, or fermented shrimp paste.

Over the years, this intermingling of ingredients and spices from nearby cultures, as well as those from faraway places such as Portugal, all led to Singapore's distinctive fusion cooking, something found nowhere else at this level in Asia. The advantages of cooking Singaporean, therefore, can be several fold. First, if you're already keen on Chinese and Indian cooking, you're probably all set as far as equipment and basic ingredients are concerned. Second, you certainly have the flexibility to present several different cuisines at the same meal. Put another way, where else could you go to cook your favorite Chinese ingredients with Southeast Asian aromatics such as lemongrass, galangal, and chiles and Indian spices such as mustard, fennel, cumin, and coriander seeds?

CHINA

It's risky to summarize a cuisine as world class, ancient, varied, and influential as China's. But disclaimers aside, Chinese cuisine is indeed one of the great mother cuisines, like those of the Mediterranean, the root from which many other cuisines are derived or influenced.

A vast country with astonishingly varied climatic and geographic conditions, China has many regional culinary cultures and subcultures. But unfortunately in the West, our knowledge of this great cuisine has been typically limited to Cantonese (and in the past, not very authentic at that), which is the style of cooking Chinese immigrants brought with them years ago. If one were to visit areas outside of the major cities in China, one would witness a world of traditions and flavors far different and more compelling than those in the West.

There are several ways of categorizing Chinese regional cuisines but for home cooks outside of China, it's more useful to think about the character of the cuisine roughly divided by four regions: the North, South, East, and West.

The best known is southern Chinese or Cantonese cooking, which is centered in Guangdong and Hong Kong and known for its extraordinary range of foods, from produce to seafood. These include such familiar and beloved foods as *dimsum* (page 18), roast pork, and innumerable noodle and stir-fry dishes. The Cantonese kitchen emphasizes the individual flavor of each ingredient with subtle, light seasonings. Meats and vegetables are quickly stir-fried with garlic, ginger, and soy sauce and fresh fish are steamed whole and seasoned with similar ingredients.

By contrast, the foods from the west and central regions, particularly those of Hunan and Sichuan, are much more vibrant and packed with intense flavors. A landlocked province with fertile land and a famously humid climate, Sichuan is the home of spicy foods. Chiles and the famed Sichuan pepper are used extensively with fava bean paste, sugar, vinegar, and other seasonings to create complex dishes such as *gong bao* chicken.

Hunan cooks also love chiles but have their own distinctive ways of using them. Their food tends to lack the sweeter notes of Sichuan and has more of a hot and sour character with fresh aromas and deep color. Chiles in all forms are combined with black fermented soybeans, vinegar, and preserved or pickled vegetables to create a more hearty fare.

Beijing, the capital city of China for centuries, may be part of the North, but its cuisine is quite different and includes lavish Mandarin and palace-style dishes as well as foods from other regions, most notably Shandong, where seafood plays a big role. The justifiably famous Peking duck, a delicacy of crispy, melt-in-your-mouth duck skin served with steamed pancakes, white leeks, and a dark, fermented sauce, has been gracing tables of the wealthy and governing class for centuries, and in recent decades has also become a favorite at family banquets.

Outside of Beijing, however, northern cuisine is much simpler and more frugal. Since the region is too cold for rice cultivation, wheat-based staples such as dumplings (page 18), pancakes, flatbreads, steamed breads, and noodles are eaten instead of rice. Seasonings are mainly limited to garlic, onions, soy sauce, and vinegar with a little chile. Because of the proximity of the Mongolian grasslands and their nomadic traditions, the North adopted lamb and mutton into their diet, something that has not been taken up elsewhere in China.

The food of the eastern, coastal region of China is prominently represented by the modern metropolis of Shanghai, one of the great engines of the rise of China in the last century, and by Hangzhou, a city of great tradition, prestige, and beauty. As centers of wealth, the food here evolved into a lavish cuisine, one that borrows heavily from other regions but capitalizes on its own bounty. The region—with its vast, fertile fields full of rice and its lakes, rivers, and sea teeming with marine life—also produces some of the country's best soy sauce, vinegar, and rice wine, which are used quite extensively in dishes such as "drunken" chicken.

Cooks from the eastern region are also known to use sugar more heavy-handedly than elsewhere and often combine it with soy sauce to impart a caramelized, savory flavor as in its many braised dishes.

Shanghai cuisine is well known for its delicious cold appetizers. These consist of roast meats, soy sauce–braised meats and seafood (page 30), as well as the many small, tasty plates of legumes (think fava beans), vegetables, tofu, and other soybean products that essentially have been stir-fried or braised in spices and served cold. You might have tasted these flavors hot, but reimagine them cold. In fact, we hope the recipes here will get you to rediscover and reimagine the whole of Chinese cooking.

THAILAND

The land of a thousand smiles, as Thailand is aptly called, deserves its reputation because Thai food is bound to make you smile with joy, be it *kao soi*, an iconic Burmeseinfluenced noodle soup eaten in the North, the *larb* salads from the Northeast, the smoky, savory noodles and stir-fry dishes of the Center, or the fiery curries of the South.

Definitely hot, tantalizing, and addictive is how many would describe Thai cuisine. Though much of it is rooted in the mother cuisines of China and India, Thai food has remained largely intact over the centuries because, unlike its neighboring countries, it has never been occupied.

One way to get grounded in Thai cuisine is through its curries, which if you've had really good ones, are truly a class of their own. Fresh aromatics and roots such as lemongrass, garlic, galangal, chiles, cilantro, and kaffir lime are pounded in a stone mortar with spices such as coriander, cumin, and peppercorn seeds and the salty, pungent *kapi*, or shrimp paste, which adds depth and savoriness. To prepare a curry, a Thai cook first "blooms" the flavors by stirring the spice paste in hot coconut milk to extract the intense flavors before adding other ingredients. The result is a luscious, creamy curry that is at once spicy, sweet, and tangy but also floral and citrusy. Thai food is often an intriguing balance of extremes.

If you're serious about learning Thai cuisine, invest in a mortar and pestle and make the curry paste from scratch at least once, since the exercise is highly instructive and revealing. Then move on to salads, especially the irresistible *miang kum*. Learn to blend *nam pla*, or fish sauce, the Thai way, using chiles, garlic, and lime juice, and make some of the best savory salads of all Asia.

INDIA

If there was such a title as the world's biggest spice kitchen, India would win, hands down. That's because everywhere you go in India, spices and aromatics rule—at the markets, on hotel reception counters, growing along highways and, of course, wafting from kitchens.

One way to navigate around the complexity of Indian cuisine is to think of spices and aromatics as the building blocks of a dish or meal. We're talking about a splendid variety, from cumin, coriander, mustard, and fenugreek to fennel and cardamom, just to name a few. They may be dried or fresh, in the form of pods or seeds, and are often roasted and ground. Certain spices are always used whole, others are always ground. Any combination of spices is referred to as "masala," with the most common and widely called *garam masala* (page 220).

But spices alone don't tell the whole story. Part of the seduction of the Indian kitchen is how spices are combined with aromatics. For example, some recipes begin with popping mustard seeds, chiles, garlic, and curry leaves in hot oil. This technique creates a multi-dimensional flavor experience, full of bright and fresh flavors as well as rounded, savory notes.

Indian cuisine is generally divided into four culinary regions: North Indian, South Indian, East Indian, and West Indian, the first two being the most popular outside the subcontinent. With a history dating back thousands of years and an influx of outside influences from Central Asia, Arabia, the Persian and Mogul empires, and later, Portugal and Britain, Indian cuisine is incredibly diverse.

North Indian cuisine is distinguished by the use of dairy products such as milk, yogurt, *paneer*, or cheese, and *ghee*, or clarified butter, which is used as cooking oil. Lamb and goat are marinated in spices and cooked in a clay tandoori oven or slowly simmered in curries, which are thick and eaten with flatbreads like *roti* and *paratha*.

In South India where the climate is warmer, the food is lighter with a tropical spirit. In the coastal cities, fish and seafood play an important role. Coconut or mustard oil is used instead of *ghee,* and rice, not bread, forms the basis of most meals. Fresh coconut is used extensively in chutneys, curries, and stews. Vegetables and legumes, the latter most often eaten in the form of *dal*, a spiced purée of lentils, peas, or beans, are an essential component of everyday meals. Rice flour–based pancakes and cakes such as *dosas, idlis,* and *palappams* (page 241) are delicious accompaniments to curries, chutneys, and raitas.

The rest of India shares many similar foods, but the cooking and seasoning styles vary, reflecting local preferences and availability of ingredients.

All told, the Indian kitchen is an invaluable culinary treasure. Looking for big, bold flavors? Try the many meat and seafood recipes. If you prefer meatless dishes, India, with the majority of its population being Hindu, has created some of the world's best vegetarian cooking.

CHAPTER ONE

Appetizers & Small Plates

STREET FOOD TRADITIONS

In many ways, Asia is the land of appetizers and small plates. From China and Japan to India, Vietnam, Thailand, and Malaysia, it's really a paradise for "street food," a term loosely coined to describe food that's typically cooked and eaten on the go, from small plates and small bowls to snacks served on skewers or banana leaves. These dishes, which are packed with bold flavors, are often small-portioned and portable, and, as such, make great appetizers.

*T*hey're served in every setting imaginable, from carts parked at street corners and on sidewalks to small counters at market stalls, train stations, and floating markets. And rarely is Asian street food just about a handful of vendors here and there. Very often it's a sea of cooks with their stands and carts filling an entire street, creating bubbly, live-fire food bazaars such as those in Bangkok's Chinatown or in Singapore's legendary hawkers' centers where street foods are brought inside into modern-day, food-court settings.

At these hawkers' centers, the selections can be overwhelming. Craving dumplings? Head over to the Chinese dumpling stand and order a few hot Steamed Pork Dumplings (page 21) from the tall stacks of bamboo steamers. If you're in the mood for something spicy, you can't go wrong with Indian Pakoras (page 38) or Spicy Fritters with Coconut Chutney (page 27). And there's no limit to the noodle dishes for your choosing.

In other parts of Asia, street food thrives in a more traditional form, scattered wherever there are hungry customers. In Guangzhou, in the middle of a construction project where hundreds of hard-hat workers gather for a lunch break, a husband and wife team stands in front of a wobbly makeshift table, their hands flying while folding *sui mai*, or pork dumplings, and steaming them in a huge propane-fired steamer.

In Seoul, at a busy outdoor market, between rows of ginseng traders and tee-shirt hawkers, shoppers wait patiently as skewers of barbecued meat and seafood are being grilled or fried in bubbling oil. At a street corner near the main post office in Saigon, office workers gather to snack on *bo bia*, a salad roll stuffed with jicama and Chinese sausage, and *cha gio*, or crispy spring rolls wrapped with lettuce and herbs.

What all of these dishes have in common is they're freshly prepared on the spot, fast, and inexpensive. Contrary to the image of Western fast food being anything but fresh and expertly prepared, traditional Asian street food is in a unique class by itself. It is art, family, and life all in one and it existed long before the restaurant culture as we know it today came into being.

Many of the recipes in this chapter are inspired by such rich street food traditions. Layered with different ingredients and packed with flavors, they tease the palate and make welcoming beginnings to a meal. Other recipes aren't necessarily street foods, but those inspired by traditional *dimsum* houses, restaurants, and home kitchens. Regardless of the origin, the selections reflect the diverse world of Asia's small plates. What follows here is a collection of must-makes. Each was chosen for its wonderful flavor, for the story it tells of a certain cuisine and the collective spirit that it shares. On the one hand, the incredibly rich and distinctive tradition behind each dish, and on the other, the refreshing notion that each can be enjoyed any way one wishes—as a snack, as the beginning of a bigger meal, or as a complete meal in itself.

CHINA

zhong crescent dumplings are traditionally eaten in northern China to celebrate the New Year. While making the wrapper dough by hand is part of the tradition, store-bought wrappers can be substituted to save time. Replace the dipping sauce with a simple combination of soy sauce and black vinegar if you prefer a less spicy finish. When boiling the dumplings, add cold water to keep the dumplings from tearing.

ZHONG CRESCENT DUMPLINGS
ZHONG SHUI JIAO

SERVES 8

FILLING
One 4-inch (10-cm) piece fresh ginger, unpeeled
1 cup cold water
1 egg
1 tablespoon Shaoxing rice wine
or medium-dry sherry
¾ teaspoon salt
Freshly ground black pepper to taste
1 pound (450 g) ground pork

DIPPING SAUCE
3 tablespoons light soy sauce
2 teaspoons sugar
1½ tablespoons chili oil
1 teaspoon sesame oil
2 cloves garlic, peeled and crushed
1 to 2 teaspoons cold water

60 to 80 circular flour-and-water
dumpling wrappers (approximately four
7-ounce/200-g packages)

1. For the filling: Smash the ginger with the flat side of a cleaver blade or a heavy object and allow it to soak for a few minutes in the water. Remove the ginger pieces from the water and discard.

2. Mix the egg, rice wine, salt, and pepper with the pork, and then gradually add the ginger-water, so it is absorbed by the meat to form a fragrant, floppy paste.

3. For the dipping sauce: Mix the soy sauce, sugar, chili oil, and sesame oil together. Combine the garlic and water in a separate bowl. Combine the dipping sauce with the water at the last minute to get the most out of the flavor of the garlic.

4. Place a dumpling wrapper flat on your hand and add a generous teaspoon of the filling. Fold one side of the wrapper over the meat, make one or two tucks in it, and then press it tightly to meet the other side and make a little, half-moon-shaped dumpling. You can seal the dumpling with a series of little pinches if you wish. Make sure you punch the wrappers together tightly so the filling can't ooze out. Lay the dumplings, separately, on a lightly floured tray, plate, or work surface.

5. Heat a large pot of water to a rolling boil over high heat. Stir the water briskly and place in a couple of handfuls of dumplings. Stir once to prevent them from sticking to the bottom of the pot. When the water has returned to a boil, throw in a coffee-cupful of cold water. Allow the water to return to a boil again, and add another coffee-cupful of cold water. When the water has returned to a boil for the third time, the dumpling wrappers will be glossy and puckered and the meat should have cooked through—cut one dumpling in half to make sure. Remove the dumplings from the pot with a slotted spoon, drain well, and serve steaming hot with the spicy, aromatic dip. Continue cooking the dumplings in batches until your guests are incapable of eating any more.

Recipe from Land of Plenty: A Treasury of Authentic Sichuan Cooking *by* FUCHSIA DUNLOP *(Michael Joseph, 2001, Penguin Books, 2003). Copyright © Fuchsia Dunlop, 2001.*

In many parts of China, you can just grab a small container of these steamed dumplings right off the steamer along the sidewalk and enjoy them as a snack. Although many versions exist, this Cantonese recipe calls for pork, shrimp, and mushrooms. The filling can be made in advance and the dumplings can be shaped closer to serving time. The accompanying ginger-soy dipping sauce provides a nice contrast.

STEAMED PORK DUMPLINGS
SUI MAI

SERVES 8

DIPPING SAUCE
3 tablespoons minced ginger

¼ cup light soy sauce

½ cup rice vinegar

¼ cup water

1 tablespoon sesame oil

2 tablespoons sugar

FILLING
8 ounces (225 g) small shrimp,
peeled and deveined

8 ounces (225 g) pork loin

4 ounces (115 g) fatty pork

1¼ cups dried shiitake mushrooms

2 teaspoons salt

1 tablespoon potato starch

2 teaspoons sugar

1½ teaspoons light soy sauce

1 teaspoon freshy ground black pepper

1½ teaspoons sesame oil

1 tablespoon Green Onion Oil (page 231)

4 large carrots, peeled

30 dumpling wrappers (*sui mai* skins)

1. *For the dipping sauce:* Whisk together all of the ingredients in a stainless-steel bowl until the sugar is dissolved. Refrigerate until ready to use.

2. *For the filling:* Drain the excess moisture from the shrimp and pat dry.

3. *Clean* the pork loin, removing any traces of veins or excess fat. Dice the pork loin into ⅓-inch (8-mm) cubes. Dice the fatty pork into ⅛-inch (3-mm) cubes.

4. *Rehydrate* the dried mushrooms in warm water until soft, about 15 minutes. Strain the mushrooms out of the water and pat dry. Dice into ⅛-inch (3-mm) cubes.

5. *Toss* the shrimp and pork loin with the salt and potato starch to form a starchy mixture. Stir in the sugar, soy sauce, and pepper. Add the mushrooms, fatty pork, sesame oil, and Scallion Oil and stir to combine thoroughly.

6. *Cut* the widest part of the carrots into ¼-inch (6-mm) thick slices. Each slice should be wide enough to place a dumpling on top and you should have 30 slices. Reserve any leftover carrots for another recipe. If desired, carve the slices in a floral design.

7. *For the dumplings:* Place 1½ to 2 tablespoons of the filling in the middle of each dumpling wrapper. Gather the outer edges of the wrapper to form a cylinder around the filling, so the filling is exposed at the top. Wrap your pointer finger and thumb around the center "waist." Dip your thumb from the other hand in water and gently push down to compact the filling. Tap the entire dumpling on the table to make the bottom flat.

8. *Place* an 8-inch (20-cm) bamboo steamer in a saucepan that will hold the steamer snugly. Add enough water to the pan but keep the level at least 1 inch (2.5 cm) below the steamer so the dumplings don't get wet. Remove the steamer from the pan and bring the water to a boil.

9. *Place* each dumpling on a carrot slice and then place in the steamer. Transfer the steamer to the pan; cover and steam for 6 minutes or until the filling is cooked through.

Adapted from a recipe prepared by CHAN CHUN HUNG, *Senior Instructor, the Chinese Cuisine Training Institute, Vocational Training Council*

JAPAN

in this modern take on the classic tempura from chef Kiyomi Mikuni, both the batter and the mayonnaise dip are flavored with *matcha*, a Japanese powder made from ground green tea leaves. With its slightly bitter flavor and a bright green color, it makes the tempura unique. This recipe calls for whole smelt so be careful with the bones. If you prefer, you can substitute fish fillets.

GREEN TEA SEAFOOD TEMPURA
MATCHA NO TEMPURA JITATE

SERVES 8

1 cup mayonnaise

1 tablespoon plus 1 teaspoon matcha green tea powder

8 *wakasagi* (Japanese smelt) (about 13 ounces/375 g)

1 quart (1 liter) milk, or as needed

8 tiger shrimp (about 5 ounces/150 g), shelled but tail attached

2 whole eggs

1 cup bread flour

¼ cup vegetable oil

6 tablespoons plus 2 teaspoons water

1 quart (1 liter) vegetable oil, for frying, or as needed

8 sea scallops (about 8 ounces/225 g)

1 carrot, cut into ¼-inch (6-mm) by 2-inch (5-cm) sticks

1 lemon, cut into 8 wedges

1. To make the matcha mayonnaise, combine the mayonnaise with 1 teaspoon of the matcha powder. Refrigerate until needed.

2. Cover the smelt with the milk and soak for 1 hour to remove the fishy smell. Drain the fish and pat dry with paper towels. Refrigerate until needed.

3. Make 3 to 4 shallow cuts on the belly side of the shrimp (this prevents the shrimp from bending).

4. In a medium bowl, whisk the eggs, flour, vegetable oil, water, and remaining matcha powder together.

5. Line a sheet pan with paper towels and place a wire rack over the paper towels.

6. Heat 3 inches (7.5 cm) of vegetable oil in a wok or saucepan over high heat to 350°F (180°C). Dip each ingredient in the batter, shake it briefly to remove excess batter, and place in the oil. This will need to be done in batches. Cook each ingredient until done, 1 minute for the shrimp, 1½ minutes for the smelt, 40 seconds for the scallops, and 20 seconds for the carrot.

7. Drain the fried items well on the rack. Serve the tempura with wedges of lemon and the matcha mayonnaise.

Adapted from a recipe by KIYOMI MIKUNI

this dish is inspired by the smoky, cumin-scented grilled meats that are sold by street-food vendors in the northwestern province of Hunan, China. It combines beef with a lot of chiles, both fresh and dried, but the flavors are quite distinctive with the addition of ginger and cumin. You can serve this with lettuce leaves as an appetizer or part of a meal. To make this less hot, reduce both kinds of chiles proportionately.

SPICY CUMIN BEEF WITH LETTUCE LEAVES

SERVES 4

1 pound 8 ounces (675 g) boneless sirloin beef

1½ teaspoons salt, or as needed

1 teaspoon freshly ground black pepper, or as needed

¾ cup peanut oil, or as needed, for frying

½ to ¾ cup dried chiles (½ to ¾ ounce/12 to 20 g), or as needed

¼ cup fresh chiles, seeded, stemmed, and finely chopped, or as needed

1 tablespoon chopped garlic

2 green onions, cut into ¼-inch (6-mm) thick slices on the bias

1½ tablespoons minced ginger

¼ cup cumin seeds, crushed

1½ tablespoons oyster sauce

16 green leaf lettuce leaves

1. Cut the beef across the grain into thin slices, about 1 x 2 inches (2.5 x 5 cm). Season the beef with salt and pepper.

2. Heat the peanut oil over medium-high heat in a wok or large sauté pan to about 275°F (140°C). Add the beef and stir gently until it separates and is slightly cooked, about 2 minutes. Remove the pieces from the oil and drain well. Reserve until needed.

3. Remove all but 2 tablespoons of the oil. Heat the oil over high heat and add the dried and fresh chiles, garlic, green onions, ginger, and cumin seeds and stir-fry briefly until the ingredients just release their aroma, about 30 seconds. Return the beef to the wok and stir well. Add the oyster sauce and season with salt and pepper.

4. Place 3 to 4 tablespoons of the beef on each piece of lettuce. Wrap the lettuce around the beef and serve.

Adapted from a recipe by LIN WANG

cha gio are most delicious when wrapped with lettuce leaves and fresh herbs. Rice paper, which has a wonderful flavor when fried, is the traditional wrapper but you can also use wheat spring-roll wrappers, which are sold in Asian markets. They brown nicely when cooked and freeze well. These rolls can be made in advance by cooking them two-thirds of the way, then reheating them at 300°F (150°C) for 15 minutes.

VIETNAMESE SPRING ROLLS
CHA GIO

SERVES 8

½ package dried bean thread noodles (1 ounce)

1 tablespoon dried tree ear mushrooms

¾ cup minced onion, squeezed dry in cheesecloth

¼ cup grated carrot or taro root, squeezed dry in cheesecloth

½ cup thinly sliced green onions

1 egg

2 tablespoons fish sauce

1½ teaspoons minced garlic

½ teaspoon salt

2 teaspoons sugar

½ teaspoon freshly ground black pepper

8 ounces (225 g) crabmeat, picked through

10 ounces (275 g) ground pork or minced pork loin

2 tablespoons cornstarch

⅓ cup water

15 thin spring roll wrappers

1 quart vegetable oil, for frying

1 cup Vietnamese Dipping Sauce (page 229)

Table Salad, as needed (page 114)

1. *S*oak the bean thread noodles in hot water for 30 minutes and drain. Cut the noodles into ½-inch (1-cm) pieces (there should be about 1½ cups).

2. *S*oak the dried mushrooms in hot water for 30 minutes and drain. Trim the stems and roughly chop the mushrooms.

3. *In* a mixing bowl, combine the bean thread noodles, mushrooms, onion, carrot, and green onions. Reserve until needed.

4. *In* another large mixing bowl, beat the egg, then add the fish sauce, garlic, salt, sugar, and black pepper. Add the crabmeat and pork and, using a fork, break up the meat so it is thoroughly mixed with the seasonings. Do not overmix. Add to the noodle mixture and mix well. Set aside.

5. *In* a small saucepan, combine the cornstarch and water. Bring to a boil over high heat, stirring often to prevent sticking. If it is too thick, add more water. This is the "glue" to seal the edges of the wrapper. Cool to room temperature.

6. *C*ut the wrappers in half diagonally. You will have 2 equal size triangles. Starting with the longest side toward you, place about 2 tablespoons of filling on the bottom area of the triangle. Using your fingers, mold the filling into a cylinder 2 inches (5 cm) long and 1 inch (2.5 cm) wide. Fold the 2 sides of the wrapper in and roll to enclose. Dab a little cornstarch mixture along the edges (do not overglue) and seal the roll. Set aside while you finish making the remaining rolls. Do not stack them.

7. *T*o fry, preheat a large wok or saucepan over medium-high heat. When hot, pour in the oil and heat to about 325°F (160°C). Carefully place the rolls in the oil. There should be enough oil in the pan to completely cover the spring rolls and the rolls should float and not touch the pan. Do not crowd the pan or place the rolls on top of each other. They may need to be cooked in batches.

8. *F*ry the spring rolls for 3 to 4 minutes on each side, turning often until they are nicely brown and crisp. If they brown before that, reduce the heat as the oil is too hot. Remove the cooked spring rolls from the heat and drain on paper towels. Serve immediately with the Vietnamese Dipping Sauce and the Table Salad.

Adapted from a recipe by MAI PHAM

INDIA

these hot fritters are made from soaking *tuvar dal*, or yellow lentils, and mashing them in a food processor to create a thick dough. Seasoned with chiles, ginger, and cilantro, the dough is shaped into rounds, then pan-fried until golden and crisp. Spicy fritters are nicely complemented when served with cool, fresh coconut chutney.

SPICY FRITTERS WITH COCONUT CHUTNEY
PARIPPU VADAS

SERVES 8

1 cup *tuvar (toor) dal*, not coated with oil
1 tablepoon salt, or as needed
1 tablespoon finely chopped cilantro leaves
⅓ cup finely diced onions
1 teaspoon minced serrano or Thai bird chiles
1 tablespoon fresh grated ginger
15 fresh curry leaves, thinly sliced
6 cups canola oil, for deep frying
1 cup Coconut Chutney (page 216)

1. Soak the *tuvar dal* in water for 3 to 4 hours. Rinse in several changes of water until the water runs clear, and then drain.

2. In a food processor, combine 6 tablespoons of the soaked *tuvar dal* and the salt and process until it achieves a thick dough. Add the remaining soaked *tuvar dal*, and grind coarsely. Since the *dal* absorbs water during soaking, there is no need to add extra water when processing. However, if necessary, add water to facilitate grinding. The ground dough should be very thick, so that it can be shaped into small disks.

3. Remove the dough from the processor, sprinkle it with the cilantro, onions, chiles, ginger, and curry leaves, and mix well.

4. Heat the canola oil in a heavy medium-sized pan to 365°F (185°C). When the oil is hot, wet the palms of your hands, and shape 2 tablespoons of the dough into a disk 1½ inches (3.75 cm) in diameter. When shaping the disks, press out any excess liquid from the dough. Slide the disks (*vadas*) gently into the hot oil. This should be done in batches. Fry the *vadas* until they are golden and crisp, 4 to 5 minutes. Remove them from the oil and drain briefly on paper towels. Serve hot or warm with the Coconut Chutney.

Adapted from a recipe by AMMINI RAMACHANDRAN. *From Grains, Greens, and Grated Coconuts by Ammini Ramachandran Copyright ©2007, 2008 by Ammini Ramachandran. Reprinted by permission of iUniverse, Inc. All right reserved.*

Korea

this fun Korean barbecue recipe features different meats such as beef ribeye, chicken, and pork belly cooked over a charcoal grill and served with a variety of sweet and savory sauces. You can make a buffet of skewers, or you can just feature one kind of meat. For the pork, cut the meat slightly larger than the garlic cloves. Serve with the Daikon and Cucumber Salad (page 105) or Stir-Fried Glass Noodles (page 182).

18 TO 24 SKEWERS

PORK BELLY SKEWERS
⅓ cup soybean paste
2 tablespoons Korean chili powder
1 tablespoon chopped garlic
2 tablespoons chopped green onions
1½ teaspoons finely grated ginger
1 tablespoon soy sauce
¼ cup sugar
1 tablespoon sesame seeds
1 tablespoon sesame oil
1 pound 2 ounces (500 g) pork belly, cut into
1-inch (2.5-cm) cubes

2½ ounces (70 g) cloves garlic, peeled
1½ tablespoons vegetable oil

BEEF SKEWERS
1½ cups soy sauce
¼ cup rice wine
2 tablespoons black or brown sugar
2 tablespoons white sugar
2 tablespoons chopped garlic
2 tablespoons chopped green onions
2 tablespoons chopped Asian pears
2 tablespoons chopped onions
Pinch of black pepper
1 tablespoon sesame seeds
1 tablespoon sesame oil
1 pound 2 ounces (500 g) rib eye, thinly sliced

CHICKEN SKEWERS
⅓ cup chili paste
2 cups chopped leek
2 tablespoons Korean chili powder
2 tablespoons chopped garlic
6 tablespoons chopped green onions
2 tablespoons soy sauce
½ cup sugar
1 tablespoon sesame seeds
1 tablespoon sesame oil, or as needed
2 tablespoons vegetable oil
1 pound 2 ounces (500 g) boneless, skinless
chicken breast, cut into long, thin slices

ASSORTED BARBECUE SKEWERS
MODEUM SANJEOK

1. *For the pork belly skewers:* Combine everything but the pork to make the marinade.

2. *Mix* the marinade with the pork and allow it to marinate overnight under refrigeration.

3. *Cut* the top third of each garlic head off and rub with vegetable oil. Bake in a 350°F (180°C) oven until soft, 30 to 40 minutes. Remove from the oven and allow to cool until the garlic heads can be easily handled. Squeeze the individual garlic cloves from the head and reserve until needed.

4. *Remove* the pork and the garlic cloves from the marinade and discard the marinade. Thread 4 pieces of pork and 3 garlic cloves, alternating pork and garlic, onto each skewer. Refrigerate until needed.

5. *For the beef skewers:* Combine everything but the beef to make the marinade.

6. *Mix* the marinade with the beef and allow it to marinate for 30 minutes to an hour.

7. *Remove* the beef from the marinade and discard the marinade. Thread 2 pieces of meat onto each skewer. Refrigerate until needed.

8. *For the chicken skewers:* Combine everything but the chicken to make the marinade. Mix the marinade with the chicken and allow it to marinate for 30 minutes to an hour.

9. *Remove* the chicken from the marinade and reserve the marinade. Thread 2 pieces of chicken onto each skewer. Refrigerate until needed.

10. *Preheat* the grill to high.

11. *Grill* the beef skewers for 3 to 4 minutes, the pork skewers for 3 to 4 minutes, and the chicken skewers for 5 minutes, or until cooked through. Brush the reserved marinade on top of the chicken 2 to 3 times while turning the chicken.

Adapted from a recipe by DR. HEE SOOK CHO

Shanghainese cuisine is known for its many cold appetizer dishes and this is one of them. For this recipe, use good quality shrimp as it is the main ingredient and flavor featured here. The shrimp are traditionally deep-fried, but you can also pan-sear them before tossing them into the sauce.

SAUTÉED SHRIMP

SERVES 8

2 cups plus 1 tablespoon vegetable oil

3 green onions, sliced ¼ inch (6 mm) thick on the bias

1½ tablespoons minced ginger

½ cup Shaoxing rice wine

¾ cup plus 2 tablespoons water

¼ cup soy sauce

½ cup sugar

1 pound 8 ounces (675 g) shrimp (26/30 count), peeled and deveined

1. Warm 1 tablespoon of the vegetable oil in a medium sauté pan over high heat. Stir fry the green onions and ginger until the aroma is released, about 1 minute. Add the rice wine, water, soy sauce, and sugar into the pan and boil for 15 minutes until it becomes thick and sticky. Keep the sauce warm.

2. Heat the remaining oil to 350°F (180°C) over high heat. Deep fry the shrimp until just cooked through, 20 to 30 seconds. Remove the shrimp from the oil and add to the sauce. Coat the shrimp with the sauce thoroughly.

3. Cool the shrimp in the refrigerator before serving.

Adapted from a recipe by LAMONT FU, *executive sous chef, Hyatt Regency Hangzhou, China*

this recipe makes clams or other mollusks, such as mussels, particularly savory and satisfying because of the distinctive flavor from fermented black beans. Look for absolutely fresh, live clams and make sure to soak and scrub them well before using. The sauce is great over rice.

CHILI CLAMS WITH GARLIC AND FERMENTED BLACK BEANS

SERVES 4

2 tablespoons vegetable oil

2 teaspoons chopped garlic

2 teaspoons fermented black beans,
soaked in water for 5 minutes and drained

2 teaspoons dried chili flakes, or as needed

2 tablespoons oyster sauce

1 cup Asian basil leaves

2 pounds (900 g) clams, scrubbed and rinsed

1 teaspoon cornstarch

⅓ cup chicken stock

1½ tablespoons rice wine

Salt, as needed

1. Heat the oil over high heat in a wok or large frying pan. Add the garlic, fermented black beans, and chili flakes and stir until fragrant, about 20 seconds. Add the oyster sauce, basil leaves, and clams and stir several times.

2. Combine the cornstarch and chicken stock, stir well, then add to the pan. While stirring, cook until the clams are all open and cooked through, 3 to 4 minutes. Just before the clams are done, stir in the rice wine. The sauce should be just slightly thickened. Adjust the seasoning with salt if necessary.

Adapted from a recipe by MAI PHAM

Asian Herbs

One way to understand the importance of herbs in Asian cooking is to visit a well-stocked produce section of an Asian market. Chances are you'll see them openly displayed alongside other leafy greens, sometimes tied like a bouquet of spring plantings with whole sprigs and tender leaves. In some instances, they're packed inside a long plastic bag filled with air to prevent bruising. Each bunch may seem like a lot but if you were to use the herb by the cupfuls in a stir-fry or a salad, which is how they're traditionally used, then the amount seems just right.

Unlike the Western style of using herbs in small amounts, Asian herbs are used abundantly, much like a vegetable. In their tropical home, many grow wild, thriving along the edges and banks of wet rice fields and rivers. Historically, they were inexpensive supplements to a meal and were often used to make staples such as rice and grains more palatable.

Although herbs show up in many Asian cuisines, their roles vary. In China, particularly in southern Cantonese cooking, very thinly slivered green onions, cilantro, and Asian celery are common on steamed fish and chicken. In Japan, red *shiso* leaves are used to make pickled plums while green *shiso* is often served with sushi, sashimi, and other seafood dishes. Other herbs used in the Japanese kitchen include *mitsuba*, which is reminiscent of parsley and celery, and *kinome*, the leaves of the *sansho* plant with an astringent peppery lemon flavor. The Koreans also love *shiso* and use them as wrappers for grilled meats and in stuffed dishes and pickling. In India, curry leaves are essential in tempering oils, curries, and stews. In Singapore, *laska* leaves and kaffir lime leaves add a distinctive citrusy, floral note to food.

In Vietnam and Thailand, herbs play a more prominent role. A Vietnamese meal often includes a platter of different sprigs of herbs, which are used to wrap foods and to add to noodles, soups, and salads. In Thailand, cooks toss cupfuls of *bai horapa*, or basil, into stir-fries, curries, and soups, or deep-fry them and use them as garnishes.

Herbs can work miracles, balancing and cutting richness in meats and refreshing and enlivening pungent sauces. They can transform a dish, giving it the distinctive character that it otherwise might not have.

When purchasing herbs, look for fresh, blemish-free sprigs. Unless you're going to use them right away, keep them in a loose plastic bag and store them in the warmest spot of the refrigerator. Before using, trim to the desired length and soak in water for 30 minutes, then pat dry with a towel. For table salads and salad rolls, use whole leaves or the entire top sprigs. For cooking, gently cut the leaves in two or three pieces.

The following list is a quick reference to the herbs called for in this book and those that are more commonly available at Asian markets, specialty stores, and farmers' markets.

• ASIAN BASIL/ THAI BASIL/ANISE BASIL
Ocimum basilicum—*rau que* (Vietnamese) and *bai horopa* (Thai)

Call it "baa-sil" or "bay-sil," either way, this herb is guaranteed to seduce with its vibrant licorice, anise flavors. With skinny, pointed oval green leaves and purplish stems and flowers, this is a must in Vietnamese noodle soups as well as Thai stir-fries and curries. Great in table salads, salad rolls, and as garnishes, basil is very versatile and can enhance just about any dish. Should you need to substitute, use sweet basil but reduce the amount by half since it is quite intense.

• VIETNAMESE CORIANDER, LASKA LEAVES
Polygonum odoratum—*rau ram*

Spicy, sharp, and tangy with a slight eucalyptus undertone, this herb is used to enhance salads and noodle soups such as the Singapore Laska Noodle Soup (page 70). Often marketed under its Vietnamese name *rau ram*, this herb has small, skinny pointed green leaves, with brown veins and slightly knobby brown stems. Probably among the sturdiest, it keeps well and can be easily propagated by rooting a sprig in water. Substitute mint or Asian basil.

• FISH MINT, FISH SCALE MINT
Houttuynia cordata—*rau diep ca*

Unlike other herbs, fish mint doesn't have much of a smell but it does have a strong flavor—tangy, almost like sorrel, with a slight fishy undertone. It has dark green, arrowhead-shaped leaves with light brown, leggy stems. It's common in table salads that accompany grilled meats and fish. Substitute mint or Asian basil.

• MINT, SPEARMINT
Mentha arvensis—*rau hung lui*

Mint has a unique quality of accentuating the flavors of meat, especially anything grilled. It is a must in Thai salads. In Asia, the mild-tasting, small, rounded variety (slightly more coriander-like than mint) is preferred, although the more common spearmint works just as well.

• RICE PADDY HERB
Limnophila aromatica—*ngo om*

This tiny herb, with its spongelike stem, is intensely aromatic and reminiscent of cumin and coriander. It's often chopped and tossed into sweet and sour soups and taro root soups. Substitute cilantro.

• RED PERILLA, SHISO
Perilla frutescens—*rau tia to*

A bit floral and anise-like, *rau tia to* has big, oval leaves that are deep purple on the bottom and dark green on top. It is a common ingredient in table salads and is also shredded and added to noodles and noodle soups. In Japanese and Korean cuisines, the ruffle-leaf red perilla is preferred for pickling. Substitute Asian basil or cilantro if need be.

• GREEN PERILLA, GREEN SHISO, VIETNAMESE BALM
Elsholtzia ciliata—*rau kinh gioi*

This lovely herb, which resembles red perilla, is a relative of the lemon balm, but has a more pronounced lemongrass flavor. With light green oval leaves and serrated edges, this herb is used extensively in Vietnamese cooking for soups and noodles as well as wrappers. In Japanese cuisine, a slightly more aromatic variety is used to garnish sashimi, rice, and noodle dishes. Substitute red perilla or cilantro.

• JAPANESE WILD PARSLEY, JAPANESE CHERVIL OR TREFOIL
Cryptotaenia japonica—*mitsuba*

Similar to Italian parsley but more delicate, this Japanese herb has a mild, sweet celery flavor. It's often cut into 1- to 2-inch (2.5- to 5-cm) lengths and used in soups, udon noodles, savory custards, and salads.

• JAPANESE PEPPER LEAVES
Zanthoxylum piperitum—*kinome*

The small, serrated leaves of the prickly ash tree are amazingly aromatic with flavors reminiscent of pepper, citrus, and fennel. Expensive even in Japan, *kinome* is revered for its beautiful shape and is used mostly in restaurants for garnish, although it's also made into pesto and added to sweet miso sauce.

• PEPPER LEAF, WILD BETEL LEAF
Piper sarmentosum—*la lot*

A relative of the betel leaf, *la lot* has large, heart-shaped leaves that are shiny and bright green. It has a slightly peppery, woody flavor and is particularly good when used to wrap meat and then grilled. In Thailand, it's used to wrap *miang kam*, an appetizer of grated coconut, lime, and chiles. When used in cooking, it's usually shredded and added toward the end. Substitute with red or green perilla or basil.

• KAFFIR LIME, MAKRUT LIME
Citrus hystrix—*bai makrut*

The leaves of this citrus fruit are used extensively throughout Southeast Asia, appearing in curries, salads, and soups. With its distinctive number eight-shaped leaves, kaffir lime is intensely citrusy and floral. For soups, use whole leaves and for salads and stir-fries, cut them into thin slivers. In Thailand, the zest and skin of this knobby fruit is used in curry pastes.

• SAW-LEAF HERB, SAWTOOTH HERB, CILANTRO
Eryngium foetidum—*ngo gai*

A member of the coriander family, saw-leaf herb has long, shiny serrated leaves that are 3 to 4 inches (7.5 to 10 cm) long. *Ngo gai*, which has an intense, cilantro-like flavor, is a must in noodle soups. To appreciate this herb's wonderful qualities, try it in any dish that calls for cilantro. Substitute cilantro or Asian basil.

JAPAN

this dish is traditionally served in Japan at the winter solstice. In the past, squash left over from a late harvest were stored as winter settled in. Kabocha, rich in carotene and packed with vitamins A, C, and E, provides excellent nourishment, particularly when combined with dried red beans, a year-round staple bursting with iron and fiber. Serve this as an appetizer in small ceramic bowls, or as a vegetable side dish.

KABOCHA SQUASH WITH RED BEANS

SERVES 4

¼ cup dried azuki beans

1 piece kombu, 1 inch (2.5 cm) square

3 tablespoons sake

1 tablespoon sugar

2 tablespoons soy sauce

¼ kabocha squash (about 10 ounces/275 g), cut into 12 chunks with seeds removed but skin intact (or peeled partially for a striped pattern)

1¼ to 2 cups Dashi Stock (page 60)

1 teaspoon light-colored soy sauce

1. *Wash* the beans well, drain, and place in a small, heavy saucepan. Add enough cold water to cover and bring to a boil. Remove the pan from the heat, cover, and let the beans cool to room temperature naturally. Transfer to a glass jar with a tight-fitting lid and let the beans sit in the refrigerator for at least 3 hours or overnight. The beans will swell to twice their original size.

2. *Return* the beans and whatever liquid remains in the jar to the saucepan. If necessary, add enough water to just cover the beans. Add the kombu and 2 tablespoons of the sake and bring the mixture to a boil. Skim away any froth that appears. Simmer the beans for 30 minutes, adding more water as necessary to keep the beans submerged in liquid. Swirl the pan occasionally to ensure even cooking.

3. *Add* 2 teaspoons of the sugar and additional water if needed to keep the beans submerged and cook for 30 to 40 minutes longer. Test for tenderness: beans should give easily when pinched. Once the beans are tender, add the soy sauce and simmer for 8 to 10 minutes. Discard the kombu. Pour the contents of the pan through a fine-mesh sieve, reserving the liquid and beans separately.

4. *Arrange* the squash pieces, skin side down, in a pot in a snug single layer. Add enough Dashi Stock to cover the squash barely. Bring the squash to a simmer. Cover the pot and swirl occasionally to ensure even cooking. Cook for 3 to 4 minutes, or until barely tender. Test with a toothpick or skewer; it should meet with some resistance.

5. *Add* the remaining sake and sugar and carefully flip the squash pieces so that the skin faces up. Replace the lid and simmer for about 2 minutes. Add the light-colored soy sauce and ¼ to ½ cup of the reserved cooking liquid from the beans. Simmer for 2 more minutes; the squash should be completely tender.

6. *Transfer* the simmered squash, skin side down, to deep individual serving dishes. Strain the cooking liquid and reduce it over high heat until about ½ cup remains. Taste and adjust seasonings if necessary. Add the beans back to the sauce and heat briefly over medium heat.

7. *Top* each portion with an equal amount of sauce. Serve hot or at room temperature.

Reprinted with permission from Washoku *by* ELIZABETH ANDOH. *Copyright 2005 by Elizabeth Andoh, Ten Speed Press, Berkeley, CA. www.tenspeed.com*

a common Thai snack, miang kum *makes a unique appetizer. It's typically presented with the fillings laid out for the diner to make little wraps at the table. Traditionally, pepper leaves are used but spinach or lettuce leaves work well too. Cut all the ingredients uniformly. If fresh coconut isn't available, substitute with dried coconut flakes but toast right before using, and reduce the sugar in the sauce.*

THAI SPINACH WRAPS WITH COCONUT AND GINGER
MIANG KUM

SERVES 8

SAUCE
¼ cup thinly sliced shallots (1 each)
¼ cup sliced ginger
One ½-inch (1-cm) piece galangal, peeled and sliced ¼ inch (6 mm) thick
2 teaspoons shrimp paste
1 cup sugar
½ cup coconut or palm sugar
1½ cups water
2¼ cups toasted fresh coconut or dried coconut flakes
¼ cup ground dried shrimp
2 tablespoons fish sauce

WRAP
½ cup small-dice shallots or red onions
½ cup small-dice ginger
½ cup unsalted roasted peanuts
2 limes, sliced thin and cut into eighths
½ cup small dried shrimp, washed and patted dry
2 bunches large spinach leaves, or as needed

1. *P*reheat the oven to 375°F (190°C).

2. *F*or the sauce: Wrap the shallots, ginger, galangal, and shrimp paste for the sauce in a piece of foil and toast in the oven for 30 minutes, or until it is softened.

3. *I*n a small pot, combine the sugar and coconut sugar with ¾ cup of the water. Bring to a boil over high heat and reduce the heat to low. Cook for about 10 minutes to make a thick syrup.

4. *T*urn the oven down to 325°F (160°C).

5. *T*oast the shredded coconut on a sheet pan in the preheated oven until golden brown and crisp, about 15 minutes. Stir occasionally to ensure even toasting. Cool to room temperature and set aside.

6. *I*n a blender, combine the toasted ingredients and ¼ cup toasted coconut with the remaining ¾ cup water to facilitate blending. Purée until the mixture is smooth.

7. *A*dd the blended mixture to the syrup, along with the dried shrimp and the fish sauce. Mix well and cook another 8 to 10 minutes over medium heat, or until it becomes thick. Cool until well chilled.

8. *F*or the wrap: Place the shallots, ginger, peanuts, limes, dried shrimp, and the remaining toasted coconut in separate mounds on a serving platter. Set aside.

9. *W*ash and cut the spinach leaves, using only large, nice-looking ones. Set aside.

10. *S*erve the filling and spinach leaves alongside the sauce. Invite guests to assemble their wraps by placing ½ teaspoon each of the filling on each spinach leaf, dull side up, and then drizzling ½ to 1 teaspoon of the sauce on top. For a burst of flavor, it's important to eat the whole packet in one bite.

Adapted from a recipe by CHAI SIRIYARN

INDIA

pakoras are Indian fritters, generally vegetarian, made with various different vegetables and fillings but always deep fried and served crisp and warm. This simple recipe calls for a staple combination of potato, onions, and spinach for extra flavor and texture. If desired, form all of the patties before frying ahead of time. Serve the pakoras with a mango, jalapeño, and ginger-flavored green chutney.

SPINACH, ONION, AND POTATO PAKORAS
PALAK PAKORAS

SERVES 8

SPICE POWDER
1 teaspoon coriander seeds
1 teaspoon cumin seeds
1 teaspoon garam masala
½ teaspoon cayenne pepper
½ teaspoon fennel seeds

FILLING
6 cups spinach, stemmed, chopped, and firmly packed
1 red boiling potato, peeled and cut into a very fine dice
1 red onion, cut into medium dice
1 fresh hot green chile, very finely chopped
⅓ cup chopped cilantro
2 cups chickpea flour
1 teaspoon salt
½ teaspoon baking powder
¼ cup water, or as needed
1 quart (1 liter) canola oil, or as needed, for deep-frying
1 cup Green Chutney (page 216)

1. *For the spice powder:* Combine the spices in a mortar and pestle or spice grinder and grind very coarsely.

2. *For the filling:* Combine the spice powder with the spinach, potato, onion, chile, cilantro, chickpea flour, salt, and baking powder. Stir until everything is uniformly coated with the flour. Add the water and stir to make a batter.

3. *Pour* 3 inches (7.5 cm) of the canola oil into a large saucepan or medium *kadai* and heat to 360°F (182°C) over medium-high heat. Use a scant ¼ cup measure or large serving spoon to measure out about 3 tablespoons of the filling (*pakora*) and slide it into the hot oil. Immediately turn the heat down to medium. Spoon several more pakoras into the oil (4 or 5 total) and cook for 1 minute. Turn the pakoras over with a slotted spoon and cook for 1 more minute. Then turn the heat back up to high and continue cooking, turning twice, until evenly browned all over, 5 to 6 minutes. Remove to a paper towel–lined platter with a slotted spoon. Repeat to cook all of the pakoras.

4. *Serve* two of the pakoras with 1 to 2 tablespoons of the Green Chutney.

Adapted from a recipe by SUVIR SARAN

there are many versions of this popular dish, from beef, chicken, mutton, and pork to the variety of spices used in the marinade. In this recipe from Thailand, the chicken is marinated in an aromatic blend of lemongrass, coconut milk, and turmeric, then grilled and served with a peanut sauce flavored with chile jam, which you can make or buy from an Asian market. Serve with Satay Sauce and Cucumber Salad.

CHICKEN SATAY
SATAY GAI

SERVES 4

1 pound (450 g) chicken tenders or boneless, skinless chicken breast

1½ tablespoons finely sliced lemongrass

1 tablespoon Thai thin soy sauce

2 tablespoons vegetable oil

1 tablespoon melted butter

1 tablespoon sweetened condensed milk

1 tablespoon coconut milk

1½ tablespoons sugar

1 teaspoon turmeric powder

1 teaspoon salt, or as needed

⅓ teaspoon ground white pepper

8 to 10 bamboo skewers, 6 to 8 inches (15 to 20 cm) long

½ cup Peanut Satay Sauce (page 222)

1 cup Thai Cucumber Salad (page 104)

1. *C*ut the chicken on the diagonal into thin slices about 1 inch (2.5 cm) wide and 2 inches (5 cm) long.

2. *C*ombine the remaining ingredients except for the skewers, Satay Sauce, and Cucumber Salad in a blender and blend well. Transfer to a bowl, add the chicken, and marinate for a few hours or overnight.

3. *P*reheat the grill to medium.

4. *T*hread the chicken onto the bamboo skewers. Grill the chicken until just done, 4 to 5 minutes total, turning the skewers as necessary. Serve with the Satay Sauce and Cucumber Salad.

Adapted from a recipe by CHAI SIRIYARN

INDIA

samosas are a beloved Indian snack eaten throughout Asia. They can be made with a variety of fillings, although the most traditional are made with a savory filling of spiced onions and potatoes. This adapted version calls for shrimp and a refreshing dipping sauce made with ginger and soy sauce.

SAMOSAS

SERVES 8

DIPPING SAUCE
5 tablespoons soy sauce
1½ tablespoons rice vinegar
2 tablespoons honey
1 teaspoon dry mustard
1 teaspoon chili sauce
2 teaspoons minced ginger
1 tablespoon minced garlic
6 tablespoons minced green onions

DOUGH
1½ cups all-purpose flour
1¼ cups vegetable oil
¼ teaspoon salt
6 tablespoons warm water

FILLING
2 tablespoons butter
¾ cup small-dice onions
1 teaspoon minced ginger
1 teaspoon minced garlic
1 teaspoon minced Serrano chiles
¼ teaspoon crushed coriander
1 teaspoon curry powder
1 teaspoon tomato paste
1 teaspoon lemon juice
¾ cup peeled, deveined, and roughly chopped shrimp
6 tablespoons fish stock or water

2 tablespoons water
5 cups vegetable oil

1. *For the dipping sauce:* Combine all of the ingredients and mix well. Reserve until needed.

2. *For the dough:* Combine all of the ingredients in the bowl of a 5-quart (5-liter) electric mixer fitted with the paddle attachment. Mix the dough on low speed until smooth, about 5 minutes. Wrap it tightly with plastic wrap and let rest for 1 hour in the refrigerator.

3. *For the filling:* Heat the butter in a large sauté pan over medium heat. Sauté the onions in the butter until translucent, about 4 minutes. Add the ginger, garlic, chiles, coriander, and curry powder and sauté until the aroma is strong, 1 to 2 minutes. Add the tomato paste, lemon juice, and shrimp. Sauté for 1 minute or until the shrimp start turning opaque without browning. Add the stock and simmer until almost all the liquid has evaporated, about 5 minutes. Transfer the filling to a bowl and refrigerate until chilled.

4. *Roll* the dough out in a pasta machine until it is 1/16 inch (1.5 cm) thick. Cut into 3-inch (7.5 cm) squares.

5. *Place* 1½ teaspoons of the filling on the middle of each square of dough and fold into a pyramid around the filling. Seal the edges with water and pinch the edges together.

6. *Heat* the oil in a medium saucepan to 375°F (190°C) over medium heat. Deep-fry the samosas until golden brown, about 3 minutes. Flip them occasionally so that they are cooked evenly. Drain on paper towels and serve with the dipping sauce while very hot.

Adapted from a recipe by THE CULINARY INSTITUTE OF AMERICA

Rice Papers, Wrappers, Nori

RICE PAPER

In Vietnam, the word for rice paper is *banh trang*, which translates into "thin pancake." A dried, paper-thin wrapper made from rice flour (and sometimes with tapioca starch), water, and salt, it's used for salad rolls and spring rolls and for foods that need to be wrapped at the table and eaten out of hand. Although indigenous to Vietnam, it's also used in Laos, Cambodia, and Thailand. Its sheer texture makes it an appealing wrapper for many other dishes such as sushi rolls and banana spring rolls. A thicker variety, made with sesame seeds or coconut or dried shrimp, is great toasted and can be eaten as a bread with salads.

Up until recent years, the process of making rice paper in Vietnam was mostly done by hand. First, a thin layer of rice flour batter is spread on a cloth tightly stretched over the rim of a large pot of boiling water. The rice sheet is allowed to steam for about 20 seconds after which, with the help of a long flat bamboo stick, it's transferred to a large bamboo mat (hence the pattern) to be sun-dried. Once fully dried, the rice paper loosens itself from the mat.

Rice paper can be a bit tricky to work with—you have to be very patient and focused, especially during the first few tries. Keep your work area well organized to roll quickly so the rice paper doesn't dry out. Before starting, set up the ingredients on a large platter in the order they will be used. Next, place a big bowl of hot water nearby for wetting the rice sheets. The thicker the rice paper, the hotter the water should be. Dampen a dish towel or cheesecloth and drape it over a cutting board—this is where you will make the rolls. To soften the rice sheet, lower it into the water and rotate to moisten the entire sheet. Proceed making the rolls as instructed in your recipe.

Rice paper–wrapped foods should be eaten soon after they're made as the skin can quickly dry out. Wrap with plastic if you need to hold them for a couple of hours.

WRAPPERS AND SKINS

There are two kinds of Chinese-style wheat wrappers—the thick wrapper used for egg rolls and wontons that is readily available in the produce section of many supermarkets and the thin varieties sold in the frozen-food section of Asian markets. The more common wrappers found in supermarkets come in large 7- to 8-inch (17.5- to 29-cm) squares or as 3½-inch (6-cm) squares or rounds, and are quite easy to use. Just add a filling, shape into any size egg roll, and seal with an egg wash or a "glue" made by cooking cornstarch and water until slightly thickened (try 1 tablespoon cornstarch with ⅓ cup water). It's best to cook the rolls soon after they're stuffed as the skin can get soggy.

However, for authentic dimsum or dumpling-style items popular in Chinese restaurants, use the thin wrappers. Sold in 14- or 16-ounce (400- or 450-g) packages, they're available in various thicknesses, depending on the kind of dumplings you want to make and their intended use (if they are to be poached, fried, or steamed). For boiled dumplings or pot stickers, wrappers of medium thickness (like ¹⁄₃₂ inch/¾ mm) work best and for steamed dumplings, use the paper-thin kind, sometimes labeled as "sui mai" or "har gow" skins.

NORI

If there's one cuisine that celebrates sea vegetables like no other, it's Japanese. (The Koreans also consume a good amount.) Packed with valuable nutrients and vitamins, they have been cultivated and eaten in Japan for centuries. There are many varieties but most common are the family of *kombu* used to flavor stocks and sauces, and *nori*, a popular seaweed harvested from the many inlets and estuaries along the country's coastlines. Nori is usually sold in the form of paper-thin sheets and is used for wrapping and flavoring sushi rolls. As a wrapper, it may well be among the most nutritious ingredient of its kind. Typically sold in packages of 7 x 8-inch (17.5 x 20-cm) sheets, it's available in two varieties: *yakinori*, or toasted, and *ajinori*, or seasoned. The latter, which is sold as small squares, is served with rice and also cut into thin strips for garnishing noodles and soup. And even though yakinori comes pre-toasted, it has better taste and texture if it's re-toasted before using. To toast, hold two sheets together (dull side on the outside) with tongs or chopsticks, and quickly pass over an open flame. Turn slightly so any unexposed area is also toasted. This process helps revitalize the sweet ocean flavor of nori.

To prevent it from absorbing moisture and air, store open bags of nori (along with the desiccant in the package) in a ziplock bag in an airtight container.

in India, this salad is made with a roti dough that's been rolled thin and cut into diamond shapes and deep-fried. This simplified version calls for store-bought flour tortillas that work just as fine and help make this dish a snap to assemble. There are two rules here—serve this immediately to avoid the chips from becoming soggy, and eat it immediately while the tortillas are still crisp. Black rock salt (*kaala namak*), a grayish, pink salt prized for its spicy, tangy taste, is traditionally used to season the dish. You can buy it anywhere you can obtain Indian groceries; if not, regular table salt is fine.

CRISP TORTILLA CHIPS WITH CHICKPEAS AND YOGURT

LUCKNOWI CHAAT

SERVES 8

2 medium red boiling potatoes

12 large flour tortillas, preferably whole wheat, 10 to 11 inches (25 to 27.5 cm) each

6 cups canola oil, for deep-frying

1¼ teaspoons cumin

2 cups plain yogurt

5 tablespoons chopped cilantro

1 hot green chile, stemmed, deseeded, finely chopped (1 tablespoon)

1 teaspoon sugar

½ teaspoon Indian black salt (*kaala namak*) or table salt

½ teaspoon cayenne pepper, plus as needed for garnish

One 14½-ounce (412-g) can chickpeas, drained and rinsed (about 1½ cups)

4½ tablespoons Green Chutney (page 216), plus extra for serving

3½ tablespoons Tamarind Chutney (page 217), plus extra for serving

3 tablespoons julienned ginger, for garnish (optional)

1. Place the potatoes in a small saucepan and cover with water. Bring to a simmer over medium-high heat and cook until tender, about 30 minutes. Peel the potatoes when they are cool enough to handle but still warm. Cut them into ¼-inch (6-mm) thick slices and then cut into 1-inch (2.5-cm) squares. Set aside, covered, until needed.

2. To make the tortilla chips, cut the tortillas into 1-inch (2.5-cm) strips. Then cut the strips on the diagonal to make diamond shapes that are about 2 inches (5 cm) long.

3. Pour about 3 inches (7.5 cm) canola oil into a large saucepan or medium *kadai* and heat to 360°F (182°C) over high heat. To gauge the temperature of the oil without using a thermometer, drop a piece of bread about 1 inch (2.5 cm) square into the hot oil; when the oil reaches 360°F (182°C), the bread should float to the surface of the oil and turn a golden brown color in about 45 seconds.

4. Turn the heat down to low, add the tortillas in 2 batches and cook, stirring every now and then with a slotted spoon, until puffed and golden brown, 4 to 5 minutes. Drain on paper towels.

5. Toast the cumin in a dry frying pan over medium heat, stirring, until fragrant and lightly browned, 2 to 3 minutes. Grind to a powder and set aside.

6. Stir together the yogurt, ¼ cup of the cilantro, the green chile, 1 teaspoon of the toasted cumin, the sugar, salt, and cayenne in a large bowl; set aside.

7. Put the potatoes in a second bowl and add the chickpeas. Add 2 tablespoons of the Green Chutney and 1 tablespoon of the Tamarind Chutney and toss together.

8. Gather the tortilla chips, the potato-chickpea mixture, the yogurt mixture, and the 2 chutneys on a work surface along with a large bowl or 8-inch (20-cm) baking dish.

9. To assemble the *chaat*: Sprinkle a handful (about 2 cups) of the tortilla chips over the bottom of a bowl or 13 x 10 x 2-inch (32.5 x 25 x 5-cm) casserole dish. Sprinkle a handful (about 1 cup) of the potato-chickpea mixture on top. Drop a handful (about 2 cups) of chips into the bowl filled with yogurt, stir to coat the chips, lift them out of the yogurt, and layer them on top of the potatoes. Drizzle 1½ teaspoons of the Tamarind Chutney over the top and then drizzle with 1½ tablespoons of the Green Chutney over the top as well.

10. Repeat this layering process 3 more times to use all of the tortilla chips, the potato-chickpea mixture, and the yogurt mixture. Pour any yogurt remaining in the bowl over the top.

11. Drizzle the remaining 1½ teaspoons of each of the chutneys over the top and sprinkle with the remaining 1 tablespoon cilantro. Sprinkle with the remaining ¼ teaspoon toasted cumin and a pinch of cayenne. Garnish with the julienned ginger, if using. Serve immediately before the tortilla chips get soggy, with more chutney on the side.

Adapted from a recipe by SUVIR SARAN

this is one of Vietnam's culinary treasures. Stuffed with shrimp, pork, and fresh herbs, *goi cuon* is traditionally eaten whole as a snack although it also makes a great appetizer, cut into smaller pieces. Make the rolls tight so the filling doesn't fall out when you're eating them. Grilled salmon and fresh basil are a great combination; you can also use chicken, beef, or tofu and mushrooms for the filling.

RICE PAPER–WRAPPED SALAD ROLLS
GOI CUON

SERVES 6 TO 8

4 ounces (115 g) *bun* (rice vermicelli or rice sticks)

Pinch of salt

10 ounces (275 g) pork shoulder, untrimmed, cut into 2 pieces

12 shrimp (16/20 count), unpeeled

Eight 8- to 10-inch (20- to 25-cm) dried rice paper rounds, or as needed

1 cup bean sprouts

½ cup mint leaves

1 small head red leaf lettuce, leaves separated and washed

½ cup Hoisin Peanut Sauce (page 230)

1. Bring a large pot of water to a boil over high heat. Boil the *bun* for 5 minutes, then drain. Rinse immediately in cool water and drain. Keep covered until needed.

2. Bring the water back up to a boil over high heat and add the salt. Cook the pork in the boiling salted water until it's cooked but still firm enough for slicing, about 30 minutes. Remove the pan from the heat.

3. While the pork is cooking, bring another small pot of water to a boil. Add the shrimp and cook until they turn pink, about 2 minutes. Rinse under running water and set aside to drain. When they're cool enough to handle, shell, devein, and cut the shrimp in half lengthwise. Set aside.

4. Remove the pork from the pot and drain. When it's cool enough to handle, slice into thin slices, about 1 x 2½ inches (2.5 x 6 cm). Set aside on a small plate.

5. Set up a salad roll "station." Line a cutting board with a damp kitchen towel. Fill a large mixing bowl with hot water and place it nearby. (Keep some boiling water handy to add to the bowl.) Arrange the ingredients in the order they will be used: the pork, shrimp, rice vermicelli, bean sprouts, mint leaves, and lettuce.

6. Working with 2 rice paper sheets at a time, dip 1 sheet, edge first, in the hot water and turn it to wet completely, about 10 seconds. Lay the sheet down on the towel. Repeat with the other rice paper and place it alongside the first.

7. Line the bottom third of the rice sheet with 3 shrimp halves, cut side up, and top with 2 slices of pork. Add 1 tablespoon rice vermicelli, 1 tablespoon bean sprouts, and 4 to 5 mint leaves. (Arrange the ingredients so the rolls will end up being about 5 inches/12.5 cm long and 1½ inches/4 cm wide.) Halve a lettuce leaf lengthwise along the center rib. Roll the lettuce up in one piece and place on top of the filling. (Trim it if it's too long.) While pressing down on the ingredients, fold the edge of the rice paper over the filling, then fold in the two sides and roll into a cylinder. If the paper feels thick, stop three-quarters of the way and trim the end piece. (Too much rice paper can make the rolls chewy.) Repeat with the remaining rice papers and filling.

8. To serve, cut the rolls into two or three pieces and place them upright on a plate. Serve with the Hoisin Peanut Sauce on the side.

Adapted from a recipe by MAI PHAM

INDIA

the use of cayenne pepper or chili powder and turmeric in this recipe evokes the flavor of masala, an Indian spice blend whose makeup varies but always results in one that is warm, bold, and often spicy. Note that the shrimp should rest for 15 to 30 minutes following their spice rub. If you choose, garnish the fried shrimp with a couple of tablespoons of fresh avocado.

MASALA SHRIMP

SERVES 8

1 teaspoon cayenne pepper
or Indian chili powder

1 teaspoon turmeric

1 teaspoon sea salt

1 pound 8 ounces (675 g) shrimp (²⁶/₃₀ count),
peeled and deveined

1 tablespoon vegetable oil

1 key lime, cut into eighths

24 cilantro leaves

1 small avocado, cut into small-dice
(optional)

1. *Combine* the cayenne or chili powder, turmeric, and salt. Rub the spice mixture onto the shrimp. Set aside for 15 to 30 minutes.

2. *Heat* the vegetable oil in a large sauté pan over medium-high heat. Fry the shrimp in the oil until they lose their translucency, 1 to 2 minutes per side. Do not overcook.

3. *Serve* at once, garnished with the lime, cilantro leaves, and avocado.

Excerpted from My Bombay Kitchen *by* NILOUFER ICHAPORIA KING, © 2007 *The Regents of the University of California. Published by the University of California Press.*

this adorable version of sushi is really easy to make and features the refreshing combination of shrimp, avocado, and cucumbers. If you need to make this in advance, wrap each uncut roll in plastic wrap and put it in a sealable container at room temperature for no longer than 2 hours. Try not to refrigerate it or keep it any longer because the rice will dry out and become hard.

INSIDE-OUT ROLL WITH SHRIMP AND AVOCADO

SERVES 6 TO 8

SRIRACHA MAYONNAISE
¼ cup mayonnaise
2 tablespoons *sriracha* (Vietnamese chile sauce)

7 half sheets nori
2 tablespoons rice vinegar
1 recipe Sushi Rice (page 202)
½ cup toasted white sesame seeds
7 ounces cooked and peeled shrimp (16/20 count),
cut in half lengthwise
4 ounces cucumber (about ½ cucumber),
cut into fourteen 4-inch-long sticks
½ large avocado (3½ ounces), pitted,
cut into 14 long sticks, and then peeled

1. *For the sriracha mayonnaise:* Combine the mayonnaise with the *sriracha* and mix thoroughly. Refrigerate until ready to use.

2. *Keep* the nori sheets covered. Combine the rice vinegar with 1 cup water in a small bowl and reserve it for moistening your hands. Keep a moistened clean cotton cloth or paper towel at hand to wipe away excess water or any rice residue stuck to your hands. Unroll a bamboo rolling mat and wrap it tightly in plastic wrap. Keep a well-sharpened cutting knife at hand.

3. *Place* one-half sheet of nori, shiny side down, on the bamboo mat with the long side facing you. Moisten your hands slightly with the vinegar water and pick up about ¾ cup of Sushi Rice, forming it into a rough egg shape without squeezing. Place the rice on the nori, ½ inch (1 cm) from the upper far left edge of the nori. Spread the rice evenly to the right leaving ½ inch (1 cm) at the far end of the nori uncovered. Using all your fingers, spread the rice toward you, until you have covered the whole area (except for the ½ inch/1 cm at the top). Sprinkle the surface of the rice evenly with 1 tablespoon of the sesame seeds to form an outer coating for the roll.

4. *Flip* the nori sheet over onto the rolling mat, lining up the bottom edge of the mat and the nori sheet evenly. The nori is now on top of the rice. Smear about 2 teaspoons of the sriracha mayonnaise across the nori from left to right, one-quarter of the way up the side nearest you. Arrange 1 ounce (25 g) of the shrimp evenly over the sauce. Place two sticks of cucumber over the shrimp and then two sticks of avocado on top. To roll, lift up the bamboo mat near you and fold it over the fillings. As you roll and the bamboo mat reaches to the surface of the nori, pull back the edge of the bamboo mat and continue to roll tightly until the whole roll is completed, leaving the seam down the roll. Now place the bamboo mat over the roll, hold it securely to firm it up, and square off the edges slightly. Unroll the rolling mat and place the roll on a cutting board. Repeat with the remaining nori sheets and filling ingredients.

5. *To* cut each roll into six to eight equal pieces, cut across the center in a sawing motion, not pushing down too hard, then cut each half roll into thirds or quarters, wiping the blade of the knife with the moist cloth to remove the rice residue when necessary. Serve the rolls with additional sriracha mayonnaise, if desired.

Adapted from a recipe by HIROKO SHIMBO

CHAPTER TWO

Soups & Noodle Soups

LIFE EVOLVES AROUND SOUP

At the crack of dawn, walk along any street in the Old Quarters of Hanoi—the small, congested shopping district of this ancient city—and chances are you'd smell star anise and ginger lingering in the cool morning air. If you see a small shop, the one with steam billowing from large pots and a long line of customers, it's yet another favorite *pho* joint in the neighborhood.

*W*hile *pho*, Vietnam's beloved noodle soup (page 59), is eaten at all hours of the day, it's really a breakfast food. People greet the day slurping noodles in beef broth perfumed with charred ginger, star anise, cinnamon, and spices. To eat, one adds slices of chiles, a squeeze of lime, and, if you have a southern palate, sprigs of fresh Asian basil. Push all that into the soup to wilt and you're in bliss.

For families who make their living off this dish, life truly evolves around a pot of *pho*. At one noodle shop on Hang Giay Street, the ritual begins at midnight when the mother starts a pot over a wood-fire stove. She fills it with beef knuckle, marrow bones, and oxtails and slowly simmers them with spices. After the first boil, she carefully skims the top so the broth stays clear. She then places the lid on top, allowing a little gap so the pot never boils since that too would make it cloudy.

During the night, she and her eldest son take turns stoking the fire, making sure it stays evenly lit. Halfway into the cooking, she adds beef chuck and tripe and allows them to simmer into the night. Before taking a nap, she makes sure a thick layer of fat has formed. This is critical as the fat traps the spice flavors and makes them permeate the broth. By sunrise, the aromatic broth is ready; the broth has been skimmed, the fresh noodles have arrived, and the stools get set up.

As you can see, in Asia, soup isn't just soup. It's either a complete meal, with all the accompanying condiments and garnishes like *pho*, or it's an integral part of a bigger meal. In either case, soup is highly regarded at the Asian table. Unlike the Western style of serving it as a first course, Asians prefer soup at the center of the table. Often delicately flavored and clear, it's enjoyed throughout the meal as a beverage and flavor balancer because it neutralizes and balances other intensely flavored dishes.

Clear soups are typically made by simmering meat or bones with vegetables and are then simply seasoned with soy sauce or fish sauce. Or the soup could be as simple as combining miso with stock. In China, for example, a family meal almost always includes soup such as pork with lotus root or chicken with greens. But it might take a more elaborate turn and become pork broth and vegetables served in a hollowed-out, carved winter melon. In Thailand, a hot and sour prawn soup served in a chimney hot pot provides needed contrast to the salty, sweet, and fiery flavors that are so typical of a Thai meal. But regardless of the ingredients, good soup is often about the broth. It can be as simple as simmering bones or meat with water, or it can be enhanced by the addition of aromatics such as onions and ginger or lemongrass. Or, it could be an ocean-flavored, Japanese-style stock with seaweed or bonita flakes.

Good soup also requires care and attention to detail. Make sure vegetables are cut correctly and attractively with sharp knives. Do not allow the soup to boil as the vegetables will lose their shape and become cloudy. If scallions and cilantro are part of the topping, cut them into very thin rings and add them just before serving.

Think of soup also as a simple way of preparing foods that you want to eat. The sweet, natural flavor of beef and vegetables, for example, really shine in a soup or light, brothy stew.

Last but not least, soup must be served piping hot, with wonderful, steamy fragrances emanating and perfuming the entire table.

a common accompaniment to Japanese meals, miso soup is simple to prepare. Its characteristic flavor is created by mixing dashi with miso, or Japanese fermented soybean paste. This traditional version features clams, but tofu is also a common ingredient. Miso should never be boiled as it's believed to lose its nutritious qualities and flavor. It's dissolved in a bowl and added back to the pot when it is off the stove.

CLAM MISO SOUP
ASARI NO MISO-SHIRU

SERVES 8

8 short-neck clams in the shell
Salt
6 cups Dashi Stock (page 60)
2 tablespoons light-colored miso
2 tablespoons dark-colored miso
½ cup thinly sliced green onions

1. **P**ut the clams into a colander and place it in a large bowl of salted water. Use the ratio of 1 tablespoon salt to each quart (liter) of water. The clams should be barely covered with the water. Let the clams stand in a cool place for 4 hours to expel any sand. Then rinse the clams under cold running tap water.

2. **A**dd the dashi and clams to a medium saucepan. Bring the mixture to a boil over medium-high heat and cook until all the clams are open, about 3 minutes. Discard any clams that do not open.

3. **P**lace the miso in a small bowl and add one ladle of hot dashi-clam liquid. Stir the mixture with a whisk, dissolving the miso. Transfer the miso liquid to the pot, add the green onion slices and give several large stirs. Turn off the heat immediately and serve ¾ cup of the miso soup with one clam in individual soup bowls while hot.

Adapted from a recipe by KUNIO TOKUOKA

in Vietnam, millions of people wake up each morning to an invigorating bowl of noodle soup called *pho*, which is made by simmering beef marrow bones and beef oxtail with spices and ginger for as long as 8 hours. This chicken version is a lot quicker but very delicious. If you like, you can also use sliced beef (steak is best) as the meat topping. The key to good *pho* is to make sure the broth is served piping hot.

VIETNAMESE RICE NOODLE SOUP WITH CHICKEN

PHO GA

SERVES 6

BROTH

One 4-inch (10-cm) piece ginger

2 yellow onions, peeled

6 star anise, lightly toasted

6 cloves, lightly toasted

3 to 4 cardamom pods

1 teaspoon fennel seeds

1 cinnamon stick

1 teaspoon whole black peppercorns

3 pounds (1.4 kg) chicken bones
(preferably backs), skin removed

One 3-pound 8-ounce (1.6-kg) whole chicken,
split in half

¼ cup fish sauce

2 tablespoons sugar

1 tablespoon sea salt, or as needed

NOODLES

1 pound (450 g) dried 1⁄16-inch-wide rice sticks

¾ cup very thinly sliced yellow onions

⅓ cup thinly sliced green onions

⅓ cup chopped cilantro

GARNISH

5 cups bean sprouts

20 Asian basil sprigs

12 saw-leaf herb leaves (optional)

3 Thai bird chiles, or 1 serrano chile,
deseeded and thinly sliced

1 lime, cut into 6 wedges

Freshly ground black pepper

1. *For* the broth: Cut the piece of ginger in half lengthwise and bruise with the flat side of a knife. Char the ginger over an open flame or under the broiler, 3 to 4 minutes. Char the onions over an open flame or under the broiler, 3 to 4 minutes.

2. *Place* the star anise, cloves, cardamom pods, fennel seeds, cinnamon, and peppercorns in a cheesecloth or spice bag and set aside.

3. *Bring* 5 quarts (5 liters) of water to a rolling boil in a large stockpot. Add the chicken bones and chicken halves. Boil vigorously for 3 minutes over high heat, then reduce the heat to medium low so that the liquid maintains a simmer. Skim the surface of the broth as necessary to remove any fat or foam. Add the charred ginger, onions, fish sauce, sugar, and salt. Cook until the chicken is just done, about 30 minutes. Remove the chicken, but not the chicken bones, and set aside to cool.

4. *Add* the spice bag to the pot and simmer the broth for another hour. Remove and discard the spice bag. Adjust the seasoning and reduce the heat to very low.

5. *Remove* the skin from the reserved chicken and discard. Hand-shred half of the chicken into bite-sized strips. Save the other half for another use; you don't need much to garnish *pho*, but you do need a whole chicken to make a good broth.

6. *For the noodles:* Soak the noodles in cold water for 30 minutes. Bring a large pot of water to a boil over high heat. Add the rice sticks and boil until soft but still resilient, 2 to 3 minutes.

7. *Place* 1 cup of the cooked noodles in each of six preheated bowls. If the noodles are not hot, reheat in a microwave or dip briefly in boiling water. Place 2 tablespoons sliced yellow onions and 1⁄3 cup shredded chicken on top. Bring the broth back to a rolling boil, then ladle 1 cup into each bowl. Top with green onions and cilantro. Invite guests to garnish their bowls with bean sprouts, fresh herbs, chiles, squeezes of lime juice, and black pepper.

Adapted from a recipe by MAI PHAM

JAPAN

dashi is a nutritious and flavorful stock made from water, *kombu* (kelp), and *kastuobushi* (bonito fish flakes), and is an essential ingredient in Japanese cuisine. It is simple, quick, and easy to make. The quality of dashi deteriorates dramatically over time, so prepare it as you need it. Many recipes call for just a small amount so freeze any extra dashi in a small container or ice cube tray for later use.

DASHI STOCK

MAKES 4 QUARTS

1½ ounces (40 g) *kombu* (about half of a
10 x 4½- inch/25 x 11-cm rectangle)
2 ounces (50 g) *kastuobushi*
(about 1¼ cups, firmly packed)
3 quarts (3 liters) cold water

1. *S*oak the *kombu* in a large bowl overnight (about 10 hours) with the water. Remove and reserve it for making a second round of dashi. This soaking liquid is the *kombu dashi* (kelp stock) and is used when a recipe calls for kelp stock.

2. *P*our the kelp stock into a cooking pot and set it over medium-high heat. When it comes to a boil, add the *kastuobushi* all at once. Count 10 seconds, then quickly turn off the heat. Remove any foam that rises. Let the stock rest with the fish flakes for 2 minutes, then strain it through a *fukin*, a tightly woven cotton cloth, or a strainer lined with strong paper towels. Discard the bonito flakes or reserve them along with the kelp for making a second round of dashi.

3. *T*o prepare a second round of dashi, combine the cold water and the reserved kelp and bonito flakes in a pot, set it over medium-high heat, and cook for 10 minutes. Strain the dashi, discarding the bonito flakes and kelp.

From The Sushi Experience *by* HIROKO SHIMBO, *copyright © 2006 by Hiroko Shimbo. Used by permission of Alfred A. Knopf, a division of Random House, Inc.*

in this lovely Japanese soup, the dumplings are made from grilled scallops and shredded lotus root, which adds a wonderful crunchy texture against the velvety scallops. Grilling makes the scallops sweet and smoky, but searing them in a pan for 1 to 2 minutes is also fine. When shaping the dumplings, make sure to squeeze to remove any excess liquid. You can buy fresh lotus root at Asian markets.

SCALLOP AND LOTUS ROOT DUMPLING SOUP
HOTATE IRI RENKON DANGO

SERVES 8

10 ounces (275 g) lotus root
10 ounces (275 g) sea scallops
2½ teaspoons salt
1 quart (1 liter) plus 1 tablespoon canola oil
16 shiitake mushrooms, cut into 1½ x ¾ x ⅛-inch (37 x 18 x 3-cm) thick rectangles (3 cups)
1 carrot, cut into 1½ x ¾ x ⅛-inch (37 x 18 x 3-cm) thick rectangles (½ cup)
8 cups arugula
1 quart (liter) Dashi Stock (page 60)
4 teaspoons soy sauce
2 teaspoons julienned lemon zest

1. Preheat the grill to high (preferably a charcoal grill).

2. Peel the lotus root and finely grate. Drain the lotus root in a strainer to remove the excess liquid, pressing if necessary.

3. Season the scallops with 2 teaspoons salt. Grill the surface of the scallops until the outside is light golden, 1 to 2 minutes per side. Allow the scallops to cool until they can be easily handled and break the scallops into rough pieces by hand.

4. Heat a large pan over medium heat and add 1 tablespoon oil. Sauté the mushrooms until light golden, about 4 minutes. This may need to be done in batches.

5. Mix the lotus root and scallops in a bowl. Shape the mixture into 8 balls about 1½ inches (4 cm) in diameter and 1½ inches (4 cm) thick. Squeeze out any excess liquid.

6. Heat the remaining cooking oil in a medium saucepan over medium-high heat to 340°F (170°C). Fry the lotus dumplings in the oil until golden brown, 3 to 4 minutes.

7. Bring a large pot of water to a boil. Place the carrot slices in boiling water and cook 30 seconds to 1 minute or until the carrots are lightly blanched and still have a slight bite to them. Remove the carrots from the water and bring the water to a boil again. Have a bowl of cold water ready.

8. Salt the boiling water and add the arugula. Cook the arugula for 30 seconds to 1 minute and then immediately plunge into the cold water. Squeeze out the excess water (you should have about 1 cup arugula).

9. Combine the Dashi Stock and soy sauce in a medium pot and add salt to taste. Bring to a gentle simmer.

10. In individual small bowls place 1 fried lotus dumpling. Arrange 4 to 5 mushrooms, 7 to 8 carrot slices, and 2 tablespoons of the arugula to the side of the dumpling. Pour ½ cup of the piping hot dashi broth into each bowl over the dumpling and garnish with ¼ teaspoon lemon zest.

Adapted from a recipe by YOSHIHIRO TAKAHASHI

Miso and Soy Sauce

MISO

Miso is one of the most important staples in the Japanese kitchen. A fermented, salty bean paste that's widely used to give umami, or savory depth, to food including soups, marinades, and sauces, miso is what makes Japanese cuisine. Like soy sauce, it originated in China centuries ago but it wasn't until it came to Japan that it became highly refined, both in the way it was manufactured and how it was used and eaten.

Miso is made by adding a yeast mold (known as "*koji*") to soybeans and other grains such as barley, wheat, and rice, and allowing them to ferment. The fermentation process, which can range from weeks to years, depends upon the specific type being produced. Once this process is complete, the fermented ingredients are ground into a paste that is similar in texture to nut butter. The color, taste, texture, and degree of saltiness depend upon the exact ingredients used, the length of fermentation, and how the soybeans were harvested and handled.

In Japan, there are hundreds, if not more, of different kinds of miso, and preferences for one type or another often boils down to the cook's regional identity and the recipes in which they'll be used. Generally, miso is classified as "*aka*" or dark, "*shiro*" or light, or somewhere in between. Miso ranges in color from beige to brown. The lighter varieties such as *saikyo* and *genmai*, are less salty and mildly flavored while the darker ones such as *hatcho* and *sendai* (and some versions of *genmai*) are more salty, pungent, and deeply flavored. Most misos are pasteurized.

Due to the growing popularity of Japanese food and the interest in the macrobiotic diet and the reported health benefits associated with this soybean product, miso is now readily available at many supermarkets and natural food stores. It's generally sold in tightly sealed plastic or glass containers, and sometimes in bulk in Japan. As a general rule, buy miso based on your personal preference as well as intended use. Darker-colored misos are stronger and more pungent in flavor and are better suited for marinades, braises, soups, and robustly flavored sauces. Lighter colored varieties are more delicate and are appropriate for soups, dressings, and light sauces. Miso can be stored in the freezer for up to one year with little loss in flavor in a tightly sealed container.

SOY SAUCE

The original soy sauce was believed to be the liquid resulting from fermented soybeans in miso-making but over the years it has evolved into a totally separate category. Today, the world of soy sauce—like the world of other culinary bedrocks such as olive oil and vinegar—is vast and complex with many different varieties and qualities from which to choose. Used extensively in China ("*see yul*") and Japan ("*shoyu*") and other Asian countries heavily influenced by Chinese cooking, soy sauce is an indispensable seasoning used to impart saltiness, savoriness, and depth—that indescribable *umami* effect—to whatever food it touches. Soy sauce has become so popular in recent decades that it is now common in non-Asian kitchens around the world.

Good soy sauce relies heavily on the production process, from the way the soybeans were grown and harvested to how they were processed and fermented, all of which could take years. While different manufacturers use different methods to produce soy sauce, the recipe is generally the same for what is termed "naturally brewed" soy sauce: Once cooked, soybeans are combined with roasted wheat and mashed, a starter mold is added to promote fermentation. Once a brine is added, the mixture is allowed to age. Depending on the style of the final product, the fermentation could take six months to more than a year before the liquid is filtered, pasteurized, and bottled. Some artisanal shoyu products, the kind you'd pair with very expensive fish, are said to have been aged for three to ten years.

What ends up on the shelves are many varieties, all boasting different applications and commanding different prices. But they fall under two general categories. One is soy sauce associated with Chinese cooking, which has a shorter fermentation and a sharp-tasting saltiness, and the other is the Japanese variety, which is generally more aged with deep, rounded flavors.

Within the Chinese group, there are three common types: a thin soy sauce (meaning light-bodied) used for both seasoning and cooking and sometimes labeled as "superior soy" or "premium soy"; a black soy sauce, which is darker, richer, and slightly sweet because of added sugar; and sweet soy sauce, which is even thicker and darker. The latter is best used for noodle dishes such as *char kway tew*, a Singapore-style wide rice noodle stir-fry that benefits from the sweet soy-stained noodles caramelizing in the hot wok or pan.

Japanese soy sauce is available in two general types—dark and light, with the former being the most popular and widely used in restaurants. The dark variety has a rich *umami* flavor and a soft sweetness that is a perfect accompaniment to a wide range of food. The lighter variety, which is light brown and saltier, is more delicate and is typically used in dishes and sauces in which you don't want the dark color or too strong of a flavor. Soy sauce is like any other seasoning ingredient—you can make your own special version by combining it with a splash of mirin, sake, and the juice from the Japanese lemon, *yuzu*.

If you're curious about good Japanese *shoyu*, it's worth perusing a specialty market and sampling all the dark and light types as well as subtypes, especially those from small, artisanal producers. Like other seasoning ingredients, the variety and the quality of soy sauce is important to the final taste of the dish. When buying this product, look for traditional brewed soy sauce, not the inexpensive seasoning sauce that resembles soy sauce.

SINGAPORE

this recipe stays true to the popular Singaporean noodle soup that uses pork fat and shrimp heads to enrich the stock. What makes this dish particularly enticing is the rich yet delicate pork broth and the fresh pork crackling garnish. The crispy shallots add a caramelized flavor if they're made fresh, but store-bought ones are also acceptable. For color, garnish the bowls with bean sprouts and water spinach or wilted green leaf lettuce.

SINGAPORE SHRIMP NOODLE SOUP

HAY MEE

SERVES 8

STOCK

7 ounces (200 g) firm pork fat,
cut into small dice

2 pounds 3 ounces (990 g) shrimp,
with shells and heads (if possible)

6 quarts (6 liters) water, or as needed

3 tablespoons vegetable oil

4 pounds 6 ounces (2 kg) pork rib bones

1 pound 2 ounces (500 g) pork belly,
with skin

2 tablespoons salt

2 teaspoons sugar

1 tablespoon white peppercorns

1 tablespoon light soy sauce

1 tablespoon sliced shallots,
deep-fried until crispy

3 cups vegetable oil

1¼ cups thinly sliced shallots

5½ cups bean sprouts, roots removed

10½ ounces (300 g) rice vermicelli
or brown rice vermicelli

1 pound 5 ounces (600 g) dried thin
yellow wheat or egg noodles

5 tablespoons light soy sauce

5 red chiles, sliced

1. For the stock: Heat a wok or a large saucepan over medium heat. Stir-fry the pork fat until the oil renders out of the pork, 4 to 5 minutes. Continue frying until the cubes are browned and crispy, about 4 minutes. Remove the cubes from the oil and place in a bowl. Drain off the fat from the pan. Do not wash the pan.

2. Remove the shrimp heads, if using, and set aside. Bring the water to a boil over high heat and add the shrimp. Simmer until they turn red, about 2 minutes. Remove from the water (but reserve the water) and allow to cool until they can be easily handled. Peel the shell from the shrimp and reserve the meat and shells separately.

3. Heat the vegetable oil in the reserved wok or large saucepan. Add the shrimp heads, if using, and shells and sauté until the shells turn bright red, about 5 minutes. Add the water used to cook the shrimp, plus the pork ribs, pork belly, salt, sugar, peppercorns, soy sauce, and crispy shallots. Bring to boil over high heat and then turn down to low and simmer for 2 hours. This is the shrimp and pork stock for the noodle soup.

4. Strain the stock and return to a boil. Add the pork belly back to the pot and, after half an hour of boiling, remove the pork belly. Cool until it can easily be handled and cut into fine julienne. Meanwhile, keep the soup simmering.

5. Heat the oil in a small saucepan to 350°F (180°C) over medium-high heat. Add the shallots and fry until crispy, 3 to 4 minutes. Drain briefly on paper towels and set aside.

6. Bring a large pot of water to a boil over high heat. Blanch the bean sprouts briefly until they are just cooked, 1 to 2 minutes. Remove the pan from the heat and the bean sprouts from the water. Reserve the pot of water.

7. Soak the rice vermicelli in hot water for 15 minutes to soften. Drain.

8. Bring the water to a boil again and cook the egg noodles until just al dente, 6 to 8 minutes. Drain the pasta and reserve.

9. For each serving, divide the egg noodles and rice vermicelli among each of 8 individual bowls. Top with the bean sprouts, shrimp, and julienne of pork.

10. Pour the stock over the top and serve with the crispy shallots and pork cracklings. Combine the soy sauce with the chiles and serve as a condiment on the side.

Adapted from a recipe by LOUIS TAY

India

this soup uses the classic Indian flavors of tamarind, cumin, tumeric, and curry to highlight the simple bold flavor of pepper. A hot soup, this dish is often served with *pappadam*, an Indian flatbread made from lentil flour, which can be either grilled or fried. The soup can be thinned further and used as a spicy broth to cook with or to serve in tiny shot glasses as welcome drinks.

BLACK PEPPER SOUP
KURUMULAKU RASAM

SERVES 8 TO 10

1½ teaspoons tamarind concentrate

6 cups water

2 teaspoons salt, or as needed

½ teaspoon turmeric powder

2 tablespoons black peppercorns

1 tablespoon cumin seeds

1 cup fresh curry leaves

2 tablespoons canola oil

2 medium beefsteak tomatoes, seeded and diced

3 fresh green chiles, cut into thin strips

2 tablespoons thinly chopped shallots

1 tablespoon finely chopped cilantro leaves

2 fried pappadams per portion (optional)

1. Mix the tamarind concentrate with the water in a saucepan, add the salt and turmeric powder, and bring to a boil over high heat. Reduce the heat to low and simmer for 5 minutes.

2. Using a mortar and pestle or a food processor, crush the peppercorns, cumin seeds, and curry leaves.

3. Heat half of the oil in a heavy medium sauté pan over medium heat. Fry the crushed ingredients for 3 to 4 minutes or until aromatic and lightly toasted. Add the diced tomatoes and green chiles and fry for another 3 minutes or until most of the liquid has evaporated.

4. Transfer the contents of the sauté pan to the simmering tamarind water and stir well. Simmer for 5 minutes and remove from the stove.

5. Heat the remaining oil in a small saucepan over medium-high heat. Fry the shallots in the oil until slightly browned, 3 to 4 minutes. Stir into the soup.

6. Garnish with the chopped cilantro leaves. Cover and set aside for a few minutes to allow the flavors to blend. Serve the soup hot or warm with fried pappadams, if desired.

Adapted from a recipe by AMMINI RAMACHANDRAN. *From Grains, Greens, and Grated Coconuts by Ammini Ramachandran Copyright © 2007, 2008 by Ammini Ramachandran. Reprinted by permission of iUniverse, Inc. All right reserved.*

there are many versions of this classic Thai soup, but the best interpretations always include the correct balance of seasonings and the perfect ratio of coconut milk to chicken stock. For this recipe, it's best to use a flavorful but light-bodied coconut milk and do include the chili jam, which gives it depth. If you prefer a richer and thicker soup, reduce the chicken stock and add more coconut milk instead.

SPICY THAI CHICKEN AND COCONUT SOUP
TOM KHA GAI

SERVES 8

1 quart (1 liter) coconut milk

3 cups chicken stock

2 lemongrass stalks, white parts only, slightly pounded and cut into 1-inch (2.5-cm) pieces

One 2-inch (5-cm) long piece galangal, peeled and thinly sliced

12 kaffir lime leaves

1 pound 8 ounces (675 g) chicken thighs, cut into ¼-inch (6-mm) thick slices

2 cups quartered fresh cremini or button mushrooms

½ cup fish sauce

10 tablespoons freshly squeezed lime juice

2 tablespoons roasted chile jam (*nam prik phao*)

4 to 8 Thai bird chiles, lightly crushed, or to taste

Salt

¼ cup cilantro, coarsely chopped (optional)

¼ cup sawtooth leaves, coarsely chopped (optional)

1. *In* a pot, combine the coconut milk, chicken stock, lemongrass, galangal, kaffir lime leaves, and sliced chicken. Bring to a boil over high heat and reduce the heat to a simmer. Simmer for 2 to 3 minutes. Add the mushrooms and continue cooking until the chicken is cooked and tender, 2 to 3 minutes.

2. *Return* the soup to a boil and stir in the fish sauce, lime juice, roasted chile jam, and chiles.

3. *Turn* off the heat and adjust the seasoning with salt. Transfer 1½ cups into each of eight soup bowls and garnish with cilantro and sawtooth leaves, if using.

Adapted from a recipe by CHAI SIRIYARN

SINGAPORE

laksa is a beloved and popular noodle soup eaten throughout the day in Singapore and Malaysia. A theory suggests that a translation of the word "*laksa*" refers to the concept of "many," referencing the number of ingredients and condiments that can be added to the soup.

SINGAPORE LAKSA NOODLE SOUP

SERVES 8

2 tablespoons vegetable oil

12 ounces (350 g) firm tofu, cut into ½-inch (1-cm) cubes

1 teaspoon salt, or as needed

1 pound 4 ounces (550 g) shrimp (16/20 count), peeled and deveined

4 cups fresh bean sprouts, roots plucked off

1 pound 4 ounces (550 g) dried rice vermicelli noodles

6 cups Laksa Gravy (see opposite page)

2 cucumbers, cut into fine julienne or into long thin slices

1⅓ cups julienned laksa or mint leaves

4 hard-boiled eggs, peeled and sliced

1. Heat 1 tablespoon of the oil in a large sauté pan over medium-high heat. Season the tofu with half of the salt. Add the tofu to the pan and sear the cubes until browned on all sides, 5 to 7 minutes. Reserve until needed. This may need to be done in batches.

2. Bring a medium saucepan of water to a simmer and place a steamer basket inside. Add the shrimp to the basket and steam until cooked through, about 5 minutes. Remove the shrimp from the pan, season with the remaining salt, and cool to room temperature.

3. Bring a large pot of water to a boil over high heat. Add the bean sprouts and blanch lightly, 1 to 2 minutes. Drain the sprouts and run them under cold water to stop the cooking process. Set aside.

4. Bring a large pot of salted water to a boil over high heat and add the rice vermicelli. Stir and cook the noodles until they are soft but still bouncy, about 1 minute. Drain and blanch in cold water if you are using them later in the day. Pour boiling water over and drain just before serving. If you are using fresh thick rice vermicelli, pour boiling water on the vermicelli, mix well, and drain.

5. Bring the Laksa Gravy to a simmer over medium heat.

6. Put 1 cup noodles into each of 8 bowls and top with ½ cup of the bean sprouts. Pour ¾ cup of the Laksa Gravy over the noodles. Alternatively pour the gravy around the noodles.

7. Serve with 3 shrimp, ¼ cup cucumber, and about ¼ cup fried tofu. Garnish with 2 to 3 tablespoons laksa or mint leaves and 3 slices of hard-boiled eggs.

Adapted from a recipe by VIOLET OON

SINGAPORE

one of the defining characteristics of *laksa* is the complex flavor that comes from simmering spices with shrimp paste and dried shrimp. If you're new to these strong, pungent flavors, try decreasing the amount of broth by half and then adjust as you like. When used in small amounts, they add a wonderful savoriness to food.

LAKSA GRAVY

SERVES 8

SPICE PASTE
15 dried Thai bird chiles, deseeded,
soaked in hot water 15 minutes, and strained
½ cup roughly chopped galangal
(about one 2-inch/5-cm piece)
¾ cup roughly chopped lemongrass stalks,
white parts only
¼ cup almonds or 3 candlenuts (*buah keras*)
¾ teaspoon ground turmeric
3 cloves garlic, peeled and thinly sliced
2 teaspoons shrimp paste (*belacan*)
¾ cup roughly chopped shallots
1 teaspoon ground white pepper

¼ cup dried shrimp
6 tablespoons vegetable oil
1½ tablespoons ground coriander
2 cups water
3 cups coconut milk
1 tablespoon salt, or as needed

1. For the spice paste: Pound or blend the first 8 ingredients in order listed until ground very fine, pounding well between each addition, about 10 minutes. Add the white pepper and mix well. Reserve until needed.

2. Wash the dried shrimp and soak in warm water for 15 minutes. Drain and blend until fine.

3. Heat the oil in a small saucepan over high heat. Add the pounded spices and dried shrimp and fry for 4 to 5 minutes or until fragrant and slightly crispy. Add the coriander and stir-fry for 30 seconds before adding the water and half of the coconut milk.

4. Bring to a boil and then reduce the heat to low. Simmer the mixture for 15 minutes or until it looks like a thin gravy. Add the remaining coconut milk and salt and bring to a boil over high heat, stirring constantly. Turn off the heat. Cool completely and reserve until needed.

Adapted from a recipe by VIOLET OON

Building Flavor in Soup

TEMPERING OIL

A soup can have many personalities. It can be mild so it can balance other foods at the table or it can be bold, robust, and stand on its own. In southern India, there's a lovely tradition of welcoming guests with small glasses of *rasam*, a hot, thin broth similar to consommé but infused with lively spices, chiles, and legumes. What makes it particularly distinctive and flavorful is the tempering oil, a technique in which you heat the oil and "bloom" the spices before adding them to the soup. This last-minute finish—this mélange of chiles, cumin, coriander seeds, and curry leaves—adds a surprising burst of fresh flavors and complexity to what is otherwise a simple dish. This technique is also common in other parts of Asia, including in Vietnam where *bun bo hue*, a spicy noodle soup enjoyed in the central region, gets a splash of lemongrass and chili oil as a garnish. *Bo kho*, a hearty Vietnamese stew of beef with carrots, potatoes, star anise, and lemongrass, gets an aromatic finish from a tempering oil made with garlic, chili powder, and annatto seeds. Similarly, if you wish to enhance your soup, make a tempering oil with spices and herbs, or a simple one made from "blooming" garlic or shallots with chiles. Just before serving a bowl of noodle soup or broth, drizzle a teaspoon or two of this aromatic oil on top.

AROMATIC BASE

Another way to create flavor in soup is to start the cooking process with an aromatic base. Heat oil and stir in garlic, chiles, and spices until they are fragrant before adding them to the pot. Some soups benefit from both techniques—use half or part of the aromatic base in the beginning and drop in the other half as a garnish. This dual approach adds complexity, imparting different levels of the same flavors in one dish.

GARNISHES

A simple technique to boost flavor is the use of garnishes and condiments. Scallions, shallots, chiles, and ginger can completely transform a soup. Slice them paper-thin so that when they are added to the hot liquid, their flavors will immediately permeate the broth and create a wonderful aroma. This technique is particularly wonderful with ginger. For interesting variations, cook the aromatics first. Scallions are completely transformed when wilted in oil and used to garnish noodles and rice. Shallots, when thinly sliced and deep-fried, have a deep, sweet, caramelized flavor and a wonderful crunchy texture. For the ultimate experience with Asian noodle soups, add both thinly cut onions and herbs and fried shallots to the hot broth before eating. Or you can emulate what many Thai cooks do to enhance noodle soups—make a tasty garnish by frying freshly chopped garlic (if the cloves are small, the whole unpeeled segment is used) in oil until it becomes golden and crispy. Then drizzle a teaspoon of this aromatic oil on top, giving the soup another layer of aroma, texture, and richness. But don't limit this garnish to just noodle soups. Creamy rice soups or puréed vegetable soups also benefit from a similar topping, along with peanuts, sesame oil, and chili sauce.

In fact, all of these tempering oils, flavored oils, and other toppings are really versatile and can be used with just about any dish, from soups and salads and steamed vegetables to grilled meats and seafood.

CHINA

if you ever get that craving for a Chinatown-style noodle soup, this recipe can be a quick fix especially if you can get freshly roasted duck or chicken. For the greens, you can use any Asian greens such as bok choy, napa cabbage, or spinach. Leftover grilled chicken or steak or even turkey make good toppings as well.

HONG KONG NOODLE SOUP WITH ROAST DUCK

SERVES 8

6 cups water

One 4-inch (10-cm) piece ginger,
peeled and sliced

6 star anise, lightly toasted in a dry pan

3 quarts (3 liters) low-sodium chicken stock

¼ cup soy sauce, or to taste

4 teaspoons sugar

2 teaspoons sea salt

¼ cup vegetable oil

4 cloves garlic, sliced thin

Two 14-ounce (400-g) packages fresh
or dried skinny Chinese egg noodles

1 pound 5 ounces (600 g) freshly roasted duck,
boned and cut into bite-sized chunks

6 cups baby bok choy or napa cabbage,
cut into 2-inch (5-cm) lengths, blanched

½ yellow onion, sliced paper thin

6 red Thai chiles, sliced, or 2 tablespoons
dried chili flakes (optional)

1. *Place* the water in a large pot over medium heat and bring to a boil. Add the ginger and star anise and simmer on low heat for 15 minutes. Add the chicken stock, soy sauce, sugar, and salt and continue to simmer.

2. *Meanwhile,* place the oil and garlic in small saucepan over low heat. Stir gently until the garlic is golden and crisp but not brown, 3 to 5 minutes, then set aside.

3. *Bring* another large pot of water to a boil over high heat. Add the noodles and cook until tender but firm, 2 to 3 minutes depending on the thickness. Drain and set aside for 2 minutes. Drizzle 1 tablespoon garlic oil on the noodles and toss gently to prevent sticking.

4. *To* serve, bring the broth back to a rolling boil. Divide the noodles among 8 large preheated bowls. If necessary, reheat the duck in the oven. Top each bowl with ⅛ of the bok choy, onion, and duck. Ladle 2 cups boiling broth into each prepared bowl. Garnish with ½ teaspoon of the reserved garlic oil and chiles, if using, and serve immediately.

Adapted from a recipe by MAI PHAM

Korea

this traditional hot noodle soup combines two cherished elements of the Korean kitchen—beef and *kimchi* (see page 110). While this dish is commonly prepared with soba or wheat noodles, this recipe uses rice noodles. *Pyogo* mushrooms refer to a Korean variety of mushrooms similar to the Japanese shiitake. For a rustic presentation, mix the vegetables with the *kimchi* and sesame oil, then divide among the noodle bowls.

Beef Broth–Braised Rice Noodle Soup
ONMYEON

SERVES 8

BROTH
2 quarts water
2 cups diced yellow onions
2 pounds (900 g) boneless beef short ribs,
cut into large dice
1 teaspoon minced garlic
2 teaspoons soy sauce
2 teaspoons salt
1 teaspoon sugar
Pinch of freshly ground black pepper

1 pound (450 g) rice noodles
½ cup julienne carrot
1½ cups julienne cucumber
1⅓ cups julienne yellow bell pepper
1 teaspoon salt
1 tablespoon vegetable oil
1½ cups julienned Pyogo or shiitake mushrooms
2 cups Baechoo Kimchi (page 110), chopped
2 teaspoons sesame oil

1. *For the broth:* Bring the water to a simmer over medium-high heat. Add the onions and beef and simmer until the broth has good flavor, about 40 minutes. Season the broth with the garlic, soy sauce, salt, sugar, and black pepper. Strain the broth and reserve warm over medium-low heat. Save the beef for another use.

2. *Bring* a large pot of water to a boil over high heat. Cook the noodles for 5 minutes or until they are cooked through. Rinse them in cold water and strain the water out.

3. *Soak* the carrot, cucumber, and yellow bell pepper with salt for 10 minutes or until they are softened. Rinse the vegetables and squeeze the excess water out.

4. *Heat* a medium sauté pan over medium-low heat and add the vegetable oil. Working with one vegetable at a time and cooking them in separate batches, sauté the carrot, cucumber, yellow bell pepper, and mushrooms until barely cooked, about 2 minutes each.

5. *Mix* the chopped Baechoo Kimchi with the sesame oil.

6. *Divide* the noodles evenly in each of 8 bowls. Pour 2 cups of boiling broth in each bowl or enough to almost submerge the noodles. Arrange the prepared vegetables in a cross pattern, place the *kimchi* in the middle, and serve.

Adapted from a recipe by MYUNG SOOK LEE

China

Wonton soup can be truly amazing especially if the dumplings are generously stuffed with a tasty filling as in this version. Many wontons are filled with pork, as shown here, but you can also use a mixture of ground pork and shrimp. For extra texture, coarsely chop the shrimp. In Asia, this soup is also garnished with blanched lettuces such as romaine or iceberg. Serve this soup as an appetizer or as a meal-in-a-bowl.

Wonton Soup

SERVES 8

WONTONS

12 ounces (350 g) ground pork

1 cup finely chopped napa cabbage

3 tablespoons thinly sliced green onions

1 teaspoon minced ginger

1½ teaspoons light soy sauce

1½ teaspoons sesame oil

¼ teaspoon salt, or to taste

1½ teaspoons sugar

⅛ teaspoon ground white pepper

24 wonton wrappers

¼ cup water

SOUP

1½ tablespoons vegetable oil

6 tablespoons thinly sliced green onions, cut on the bias

½ teaspoon minced ginger

2 quarts chicken stock

3 tablespoons dark soy sauce, or as needed

¼ teaspoon salt

⅛ teaspoon ground white pepper

2½ cups spinach leaves, stems removed

2 beaten eggs

½ cup julienned ham

1. For the wontons: Combine the pork, cabbage, green onions, ginger, soy sauce, sesame oil, salt, sugar, and white pepper and mix well with a spoon or by hand until thoroughly combined. Keep chilled until ready to fill the wontons.

2. Spoon 1½ tablespoons of the filling in the center of each wrapper and brush the edges of the wrapper lightly with the water. Fold the wonton in half to make a triangle and then overlap the points, pressing them in place. Cover the wontons and refrigerate until needed.

3. For the soup: Heat 1 tablespoon of the oil in a large soup pot over medium-high heat. Add the green onions and ginger and sauté, stirring frequently, until aromatic, about 2 minutes. Add the stock, bring to a boil, and season with soy sauce, salt, and white pepper. Reduce the heat to medium-low, keeping the soup at a simmer.

4. Bring a large pot of salted water to a rolling boil. Add the spinach and blanch for 30 seconds. Drain and rinse in cold water until chilled. Drain again, squeeze out the excess water, and chop coarsely.

5. Heat the remaining vegetable oil in a medium skillet or omelet pan over low heat. Add the eggs and scramble until they are just beginning to set. Spread the eggs in an even layer, cover the pan, and cook until the eggs have set but not browned, 2 to 3 minutes. Roll the omelet out of the pan. Allow it to cool slightly and then cut it into a fine julienne.

6. Bring a large pot of salted water to a boil over high heat. Boil the wontons until the filling is cooked through, 2 to 3 minutes. Place 3 wontons into each of 8 heated soup bowls.

7. Add the spinach, ham, and omelet to the soup. Simmer just long enough to heat, about 2 minutes. Ladle 1 cup of the hot soup over the wontons. Serve immediately.

Adapted from a recipe by The Culinary Institute of America

CHAPTER THREE

Salads & Vegetables

AN INTEGRAL PART OF A MEAL

Against the glow of the late afternoon sun, the rice barge glides down the narrow waterway, cutting through the velvety water almost like butter, effortlessly and noiselessly. At this time of day, the backwaters of Kerala in southern India are picture perfect: swaying palm trees, people washing clothes and tending their boats against the magenta sky.

*I*nside the rice barge-turned-tourist boat, the chef is busy preparing vegetables in his *kadai*, an Indian wok. He starts by heating coconut oil, then adding chiles, mustard seeds, cumin seeds, yellow split peas, and curry leaves. Within seconds, a series of pops and crackles erupt and a wonderful, spicy aroma wafts through the cabin. He throws in green beans and freshly grated coconut, then stirs and turns, splashing a little water here and there to help cook the vegetables. What follows is utterly delicious: a green bean dish that is like no other, laced with nutty coconut and crusted with spices.

With more than half of India's population choosing a vegetarian lifestyle because of religious and cultural reasons, it's no wonder the country puts out some of the world's best vegetable cuisine. But good vegetable cooking is prevalent elsewhere as well. Certainly one of the greatest hallmarks of Asian cuisine is its abundant use of produce—from leafy greens to fleshy vegetables such as gourds and melons; roots and tubers such as lotus and taro; aromatic herbs such as basil and rice paddy; and legumes such as soybeans and red beans.

In Asia vegetables show up at practically every meal. In the most basic form, they're sliced and served as raw accompaniments to dipping sauces as in the Thai manner, or simply boiled as in a wedge of cabbage and eaten with rice. Southeast Asian salads are particularly savory, spiked with chiles, fish sauce, and kaffir lime and served not as a first course but as an integral part of a meal. The ingredients can run the gamut of shaved cabbage, water spinach, green papaya, and green mango. In other instances, they're made with grilled eggplant dressed in coconut and lime. Nuts such as peanuts and

cashews as well as other legumes are often layered between greens. In Vietnam, lettuces and young mustard leaves are often served with herbs for wrapping foods and are eaten out of hand.

In more common applications, vegetables are also valuable ingredients added to soups, salads, appetizers, stir-fries, and stews, and to make pickles. In Japan, beautiful greens, mushrooms, and noodles are simmered or poached and served in hot pots, making hearty yet light meals. The Koreans have a distinctive way of enjoying vegetables in *mit banchan*, or pickled or seasoned vegetables such as soybean sprouts, cucumbers, daikon, and fern, all of which are served as side dishes.

Tofu, made from soybean milk that has been boiled, coagulated, and pressed into blocks, has been eaten for religious or cultural reasons for centuries. An essential source of protein, it's inexpensive and easily available. When combined with vegetables and pungent seasonings and spices, tofu can really transform a dish, making it remarkably scrumptious and satisfying. Whether it's soft-, medium-, or firm-textured, tofu can be used in soups, salads, stir-fries, stews, and even desserts.

Perhaps one good way for avid home cooks to discover this vast world of vegetables is just to try as many different varieties as available. Peruse Asian markets and specialty stores as well as the farmers' markets in your area. Make it simple by cooking the vegetables first in soup or enjoying them raw in salads as a way of getting acquainted with their flavors. Then experiment with more elaborate preparations. Whether you're a vegetarian or a meat eater, you might be pleasantly surprised to find so many new favorites.

this refreshing salad exemplifies the simplicity of Vietnamese cooking. Here cucumbers and mint are combined with shrimp and a classic Vietnamese dipping sauce to create this wonderfully vibrant-tasting dish. Serve this with toasted sesame-flavored rice paper, which you can find next to dried rice paper at Asian markets.

VIETNAMESE SHRIMP AND CUCUMBER SALAD

GOI TOM

SERVES 8

DRESSING
4 to 5 tablespoons fish sauce, or to taste
¼ cup sugar
4 to 5 tablespoons lime juice
2 to 4 Thai bird chiles (optional)

2 hothouse cucumbers, julienned
2 cups carrots, cut into very thin strips
1 pound (450 g) shrimp (16/20 count), peeled and split lengthwise
2 cups coarsely chopped mint leaves
⅔ cup chopped, roasted peanuts

1. For the dressing: Combine the fish sauce and sugar in a small bowl and stir well to dissolve. Just before serving, stir in the lime juice and chiles, if using.

2. Place the cucumbers and carrots in a mixing bowl with cold water. Let the vegetables soak for 30 minutes. Remove and drain completely in a colander lined with a kitchen towel.

3. Bring a medium saucepan of water to a simmer and place a steamer basket inside. Add the shrimp to the basket and steam until cooked through, about 5 minutes. Remove the shrimp from the pan and cool to room temperature.

4. To serve, combine the vegetable mixture, shrimp, mint, and peanuts in a mixing bowl. Add two-thirds of the dressing and toss gently. Taste the salad and add more dressing, if desired.

Adapted from a recipe by CHEF NGUYEN DZOAN CAM VAN

the northeastern region of Thailand, referred to as Esarn or Isaah, is well known for its many fiery, savory, and utterly delicious salads such as *larb* and *goi*. In this refreshing recipe, the shrimp is blanched and then "cooked" in lime juice. You can serve this salad as is or, as with many other Thai salads, with cabbage or lettuce leaves for wrapping.

NORTHEASTERN THAI SHRIMP SALAD

GOI GOONG

SERVES 4

2 cups raw medium shrimp, chopped into 3 to 4 pieces each

6 tablespoons freshly squeezed lime juice

3 to 4 tablespoons fish sauce, or to taste

10 Thai bird chiles, thinly sliced

2 tablespoons finely pounded toasted rice

½ cup thinly sliced shallots

½ teaspoon sugar (optional)

½ cup cilantro leaves

½ cup mint

1. **Bring** a saucepan of water to a simmer over medium heat. Add the shrimp and lightly blanch, 15 to 30 seconds. Remove and run under cool running water to stop the cooking. Drain completely and transfer the shrimp to a bowl.

2. **Add** the lime juice, fish sauce, chiles, toasted rice, and shallots to the shrimp.

3. **Toss** gently; adjust the taste by adding more fish sauce or sugar, if using, as necessary.

4. **Combine** the salad with the cilantro and mint.

Adapted from a recipe by ASSISTANT PROFESSOR KOBKAEW NAIPINIJ

INDIA

An homage to the restaurant recognized for creating this dish, "Kwalitys" chickpeas are simple in presentation and full of flavor. The mango and pomegranate powders are used as souring agents so lemon juice will do as a substitute. Be careful of the cardamom pods when eating the chickpeas. This dish makes a great appetizer with Naans (page 206) or other breads, or as a vegetable side.

"KWALITYS" CHICKPEAS

SERVES 8

1½ tablespoons canola oil

½ teaspoon cumin seeds

¼ teaspoon black peppercorns

2 whole cloves

2 cardamom pods

2 dried red chiles

2 teaspoons minced ginger

2 curry leaves, torn into pieces (optional)

1 cup finely chopped red onions

2 fresh hot green chiles, slit

¾ teaspoon salt

1 teaspoon dried mango powder
or the juice of ½ lemon (3 tablespoons)

1 teaspoon dried pomegranate powder or the
juice of the other ½ lemon (3 tablespoons)

1 teaspoon toasted ground cumin

¼ teaspoon ground turmeric

½ teaspoon Garam Masala (page 220)

¼ teaspoon cayenne pepper

⅕ teaspoon black pepper

¾ cup water

3 cups canned chickpeas,
drained and rinsed

1. *Combine* the oil, cumin seeds, peppercorns, cloves, cardamom, and red chiles in a large saucepan and place over medium-high heat. Cook, stirring, until the cumin begins to brown, 1 to 2 minutes.

2. *Add* the ginger and curry leaves, if using, and cook, stirring, about 30 seconds, or until it looks crispy and brown. Add the onions, green chiles, and salt and cook on medium heat, stirring often, until the onions turn a uniformly dark brown color, 15 to 20 minutes. Keep a cup of water beside the stove as the onions cook. As the onions begin to stick to the bottom of the pan, add water, about 1 teaspoon at a time, and stir and scrape the bottom of the pan with the spoon to pull up the browned bits and keep the onions and spices from burning. Do this as often as necessary (5 or 6 times) until the onions are well browned.

3. *When* the onions are cooked, add the mango and pomegranate powders or lemon juice, as well as the toasted ground cumin, turmeric, and ¼ teaspoon of the Garam Masala. Cook, stirring, about 30 seconds.

4. *Stir* in the cayenne and black pepper. Immediately add the water and all but about ¼ cup of the chickpeas.

5. *Mash* the reserved chickpeas to a purée with the back of a fork and add them to the pan along with the remaining ¼ teaspoon Garam Masala. Bring to a simmer, stirring, and cook gently, partially covered, for 15 minutes. Do not overmix the chickpeas. Adjust the seasoning and serve hot.

Adapted from a recipe by SUVIR SARAN

Korea

in the Korean tradition of preparing vegetables with minimal handling, the spinach here is quickly blanched, then cut into bite-sized pieces and served cold or at room temperature. Tossed in a simple soy, garlic, and sesame dressing, this is a perfect accompaniment to other vegetable or meat dishes.

SPINACH SALAD
SHE GHUM CHI NAMUL

SERVES 8

4 bunches spinach, stems removed and washed

3 tablespoons light soy sauce

3 cloves garlic, peeled and minced

2 green onions, thinly sliced

2 teaspoons sugar

2 teaspoons dark sesame oil

1 tablespoon sesame seeds

1. *Bring* a large pot of salted water to a boil over high heat. Blanch the spinach until just tender, 1 to 2 minutes. Do this in batches if necessary. Rinse the spinach in cold water to stop the cooking.

2. *Drain* the spinach and squeeze out the excess water. Transfer to a cutting board.

3. *Cut* the spinach into thirds and set aside. Mix the remaining ingredients together in a small bowl. Add to the spinach and toss well.

Adapted from a recipe by THE CULINARY INSTITUTE OF AMERICA

Horenso no Ohitashi is a blanched spinach dish typically served as an appetizer in Japan. A small amount of mirin, a Japanese cooking wine similar to sake but with less alcohol, is added to sweeten the greens and balance the dashi and soy sauce. The spinach may be garnished with sesame seeds, dried bonito flakes, or crumbled nori, a form of dried seaweed. This is a refreshing way of highlighting the natural flavor of spinach.

SPINACH SALAD
HORENSO NO OHITASHI

SERVES 8

1 pound (450 g) spinach leaves
1¼ cups Dashi Stock (page 60)
2 tablespoons light soy sauce
1 tablespoon plus 1 teaspoon dark soy sauce
1 teaspoon mirin or sweet cooking wine

1. Rinse the spinach leaves thoroughly under cold tap water.

2. Have a large bowl of cold water at hand. Bring a large pot of salted water to a boil over high heat. Cook the spinach until wilted, 1 to 1½ minutes. Quickly drain the spinach and put it into the bowl of cold water to cool.

3. Drain the spinach and gently squeeze to remove any excess water. Cut the spinach into 1¼-inch (3-cm) pieces.

4. Transfer the spinach to a bowl and add the Dashi Stock, light and dark soy sauces, and mirin. Serve in individual small bowls.

Adapted from a recipe by YOSHIHIRO TAKAHASHI

Making Great Asian Salads

CUTTING AND SLICING

One of the key factors in making Asian salads is the way the vegetables are cut. For recipes that call for thinly shaved or sliced vegetables, it's especially important to use proper tools. While a sharp knife also works, a Japanese Benriner or a mandoline slicer does a much better job, creating uniform cuts with even thickness. In Asia, different tools are used to make different cuts such as a double-bladed knife for paper-thin slices and a vegetable peeler-type tool for juliennes or thin strips. The Japanese mandoline, which comes with different blades, is inexpensive and is a great tool to have on hand. It can take carrots, cucumbers, cabbage, and green papaya and turn them into slices and strips of any size and thickness. Soak these thinly shaved vegetables in cold water first to make them firm and feathery. Then drain completely before tossing into a salad.

If you prefer to use a knife, apply a gentle, slicing motion, especially with lettuces and leafy greens because they can bruise easily. Avoid big heavy knives and refrain from chopping because that will easily bruise the vegetables. A light, Japanese-style knife, commonly found in sushi restaurants, is great for vegetables. Except for lettuces and greens, which can be cut or torn into large pieces, most ingredients, including onions, benefit from being very thinly sliced. Small pieces absorb flavors better and quicker, and are easier to pick up with chopsticks or forks.

VINEGARS/SOURING AGENTS

The Asian pantry consists of many types of vinegar but aside from the stronger and darker ones used in Chinese braises and stews, a smooth, mild Japanese rice vinegar is a good all-purpose one to use for salads. Store open bottles in the refrigerator and use within six months or so. Like other condiments, a bottle of vinegar will gradually lose its flavor and become discolored if it sits for too long. For a simple salad of tossed greens or vegetables, a dressing made with rice vinegar, sesame oil, and sesame seeds is ideal because it's light enough to allow the natural flavors of vegetables to come through. For a refreshing flavor, wait to toss the salad until just before eating. For a more intense flavor, allow the tossed salad to sit for 20 minutes before serving.

LIME

Some of the most savory salads are from the Thai and Vietnamese kitchens. Boldly seasoned and highly tangy, they're made not only with lime juice but also the pulp and skin of the fruit. For a real authentic flavor, use a mortar and pestle to pound together the garlic, chiles, and sugar before adding fish sauce, lime, and any other ingredients called for. This technique bruises the chiles and garlic and releases their oils, thereby creating an intense base for the dressing. If possible, use key lime, which is more aromatic and smooth, and scrape the pulp into the dressing. This adds wonderful bursts of flavor.

TAMARIND

Tamarind is a fruit used to impart rounded, sour flavors to salads as well as curries and soups. With undertones of raisins and dried prunes, tamarind is available as blocks and as dried whole pods. To use the block, break off a piece and soak it in hot water. A good rule of thumb is to dilute 1 tablespoon of tamarind with ¼ cup of hot water. If you want more sourness, increase the tamarind. Allow the mixture to sit for 10 minutes, then push it through a sieve to strain. To use the whole pods, which are usually more ripe and sweet, remove the seeds and scrape the pulp into a bowl. Add some hot water to create a thick sauce and strain if necessary. The tamarind liquid is now ready for use. For a more intense flavor, use whole pods as opposed to blocks because they are not as sour and you can use more.

LEMONGRASS

A common and defining ingredient in Southeast Asian salads as well as curries and soups, lemongrass is used to impart a lovely citrusy flavor to food. When purchasing, look for fresh, juicy-looking stalks with fat bulbs. To use, peel and discard the first two to three outer layers as they tend to be quite woody and fibrous. Using only the tender bottom part of the bulb, cut into very thin slices, or mince them and add to salads. The upper stalks can be used to flavor soups and curries or to make teas.

KAFFIR LIME

Extremely floral and citrusy, kaffir lime is used extensively throughout Southeast Asia, especially in Thailand, to flavor and perfume salads, curries, and soups. It has thick, waxy leaves and freezes quite well. Kaffir lime can be easily grown in mild climates and the fresh leaves are becoming more common in the West at Asian and specialty markets. If fresh kaffir lime leaves are available, buy extra and keep some handy in the freezer. For that impromptu Thai curry, a small amount makes a big flavor impact. To use, remove the ribs from the center of the leaves. Stack, then roll them together, and cut into thin slivers, as in a French chiffonade. Sprinkle these on salads or curries. For a more rustic look, you can also tear the leaves in two or three pieces and add to the pot. The fruit of kaffir lime is not as valuable as it's quite dry. In Thailand, the zest is used in making curry pastes, and sometimes the whole fruit is floated in curries.

when working with tofu, it's important to remember that tofu holds up better if you first pan-sear or pan-fry it until a golden skin develops. Not only does this improve the texture but it helps the tofu absorb seasonings and sauces. In this recipe, use firm tofu, as any other type will not hold up to the slicing and baking required. Tofu can be paired with fresh seasonal vegetables, herbs, and spices to make a healthy meal.

GINGER TOFU WITH VEGETABLES

SERVES 4

1 pound (450 g) firm tofu

1 teaspoon salt, or as needed

¼ teaspoon ground white pepper, or as needed

2 eggs, beaten

1 cup all-purpose flour

1½ cups plus 1 tablespoon vegetable oil, or as needed

2 tablespoons julienned ginger

¼ cup julienned green onions

1 ounce (25 g) dried shiitake mushrooms, thinly sliced

1½ cups snow peas, cleaned

1 cup julienned carrots

3 cloves garlic, peeled and chopped

One ½-inch (1-cm) piece ginger, peeled and chopped

¼ bunch green onions, sliced

½ teaspoon sugar

1 tablespoon soy sauce

1½ teaspoons sesame oil

1. Slice the tofu into ¼-inch (6-mm) thick slices. Season with salt and white pepper. Dip the tofu in the beaten eggs and coat lightly with flour.

2. Heat 1½ cups of the oil in a medium saucepan over medium heat to 350°F (180°C). Add the tofu to the oil, in batches if necessary, and fry until evenly browned on both sides, 5 to 6 minutes. Remove the tofu from the oil and drain briefly on paper towels.

3. Cut the tofu pieces on the diagonal to form triangles. Place the tofu in an ovenproof dish and sprinkle with the ginger and green onions. Reserve warm until needed.

4. Rehydrate the dried mushrooms in 2 cups warm water until soft, about 15 minutes. Drain the mushrooms and pat dry.

5. Bring a large pot of salted water to a boil. Blanch the snow peas until just tender, 3 to 4 minutes. Drain and run under cool water to stop the cooking. Bring the water back up to a boil and blanch the carrots until just tender, 3 to 4 minutes. Pat the snow peas and carrots dry.

6. Heat the remaining tablespoon of oil in a large sauté pan or wok over high heat. Stir-fry the garlic, ginger, and green onions until the onions are wilted, about 30 seconds. Add the mushrooms, snow peas, and carrots and stir-fry until tender crisp, 2 to 3 minutes.

7. Remove the tofu from the baking dish and add to the pan. Toss with the vegetables and add the sugar, soy sauce, and sesame oil. Toss to coat with the sauce and serve.

Adapted from a recipe by THE CULINARY INSTITUTE OF AMERICA

Korea

in this simple Korean salad, the bean sprouts are briefly steamed before being tossed with garlic, green onions, and red pepper powder. The sesame seeds add crunch and a nutty flavor. For an authentic Korean meal, serve this with Spinach Salad (page 90) and marinated Daikon and Cucumber Salad (page 105).

MARINATED BEAN SPROUTS SALAD

SERVES 8

3 cups bean sprouts

2 teaspoons salt, or as needed

2 teaspoons red pepper powder, or as needed

2 tablespoons minced green onions

2 teaspoons minced garlic

2 teaspoons ground sesame seeds, or as needed

2 teaspoons sesame oil, or as needed

1. Wash the bean sprouts under running water. Put the bean sprouts into a medium saucepan, add 1 to 2 cups of water, and 1 teaspoon of salt. Turn the heat to medium.

2. Steam the bean spouts, covered, for 10 to 12 minutes or until they are just soft and look transparent. Drain the sprouts and rinse under cold water. Dry thoroughly.

3. Put the bean sprouts into a bowl and add the following ingredients in order: red pepper powder, green onions, garlic, and sesame seeds. Mix them well. Season the mixture with the remaining salt, sesame oil, and additional red pepper powder, if desired, and mix well.

Adapted from a recipe by ANGIE HEAJUNG

in Asia, the entire banana tree is used: the leaves are used for wrapping and the blossoms, fruits, and stems are all eaten. Besides the banana fruit, the blossom, which is burgundy on the outside and pale yellow in the center and has a delightful floral flavor, is most versatile, showing up in salads, soups, and stews. For the best flavor and texture, the blossom should be thinly sliced. Cabbage can be substituted.

BANANA BLOSSOM SALAD WITH CHICKEN
GOI BAP CHUOI GA

SERVES 8

1 tablespoon vegetable oil

1 pound (450 g) boneless skinless chicken breasts

2 banana blossoms (about 1 pound 5 ounces/600 g)

1 tablespoon lemon juice

½ cup Ginger-Lime Dipping Sauce (page 229), or as needed

1 cucumber, seeded and cut into thin strips

½ yellow onion, peeled and cut lengthwise into paper-thin slices

½ cup julienned pineapple

2 tablespoons thinly slivered ginger

2 cups *rau ram* or Asian basil leaves, cut in half and loosely packed

¼ cup sliced shallots, deep-fried until crispy

¼ cup roasted, chopped peanuts

1. Heat the oil in a medium sauté pan over medium heat. Sauté the chicken breasts until cooked through, 8 to 10 minutes. Cool the chicken until it can be easily handled and shred into bite-sized pieces. Set aside.

2. Peel the two or three tougher outer layers off of the banana blossoms and discard. Remove the bottom core. Using a Japanese mandolin or a sharp knife, slice the blossoms crosswise into 1/16-inch (1-mm) thick pieces. Shake to remove the seeds from the slices and place the slices in a bowl filled with cold water. Stir in the lemon juice and let soak for 15 minutes.

3. Remove the sliced blossoms from the water and let drain in a colander. Leave any seeds and small pieces that have sunk to the bottom of the bowl. Pat the blossoms dry with paper towels and set aside.

4. Place the chicken in a mixing bowl and add half the Ginger-Lime Dipping Sauce. Let marinate for 5 minutes then add the banana blossoms, cucumber, onion, pineapple, ginger, *rau ram*, fried shallots, half of the peanuts, and the remaining Ginger-Lime Dipping Sauce. Toss gently, then transfer to a serving plate. Garnish with the remaining peanuts and serve.

Adapted from a recipe by CHEF HOANG TRANG NGUYEN *and* NGOC TINH PHAM

JAPAN

this is an excellent way to serve eggplant in the summer and autumn. The eggplant is cooked directly on a gas flame until the outside is smoky and the flesh is tender and creamy. This dish is simple, but it does require flavorful eggplants, preferably fresh from your local farmer's market.

GRILLED EGGPLANT WITH YUZU-KOSHO DRESSING

SERVES 8

4 medium eggplants
(each 5 to 6 ounces/150 to 175 g)
⅔ cup ponzu sauce
4 teaspoons vegetable oil
2 teaspoons *yuzu kosho* (salt-cured green chile spiced yuzu paste), or as needed
¼ cup green onion rings or chopped cilantro

1. Remove the frill around the stem of each eggplant and then make a very shallow cut through the skin where the frill was located. Make 4 to 5 more very shallow cuts along the length of the eggplant to make peeling the eggplant easier. Place the eggplant on a steel grill and place directly over a gas flame.

2. Cook the eggplant over medium heat, rotating from time to time, until the whole surface is lightly charred and the flesh is cooked through and tender (poke with a small knife to check).

3. Transfer the eggplant to the sink and peel it—but do not rinse with water. Cut each eggplant in half lengthwise, then cut into thirds lengthwise. Now cut the eggplant strips into thirds crosswise. Mound up equal amounts of eggplant in 8 small bowls.

4. Whisk the ponzu sauce, vegetable oil, and *yuzu kosho* to taste in a bowl. Spoon the dressing over the eggplant. Garnish the top of the eggplant with the green onion rings or cilantro before serving.

From The Sushi Experience *by* HIROKO SHIMBO, *copyright © 2006 by Hiroko Shimbo. Used by permission of Alfred A. Knopf, a division of Random House, Inc.*

in this Thai classic, the eggplant is roasted over an open flame until it's soft but still intact. It is then peeled and combined with cooked shrimp and pork. But it's the dressing—the spicy, tart, and salty flavors that come from both fish sauce and dried shrimp—that pulls the dish together. Regular Japanese or Chinese eggplant would work fine here. You can also sauté the eggplant, but it's very hard to beat the grilled flavor.

THAI GRILLED EGGPLANT SALAD

YUM MAKUA YAO

SERVES 8

SAUCE
10 Thai bird chiles, stemmed and seeded, or to taste
¼ cup fish sauce
¼ cup lime juice
¼ cup sugar

SALAD
1½ tablespoons vegetable oil
½ teaspoon salt
7 ounces (200 g) minced pork loin
¼ cup water
10 shrimp (16/20 count), peeled and deveined
4 Thai eggplants (green and long)
1 shallot, thinly sliced
6 tablespoons finely ground dried shrimp
½ cup chopped cilantro leaves

1. *P*reheat the grill to high.

2. *F*or the sauce: Pound the chiles in a mortar to a fine paste. Blend all of the ingredients together; check the seasoning and adjust accordingly. Alternatively, grind the chiles in a food processor until fine, then add the remaining sauce ingredients.

3. *H*eat a large sauté pan over high heat and add the oil. Sprinkle the salt over the pork and add it to the pan. Sauté the pork until caramelized, stirring frequently with a wooden spoon, about 3 minutes. Remove the pork from the pan. Discard the oil from the pan and add the water. Scrape the brown bits from the bottom of the pan and reduce the liquid until it's dark brown and about 2 tablespoons. Add to the cooling pork, cover, and set aside.

4. *B*ring a medium saucepan of water to a simmer and place a steamer basket inside. Add the shrimp to the basket and steam until cooked through, 3 to 4 minutes. Remove the shrimp from the pan and cool to room temperature.

5. *G*rill the eggplant until charred on all sides, 4 to 5 minutes. Clean off the burnt (dark) skin.

6. *C*ut the grilled, soft eggplant into ½-inch (1-cm) slices and place on the plate. Garnish the slices with the shallot, pork, shrimp, and dried shrimp.

7. *T*op with the sauce and sprinkle the cilantro on top. Serve immediately.

Adapted from a recipe by ASSISTANT PROFESSOR KOBKAEW NAIPINIJ

Tofu

Made from soybeans—perhaps the most important legume in all of Asia—tofu and tofu-related foods have long been regarded as essential foods, providing not only a precious and inexpensive source of protein and calcium but also giving balance and harmony to a meal because of its *yin*, or cooling qualities.

The earliest forms of tofu were made and eaten at Buddhist temples and over time became a staple in vegetarian cooking. It's been used to make every dish imaginable. From simple, straightforward methods of cubing and adding it to food, or crumbling it and using it in fillings and stuffings, tofu is very versatile and can be used instead of meat in any recipe. It's

a key ingredient in "mock meat" dishes, a tradition of using tofu and tofu-related products to resemble meat or fish.

In Asia, tofu is still made much like it was centuries ago. The soybeans are soaked overnight before they're mashed and the extracted liquid is strained and boiled. When a coagulant such as *nigari* (calcium chloride) is added, the soymilk curdles. The curds are transferred to a mold where they are drained and pressed into blocks or loaves. Freshly made tofu tastes naturally sweet, nutty, and creamy. In Asia, there are many variations made from a similar process, including pressed tofu, seasoned tofu, tofu skin (also called dried bean curd skin), and fermented tofu.

In the West, however, the most common is fresh tofu, which is packed in water in plastic tubs and sold in the produce section of supermarkets. It's available in three basic textures: soft, medium, and firm. The soft variety is best for soups, steamed dishes, and salads while the medium and firm tofu are suitable for stir-frying, braising, and stuffing. A fourth but not as popular is silken tofu, which is enjoyed as a dessert, often served with a light ginger-flavored syrup.

By itself, tofu can be delicate tasting but when combined with sauces, aromatics, and spices, it's completely flavorful.

In the Japanese kitchen, tofu is often drained and pressed to remove excess water so that the flavor is more concentrated and pronounced. This can be easily done by sandwiching blocks of tofu between two plates and propping them at an angle inside a larger bowl. In China and other parts of Asia, however, tofu is used as is or it's deep-fried or pan-seared before being added to stir-fries, stews, or soups. This technique creates a slightly chewy skin that helps the tofu better absorb flavors and keep its shape during cooking.

Tofu is highly perishable so once you open a package it's best to use the whole piece right away. If you absolutely need to hold it for a day or so, rinse the tofu, then transfer it to a clean container with a tightly fitted lid. Add some fresh cold water to cover and store in the coldest part of your refrigerator. To pre-cook tofu, drain it and cut it into manageable chunks. Heat about 2 or 3 tablespoons of vegetable oil in a nonstick frying pan over moderate heat. Carefully add the tofu pieces and brown on two sides until golden, 5 to 7 minutes total. Drain on paper towels. The tofu is now ready for the next step in cooking.

this refreshing cucumber salad is usually served with satays but it's great with any grilled food, even rice dishes. Let the cucumbers marinate for at least 15 minutes before eating. For a full satay experience, add one or two of these cucumbers to a skewer of satay. Roll the skewer in peanut sauce, then pop the whole thing in your mouth. You will be rewarded with a burst of sweet, sour, spicy, and salty flavors.

THAI CUCUMBER SALAD
AR-JARD

SERVES 4

4 pickling cucumbers or 1 hothouse cucumber
2 shallots, thinly sliced
1 fresh chile, thinly sliced
⅓ cup vinegar
⅓ cup sugar
½ teaspoon salt
Cilantro sprigs as garnish

1. Cut the cucumbers in half lengthwise and then cut crosswise into thin slices. Place the sliced cucumbers in a bowl and add the shallots and chile.

2. Bring the vinegar, sugar, and salt to a boil over medium heat in a small saucepan and stir until the sugar dissolves. When the mixture comes to a boil, reduce the heat and simmer for 2 to 3 minutes. Remove the pan from the heat and let cool to room temperature.

3. Toss the cucumber mixture with the dressing and garnish with the cilantro sprigs.

Adapted from a recipe by CHAI SIRIYARN

KOREA

this crisp salad gets its refreshing flavors from daikon, cucumber, and carrots. Julienned and lightly seasoned, the vegetables provide a wonderful contrast to other foods, especially grilled meats. If you like a more intense flavor, increase the seasonings and chili powder.

DAIKON AND CUCUMBER SALAD

MU CHAE

SERVES 8

1 pound (450 g) daikon, peeled and julienned
1 European cucumber, peeled and julienned
1 carrot, peeled and julienned
1 teaspoon kosher or sea salt, or as needed
¼ cup light rice vinegar
2 tablespoons sugar
1 teaspoon Korean red pepper powder

1. *Toss* the daikon, cucumber, and carrot with the salt and set aside until the daikon is pliable, about 30 minutes.

2. *Gently* squeeze out any excess water from the mixture and transfer to another bowl.

3. *Add* the remaining ingredients and mix well. Cover and refrigerate until chilled. Taste the salad and adjust the seasoning with salt and red pepper powder.

Adapted from a recipe by THE CULINARY INSTITUTE OF AMERICA

this Japanese vegetable dish gets its balanced flavor from toasted walnuts and the sweetness of mirin and miso. While the recipe calls for green beans, vegetables such as spinach, broccoli, or asparagus may be substituted. *Saikyo miso* is made with more rice and less soybeans than regular miso and has a short fermentation period. It is pale yellow with a distinctive sweet flavor and is very complementary to fish and vegetables.

GREEN BEANS WITH WALNUT-MISO DRESSING

SERVES 4

7 ounces (200 g) green beans, stemmed
½ cup walnuts
1 tablespoon *saikyo miso* (sweet wine miso)
1 tablespoon mirin or sweet cooking wine
2 teaspoons *shoyu* (soy sauce)
1 teaspoon sugar
2 to 3 tablespoons Dashi Stock (page 60)
Salt, as needed

1. *In* a large pot of salted boiling water, parboil the beans for 2 minutes. Drain them and spread them to cool in a flat-bottomed colander.

2. *Heat* a medium sauté pan over low to medium heat, add the walnuts, and toast them until they are heated through, about 2 minutes. Reserve $1/5$ of the walnuts, and transfer the rest to a *suribachi*, a mortar and pestle, or a food processor. Grind the walnuts until they are smooth and oily-looking.

3. *One* at a time, add the miso, mirin, shoyu, sugar, and 2 tablespoons Dashi Stock and grind the mixture until it is smooth. The texture should be like that of hummus. If the mixture is too thick, loosen it with another tablespoon of Dashi Stock.

4. *Season* the dressing with a little salt. The dressing can be made a day ahead and stored in the refrigerator, covered.

5. *Cut* the reserved walnuts into small pieces. Immediately before serving, toss the beans with the dressing. Serve the salad garnished with the walnut pieces.

Excerpted from The Japanese Kitchen *by* HIROKO SHIMBO, © 2000. *Used by permission of The Harvard Common Press.*

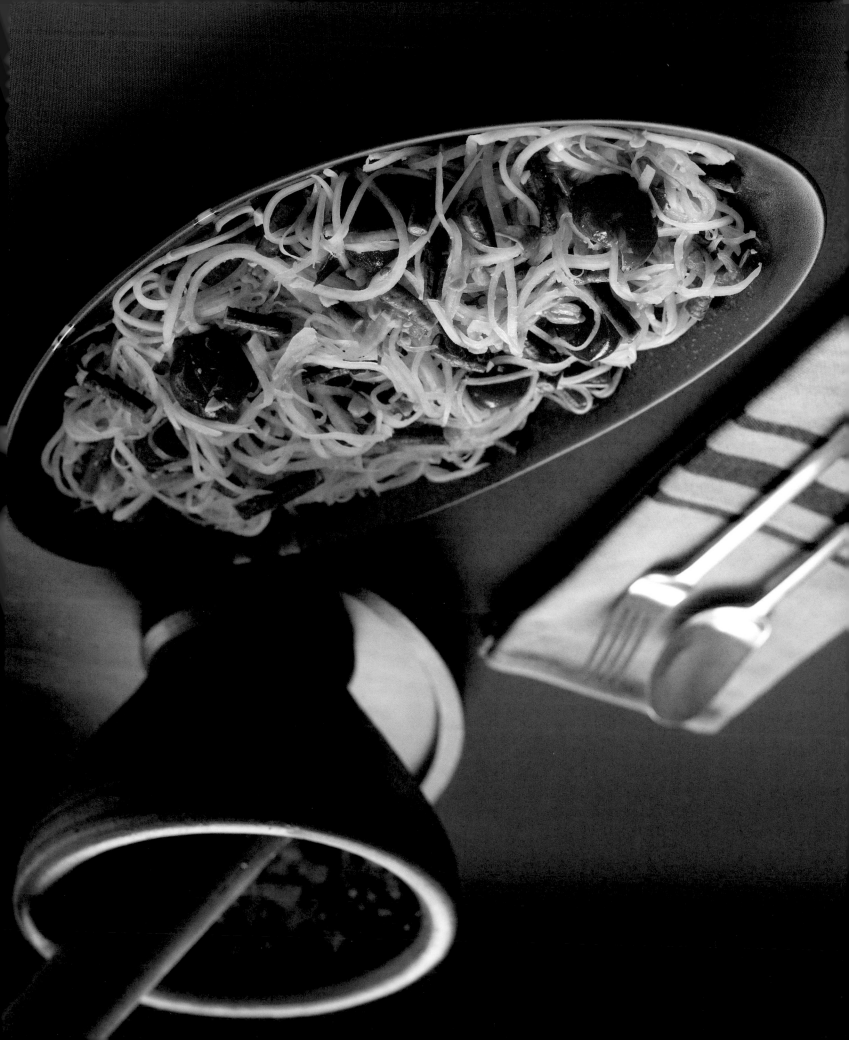

som tam **is eaten throughout Thailand** as a snack or part of a meal. The unique flavors come from the gentle mashing of green papaya with fish sauce, chiles, and dried shrimp. This classic salad can be eaten alone with cabbage leaves as a scoop, or with sticky rice. Make the salad in a mortar and pestle, in batches, as directed here, or prepare the dressing first and combine it with the remaining ingredients.

GREEN PAPAYA SALAD
SOM TAM

SERVES 8 TO 12

½ cup tamarind pulp

1 ½ cups warm water

8 small cloves garlic, thinly sliced

8 Thai bird chiles

1 pound (450 g) long beans,
cut into 1-inch (2.5-cm) pieces

½ cup roasted, chopped peanuts

½ cup palm sugar

½ cup fish sauce, or as needed

½ cup lime juice, or as needed

1 green papaya, peeled and shredded
(1 quart/liter)

24 cherry tomatoes (about 2 cups)

3 tablespoons dried shrimp,
washed with warm water

1. *Dissolve* the tamarind pulp in the warm water. Strain the resulting pulp, discard the seeds, and reserve until needed.

2. *Using* a large, deep pestle and mortar, pound the garlic and chiles into a paste. Add the long beans and roasted peanuts and pound roughly together. Add the palm sugar, fish sauce, lime juice, and tamarind and mix until the sugar has dissolved.

3. *Add* the papaya, cherry tomatoes, and dried shrimp and pound lightly, using a spoon to scrape down the sides, turn, and mix well.

4. *Taste* the sauce on the bottom of the mortar and adjust the seasoning if necessary. It should be a balance of sweet and sour, with a hot and salty taste.

Adapted from a recipe by BANSANI NAWISAMPHAN

KOREA

of the many varieties of *kimchi*, baechoo is one of the most common. Generally salty and very spicy, it is traditionally made by stuffing napa cabbage or Chinese cabbage leaves with a filling (the ingredients vary). This version is usually prepared in the fall. *Kimchi* can be used as an ingredient in a variety of dishes, served as *mit banchan,* or as a vegetable side dish.

BAECHOO KIMCHI

SERVES 16

SOAKED CABBAGE
1 napa cabbage (about 2 pounds/900 g)
1 cup salt
2 cups cold water

STUFFING
1 tablespoon minced garlic
1½ teaspoons minced ginger
1 cup apple juice
¼ cup fish sauce
¼ cup salt
1 cup Korean red pepper powder
1 tablespoon toasted sesame seeds
¼ cup sugar
2 cups shredded Korean white radishes
2 cups peeled and shredded Asian pears
2 cups horseradish leaves, cut into
2-inch (5-cm) wide strips (optional)
3 green onions, cut into 2- to 3-inch
(5- to 7.5-cm) lengths

1. **For the soaked cabbage:** Cut the cabbage in half lengthwise. Mix ½ cup of the salt in the cold water in a large bowl. Dip each cabbage half in the salt water and place in another bowl.

2. **Sprinkle** the remaining ½ cup of salt on the cabbage halves and stack the cabbage halves on top of each other, cut side up. Cover and let stand for 6 hours at room temperature. The cabbage should be soft and pliable.

3. **Rinse** the cabbage under cold running water twice to remove the excess salt. Stack the rinsed cabbage halves, cut side down, in a large strainer and let them drain for 30 minutes. Gently squeeze out any remaining excess liquid.

4. **For the stuffing:** Mix the garlic, ginger, apple juice, fish sauce, salt, red pepper powder, sesame seeds, and sugar in a bowl and allow the flavors to blend for 30 minutes.

5. **Add** the radishes, pears, horseradish leaves (if using), and green onions to the mixture and mix thoroughly. Allow the flavors to blend for 30 minutes.

6. **Place** each cabbage half on a cutting board with the cut side facing up. Starting with the topmost leaf, pull each leaf back and stuff ½ to ¾ cup of the stuffing on the leaf behind it. Concentrate the seasonings at the root of the leaf and thin out toward the top.

7. **After** stuffing each half, fold the tops of the cabbage leaves toward the cut sides to keep the seasonings from falling out. The cut side of the cabbage should be encased by the outer leaves of the cabbage.

8. **Stack** the cabbage halves in a glass container cut side up. Pour the leftover stuffing on top. Press the cabbage down with a wooden spoon and cover. Let stand for 24 hours at room temperature.

9. **Store** in a cool place or refrigerate until needed. Place the cut *kimchi* in a glass bowl and serve as a side dish.

Adapted from a recipe by MYUNG SOOK LEE

in this creative vegetarian dish, chef Masaharu Morimoto of the acclaimed Morimoto restaurants uses sliced ribbons of daikon to imitate fettuccine noodles. For the daikon, use a good, sharp vegetable peeler and peel down the length of the radish. The spicy, peppery taste of the daikon radish is a flavorful accompaniment to the tomato basil sauce.

DAIKON "FETTUCCINE" WITH TOMATO BASIL SAUCE

SERVES 4

1 pound (450 g) daikon
One 14½-ounce (410-g) can plum tomatoes
3 tablespoons extra virgin olive oil
1 small onion, finely chopped
2 cloves garlic, minced
1½ to 2 teaspoons sugar, depending on the ripeness of the tomatoes
1 teaspoon salt, or as needed
1 tablespoon chopped fresh basil
½ teaspoon salt
Pinch of freshly ground black pepper, or as needed

1. With a swivel-blade vegetable peeler, remove the outer skin of the daikon and discard.

2. Continue to peel down the length of the vegetable, removing the daikon in long, narrow ribbons, which look like noodles. Soak the "fettuccine" in a bowl of cold salted water for 15 to 20 minutes.

3. Meanwhile, make the tomato basil sauce. Drain the canned tomatoes, reserving half of the juice. Squeeze the tomatoes through your fingers to mash them, and combine with the juice. There should be about 2 cups.

4. In a heavy medium saucepan, heat the oil over medium-high heat. Add the onion and garlic and sauté until softened but not browned, about 3 minutes. Add the tomatoes and their reserved juice, the sugar, and salt. Boil vigorously, stirring often, until the sauce is thick, 10 to 15 minutes. Stir in the basil and season with salt and pepper.

5. Drain the "noodles" and dry them on a kitchen towel. Add to the sauce and toss gently over medium heat, taking care not to break the daikon fettuccine. Cook until just heated through, about 1 minute. Divide among individual plates, teasing the fettuccine into mounds. Serve immediately.

a table salad is a prerequisite at the Vietnamese table especially if spring rolls, grilled meats, or Saigon crepes are served. Any of the leaf lettuces work, including red or green, and the tender Asian mustard variety available at Asian markets. The latter has a slight peppery bitter flavor and is especially complementary to grilled meats. You can also dress up this salad with thinly sliced pineapple, starfruit, or green banana.

TABLE SALAD
RAU SONG

SERVES 8

½ head red or green leaf lettuce, leaves separated, washed and drained

1 cucumber, thinly sliced

2 cups bean sprouts

5 to 6 mint sprigs

5 to 6 Asian basil sprigs

5 to 6 *rau ram* sprigs, if available

5 to 6 green perilla sprigs, if available

1. Arrange the lettuce leaves in an attractive manner on one side of a large platter.

2. Place the cucumber, bean sprouts, and herbs on the other side. Place the platter in the center of the table and serve with foods that need to be wrapped.

Adapted from a recipe by MAI PHAM

Vietnam

one of the most valuable attributes of tofu is its ability to absorb flavors and sauces. This recipe, which is inspired by a tofu dish prepared at many temples in Vietnam, calls for medium-firm tofu. Drain it completely and pat it dry before using to allow the spices to adhere to the surface. This is the vegetarian version of the classic Vietnamese stir-fry that builds on the holy trinity of garlic, chiles, and lemongrass.

SPICY LEMONGRASS TOFU
TAU HU XA OT

SERVES 4

¼ cup finely chopped lemongrass stalks, white parts only

3 tablespoons soy sauce

4 teaspoons chopped Thai bird chiles

1 teaspoon dried chili flakes

2 teaspoons ground turmeric

4 teaspoons sugar

1 teaspoon salt

1 pound 8 ounces (650 g) medium-firm tofu, drained and patted dry, cut into ¾-inch (18-mm) cubes

6 tablespoons vegetable oil

1 yellow onion, thinly sliced lengthwise

¼ cup minced shallots

2 teaspoons minced garlic

1 cup Asian basil leaves

½ cup roasted, chopped peanuts

1. Combine the lemongrass, soy sauce, chiles, dried chili flakes, turmeric, sugar, and salt in a mixing bowl. Add the tofu cubes and turn so they're evenly coated. Marinate for 30 minutes.

2. Heat 3 tablespoons of the oil in a large nonstick frying pan over medium heat until hot. Carefully add the tofu cubes (be careful as the oil may splatter) and let them brown without disturbing until they're golden around the edges, 3 to 4 minutes. This may need to be done in batches. Using a spatula, turn the tofu over just once and brown the other side, about 3 minutes. When done, transfer the tofu to a plate and keep warm. Discard the oil, wipe the pan clean, and place the pan back on the stove.

3. Heat the remaining oil in the nonstick pan over moderate heat. Add the onion, and stir until translucent, about 2 minutes. Add the shallots and garlic and stir another 30 seconds. Add the tofu and cook, carefully stirring once or twice (so the tofu doesn't break) until thoroughly hot. Add the Asian basil and half of the peanuts.

4. Remove from the heat and transfer to a serving plate. Garnish with the remaining peanuts and serve.

Adapted from a recipe by MAI PHAM

CHAPTER FOUR

Meats

BIG, BOLD FLAVORS

At first it seems a bit odd to walk into a restaurant that looks more like a kitchen than a dining room. In this packed barbecue eatery in Seoul, every table is equipped with an open grill and a ventilation system. It's noisy and smoky but, for the customers, it's an evening of celebration. Most are feasting on *galbi*, a local favorite of grilled short ribs, and *bulgogi*, a barbecued beef dish eaten with an array of accompaniments, including lettuce, rice, *kimchi*, and *mit banchan*.

*T*o eat, one takes a piece of meat right off the sizzling grill and enjoys it with rice or wraps it with lettuce and dips it in a fermented bean sauce. While pork and chicken are also offered, most diners are happy savoring beef, either flipping it over the grill or pulling it from steaming hot pots. The Koreans indeed have a special affinity for beef, perhaps in large part because of their historical ties to the cattle-grazing Mongul and Manchu cultures. They consume it more than other Asians, but the amount they eat is still relatively small compared to their overall diet of seafood, rice, and vegetables. A prized and fairly expensive protein, beef is eaten in small amounts and often reserved for holidays and special occasions. This also holds true for much of Asia. In neighboring Japan, the widely acclaimed kobe beef, as well as pork and other meats, is eaten but not nearly as much as fish and seafood.

In China and Southeast Asia, if you are serving meat, it is usually pork, the most common animal protein, followed by chicken, duck, and other fowl. The pig is a highly revered animal. Anyone born in the year of the pig is believed to be blessed with good luck. Many families, especially those in rural areas, can easily earn a living by raising a pig or two in the backyard since they require little space and can eat practically anything. Pork is well suited to all methods of cooking from grilling, roasting,

and stir-frying to stewing and boiling, as well as different forms of curing, including hams, sausages, patés, and dried "cotton" pork, in which the meat is cooked until dried, then pounded, fluffed, and air-dried.

In other parts of Asia, religion and culture are deeply connected with the choices of meat eaten and not eaten. In India, where more than half of the population is vegetarian, meals are generally built around legumes, vegetables, and breads or rice. The Muslim community, both in India and throughout Asia, abstains from pork but enjoys goat and lamb.

No matter which protein you end up cooking, the recipe choices are endless. One of the best ways to cook meat and poultry is in curries, from the regional Indian styles of preparation to the different variations of Thai curries. They're great comfort food, laced with spices and herbs, and are delicious with rice or bread. A simple salad or a chutney would make a great meal, especially for the cooler days. For grilled foods, you can't go wrong with Korean barbecues such as *galbi* or *bulgogi*, or Vietnamese lemongrass pork, especially if they're served in the true spirit of the dish with all the fanfare of accompanying vegetables, herbs, and condiments.

Another note about the traditional Asian way with meat: Cook the meat with big, bold flavors but treat them more like precious foods, perhaps eating slightly less.

yakitori, a favorite Japanese snack or appetizer, translates loosely to "grilled bird." It usually includes some form of grilled skewered chicken. In this modern version, chef Mikuni expands beyond chicken to include duck and quail. The meat of the three birds is sautéed with mushrooms and ultimately plated and served with a slightly thickened, savory sauce.

YAKITORI OF DUCK, YOUNG CHICKEN, AND QUAIL
KAMO TO WAKADORI TO TSUGUMI NO YAKITORI

SERVES 8

½ cup butter

1 pound 8 ounces (675 g) assorted mushrooms (such as shiitake, oyster, and cremini), cut into ¼-inch (6-mm) thick slices

3 tablespoons plus 1 teaspoon salt

½ teaspoon freshly ground black pepper

¾ cup finely diced onions

⅓ cup finely dice carrots

½ cup finely diced cucumbers

1 teaspoon minced garlic

2 tablespoons minced shallots

2 tablespoons sugar

½ cup plus 2 tablespoons white wine vinegar

2 cups chicken stock

¾ cup plus 1 tablespoon commercial *fond de veau*

2 tablespoons soy sauce

1 duckling (about 3 pounds/1.4 kg)

1 young chicken (about 3 pounds/1.4 kg)

4 semi-boneless quail (about 4 ounces/115 g each), cut in half

¼ cup vegetable oil

16 lemongrass leaves as garnish (optional)

1. *Heat* 2 tablespoons of the butter in a large sauté pan over high heat. Add one-third of the mushrooms and sauté for 1½ minutes, or until they look wilted and caramelized. Season the mushrooms with 1 tablespoon salt and 2 pinches of pepper while the mushrooms are cooking. Repeat with the remaining mushrooms in two batches.

2. *Soak* the onions, carrots, and cucumbers in a bowl of cold water for 15 minutes to make them crispy. Drain the vegetables and refrigerate until needed.

3. *Heat* a medium saucepan over high heat and add the remaining butter. When it is hot, add the garlic, shallots, and sugar and cook until they are light golden and release a slightly caramelized aroma, about 3 minutes. Add the vinegar and cook until the mixture is slightly thickened, about 2 minutes.

4. *Add* the chicken stock and *fond de veau* and cook until the mixture is reduced to ⅓ of the original volume, 10 to 15 minutes. Add the soy sauce, 1 teaspoon salt, and 1 pinch of black pepper to taste. Keep the sauce warm.

5. *Separate* the duck and chicken into 2 legs, 2 thighs, and cut each breast into 2 pieces. Each of the pieces should weigh about 2 ounces (50 g).

6. *Season* the duck, chicken, and quail with 2 tablespoons salt and ¼ teaspoon pepper. Heat a large sauté pan over medium-high heat and add the oil. Sauté the meat until they are almost cooked through, about 7 minutes for the duck pieces, 12 to 13 for the chicken, and 6 to 8 for the quail. This may need to be done in batches, depending on the size of the pan. Whatever size the pan, be careful not to crowd it or the meat will not achieve a uniform deep brown.

7. *Rest* the meat for 5 minutes before serving.

8. *Arrange* one piece of the duck, chicken, and quail and 3 heaping tablespoons of the sautéed mushrooms on each of 8 plates. Sprinkle 1 tablespoon of the vegetables on top of each plate. Pour about 3 tablespoons of the sauce over the meat. Garnish the top of each plate with 2 lemongrass leaves, if using.

Adapted from a recipe by KIYOMI MIKUNI

KOREA

what makes this dish particularly refreshing and yet savory is the grilled meat next to the rice with a dab of *ssamjang,* or Korean chili bean paste. For this recipe, it's best to grill or cook the beef just before eating, or even at the table, and place the lettuce leaves and chili paste on the table for diners to assemble and eat out of hand. It's a wonderful dish for outdoor cooking and dining.

KOREAN LETTUCE WRAP WITH SPICY BEEF
BULGOGI SSAMBAP

SERVES 8

MARINADE
½ cup soy sauce
¼ cup sugar
2 cups Korean pear purée
2 tablespoons chopped garlic
½ cup chopped green onions
2 tablespoons sesame oil
2 teaspoons black pepper

2 onions, peeled and thinly sliced
2 carrots, peeled and thinly sliced
2 bunches green onions, white and light green parts only, thinly sliced
2 pounds (900 g) beef sirloin, thinly sliced
2 tablespoons vegetable oil
1 head green leaf lettuce, separated into leaves
1 quart (1 liter) steamed white rice
3 tablespoons Spicy Bean Paste (*ssamjang*) (page 233)

1. *For the marinade:* In a large bowl, mix all of the ingredients for the marinade.

2. *Toss* the onions, carrots, green onions, and beef with the marinade. Marinate for 30 minutes before cooking.

3. *Heat* the vegetable oil in a large sauté pan over medium-high heat. Pan-fry the marinated meat and vegetables until cooked through, about 5 minutes. This may need to be done in batches. Do not overcrowd the pan.

4. *Place* a leaf of lettuce or other vegetable in the palm of your hand. Add enough steamed rice, beef, and Spicy Bean Paste to fill the lettuce leaf, but can still be eaten in 1 to 2 bites. Roll up the lettuce leaves and eat.

Adapted from a recipe by MYUNG SOOK LEE

INDIA

this comfort dish features chicken simmered in a luscious sauce of almond, cream, and Indian spices. Before simmering the chicken, prepare an aromatic base with whole spices and ghee, a form of clarified butter used frequently in Indian cooking. (If you like, you can substitute vegetable oil.) When blending the almonds and cream for the sauce, add some dried red chiles for an element of heat.

ALMOND CREAM CHICKEN

SERVES 8

8 chicken thighs
3 tablespoons ghee or vegetable oil
3 to 5 dried red chiles
Two 2-inch (5-cm) long cinnamon or cassia sticks
6 cloves
4 cardamom pods
1 large onion, finely sliced
2 teaspoons finely minced ginger
2 teaspoons finely minced garlic paste
2 teaspoons salt, or as needed
½ cup blanched almonds
½ cup heavy cream

1. *H*eat a large, heavy sauté pan over medium-high heat. Sear the chicken until the pieces are browned and have rendered their excess fat, 6 to 8 minutes. Set aside.

2. *In* a Dutch oven or similar pan, heat the ghee or oil over medium-low heat. Add the whole spices and let them sizzle, about 1 minute. Add the onion and raise the heat to medium. Cook until it has softened and turned brown, 10 to 12 minutes.

3. *A*dd the ginger and garlic and stir for about a minute. Add the browned chicken thighs. Gently toss the chicken with the aromatics and onion, adding a splash of water if the thighs start to stick.

4. *P*our in enough water to barely cover the chicken (about 3 cups). Add the salt. Bring to a boil over medium-high heat. Reduce the heat, cover, and simmer until the chicken is just tender, 20 to 25 minutes. Remove the chicken from the pan and set it aside while you make the sauce.

5. *P*ut the almonds, cream, and about 1 cup of the cooking liquid into a blender or food processor. Be sure that the whole spices are left in the pan. If you want a piquant effect, you can add the whole red chiles to the food processor. Process to a creamy consistency. Scrape the mixture into the cooking liquid still in the pan and whisk until well combined. The sauce should be fairly thick and will thicken further as it stands.

6. *R*eturn the chicken to the pan. Adjust the seasoning with salt.

7. *W*hen you are just about to serve, bring the chicken to a simmer over very low heat so that the sauce doesn't stick to the bottom of the pan and burn. Alternatively, you can rewarm the chicken in the oven. To do so, place the chicken in a baking dish in a single layer and pour the sauce over it. Cover the dish with a loose tent of aluminum foil and bake in a 350°F (180°C) oven for about 30 minutes. Taste the sauce again and adjust the seasoning with salt, then serve.

Excerpted from My Bombay Kitchen *by* NILOUFER ICHAPORIA KING, © 2007. *The Regents of the University of California. Published by The University of California Press.*

a signature dish at New York's Kittichai Restaurant, these short ribs set the stage for a dressing that features 17 different Thai herbs and aromatics. The ingredients list may appear daunting but this isn't a difficult dish to make. The low-temperature slow roasting and the myriad of spices make this a most hearty and memorable dish. You can braise the short ribs the day before, then reheat them when you're ready to serve.

SIMMERED SHORT RIBS WITH THAI SPICE DRESSING

SERVES 8

THAI SPICE DRESSING

5 tablespoons shallots, roasted and minced
1 cup short-grain rice, ground and roasted
3 tablespoons minced garlic
3 tablespoons minced kaffir lime leaves
3 tablespoons minced lemongrass
2 tablespoons ground cumin
1 tablespoon ground turmeric
5 tablespoons curry powder
5 tablespoons ground coriander seeds
5 tablespoons ground fennel seeds
1 tablespoon smoked paprika
3 tablespoons ground dried oregano
3 tablespoons ground dried thyme
2 tablespoons ground red chile flakes
¼ cup fish sauce, or as needed
1 cup fresh lime juice
1 cup canola oil
5 tablespoons finely chopped mint
5 tablespoons finely chopped cilantro
5 tablespoons thinly sliced shallots

2 pounds (900 g) boneless beef short ribs
3 quarts (3 liters) pineapple juice
2 teaspoons salt, or as needed
½ teaspoon ground black pepper, or as needed
½ cup canola oil
6 lemongrass stalks, smashed
28 fresh kaffir lime leaves
1½ small galangal knobs, smashed
1 gallon (3.75 liters) chicken or white beef stock

1. *For the Thai Spice Dressing:* Combine all of the ingredients in a large bowl using a wooden spoon. If the dressing is too thick, add some water or stock until it is a workable consistency. Refrigerate until needed.

2. *Marinate* the short ribs in the pineapple juice for 1 hour to help tenderize the meat and remove the impurities. Remove the meat from the juice and pat dry.

3. *Preheat* the oven to 350°F (180°C).

4. *Heat* a large roasting pan on the stove over medium-high heat. Season the beef with salt and pepper. Pour the canola oil into the roasting pan. Sear the beef in the pan until golden brown, about 4 minutes per side. This may need to be done in batches.

5. *Remove* the beef from the heat and let rest. Discard the excess oil from the pan.

6. *Add* the beef back to the roasting pan along with the lemongrass, kaffir lime leaves, and galangal. Add enough stock to cover the beef. Bring to a boil on the stove top. Remove from the heat and cover with foil. Place the roasting pan in the oven and braise for 3 hours or until the ribs are fork tender.

7. *Remove* the beef from the roasting pan and let cool to room temperature. Refrigerate the beef and the braising liquid separately for at least 5 hours.

8. *Cut* the beef into bite-sized pieces and reheat in the braising liquid over medium heat. Remove the beef from the liquid. Dress the beef with enough Thai Spice Dressing to coat before serving.

Adapted from a recipe by IAN CHALERMKITTICHAI

Stir-Frying

Stir-frying is a great technique because the high heat cooks food quickly and seals in the natural flavors. It's not a hard technique to learn as long as you keep a few tips in mind.

First, successful stir-frying is very fast so it's critical that all of the ingredients are ready before you begin. That means all the vegetables and meat or seafood should be cut into the even bite-sized pieces. If you need to marinate the meat, do so, but make sure to drain the excess liquid before cooking.

One good way for handling protein for stir-fries is the Chinese technique of "velveting," a process by which meat or seafood is marinated in egg whites and cornstarch so that they stay moist and succulent when cooked. Foods that need to be stir-fried in a wok benefit tremendously from this technique. For 1 pound (450 g) of meat or seafood, whisk 1 egg white with 1 tablespoon each of cornstarch and oil and, if desired, a splash of rice wine or dry sherry. Add the meat and marinate for about 30 minutes. Heat the oil to about 300°F (150°C) but not hotter since the meat only needs to be par cooked. Using a sieve or wire basket, dip the meat (preferably one layer at a time) into the oil just long enough to cook the outside, about 30 seconds. Remove from the oil and set aside to drain on paper towels until you're ready to finish stir-frying the dish. Dishes such as General Tso's Chicken (page 128) are great when prepared this way.

Second, make sure that the wok or frying pan is adequately hot before adding the oil. Stir-frying is about high heat, and to achieve this throughout the cooking, start with a hot pan and don't crowd it. If necessary, cook in batches. For home cooks, stir-frying outdoors is ideal because you can get the pan smoking hot without worrying about excessive smoke inside the kitchen.

Third, stir-frying is about dry-heat cooking over high heat with no liquid. This is why it is important that the vegetables are completely dry. If not, the oil will splatter and the vegetables will steam as opposed to stir-fry. *Wok hay*, that wonderful smoky flavor that one experiences at good Chinese restaurants, happens when food is correctly cooked in a blazing hot wok. It is possible to achieve this flavor at home if your stove generates enough heat and you have a good wok and have followed all of these stir-fry techniques and tips.

For most home cooks, though, investing in a 12- to 14-inch (30- to 35-cm) flat-bottomed, cast-iron or stainless-steel wok is a good idea if you like to stir-fry. If you have one of those professional-style gas stoves with a wok ring, you might want to try the more traditional one-handle 14-inch (30-cm) wok. The advantage to this round-bottomed wok, which is restaurant grade, is that it will get extremely hot and the high sides allow you to move ingredients vigorously without spilling.

To season a wok, heat it over low heat and apply a thin coat of vegetable oil. Place it in a 300°F (150°C) oven and season for about an hour. You can also do this on the stove over medium heat. Make sure to move it around so that the wok bottom and sides are evenly seasoned and darkened.

CHINA

this popular dish has its roots in Hunan and was rumored to be named after a dish loved by 19th-century General Tso Tsung-t'ang. It was actually the creation of chef Peng Chang-kuei, who came up with the sweet and spicy chicken dish in the late 1970s at his New York City restaurant in an effort to please the American palate. This recipe by Fuchsia Dunlop pays homage to the less sweet Hunan-style version.

GENERAL TSO'S CHICKEN

SERVES 4

CHICKEN
4 chicken thighs, boned with skin
(about 12 ounces/340 g total)
6 to 10 dried red chiles
Peanut oil, for deep-frying
2 teaspoons finely chopped fresh ginger
2 teaspoons finely chopped garlic
2 teaspoons sesame oil

MARINADE
2 teaspoons light soy sauce
½ teaspoon dark soy sauce
1 egg yolk
2 tablespoons potato flour
2 teaspoons peanut oil

SAUCE
1 tablespoon double-concentrate tomato paste
(mixed with 1 tablespoon water)
½ teaspoon potato flour
½ teaspoon dark soy sauce
1½ teaspoons light soy sauce
1 tablespoon clear rice vinegar
3 tablespoons water

Thinly sliced green onions as garnish

1. *For the chicken:* Unfold the chicken thighs and lay them, skin side down, on a chopping board. (If some parts are very thick, lay your knife flat and slice them in half, parallel to the board.) Use a sharp knife to make a few shallow crisscross cuts into the meat—this will help the flavors to penetrate. Cut each thigh into bite-sized slices, approximately ¼ inch (6 mm) thick. Place the chicken slices in a bowl.

2. *For the marinade:* Add the soy sauces and egg yolk to the chicken and mix well, then stir in the potato flour and the oil; set aside while you prepare the other ingredients.

3. *For the sauce:* Combine all of the ingredients in a small bowl and set aside.

4. *Use* a pair of scissors to snip the dried chiles into ¾-inch (18-mm) pieces, discarding the seeds as much as possible.

5. *In* a wok or medium saucepan, heat enough peanut oil to deep-fry the chicken over medium heat until it reaches 350 to 400°F (180 to 200°C). Add the chicken and deep-fry until it is crisp and golden, 3 to 4 minutes. If you are deep-frying in a wok with a relatively small volume of oil, fry the chicken in batches. Remove the chicken from the pan and drain briefly on paper towels.

6. *Return* the wok to a high flame with 2 to 3 tablespoons of the peanut oil. Add the dried chiles and stir-fry briefly until they are fragrant and just changing color, about 30 seconds (do not burn them). Toss in the ginger and garlic and stir-fry for a few seconds longer, until fragrant. Then add the sauce and stir as it thickens, about 1 minute.

7. *Return* the chicken to the wok and stir vigorously to coat the pieces in the sauce. Remove from the heat, stir in the sesame oil, and then serve, sprinkled with green onions.

From Revolutionary Chinese Cookbook *by* FUCHSIA DUNLOP, *published by Ebury Press. Reprinted by permission of The Random House Group Ltd.*

"Pad Kaprao" is one of the most popular lunch street foods in Thailand. It's served everywhere from food carts to restaurants to five-star settings. Traditionally, the stir-fried chicken is served on steamed jasmine rice along with a fried egg on top, for added protein. Intensely flavorful in large part because of the garlic, chile, and holy basil used in the stir-fry base, this is usually eaten with more chiles on the side as well as fish sauce.

STIR-FRIED CHICKEN WITH HOLY BASIL
PAD KAPRAO GAI

SERVES 4

⅓ cup vegetable oil

⅓ cup chopped garlic

4 teaspoons chopped fresh Thai bird chiles, or as needed

14 ounces (400 g) minced chicken

2 tablespoons fish sauce, or as needed

2 tablespoons soy sauce

1 cup green beans, cut in half and blanched

1 cup holy or Thai basil leaves

4 eggs

1 quart (1 liter) steamed rice

1. Heat 3 tablespoons of the vegetable oil in a wok or medium saucepan over high heat. Stir-fry the garlic and chiles until the chiles turn yellow, 1 to 2 minutes.

2. Add the chicken to the wok and stir-fry until cooked, about 2 minutes.

3. Remove the wok from the heat and season the chicken with the fish sauce and soy sauce.

4. Add the green beans to the mixture and stir in the holy basil leaves. Reserve warm.

5. Heat a small sauté pan over medium heat and add 2 tablespoon of oil. Once the oil is hot, add the eggs to the pan and fry until the whites are cooked through but the yolks are still runny, 2 to 3 minutes.

6. Place the stir-fried chicken with the holy basil and fried egg on top of the steamed rice. Serve together with extra fish sauce and sliced chiles, if desired.

Adapted from a recipe by ASSISTANT PROFESSOR KOBKAEW NAIPINIJ

INDIA

named after the bare rib bones of "frenched" lamb chops, this lamb is marinated overnight in a drained yogurt sauce and grilled. To mimic tandoori charcoal cooking, use a really hot grill to achieve the lamb's flavorful char-grilled exterior. This recipe is based on the interpretation of Suvir Saran and Hemant Mathur of New York's Devi Restaurant of the amazing dish served at Karim's, a food stall in old Delhi.

LAMB LOLLIPOPS

SERVES 8

2 cups plain yogurt

4 pounds (1.8 kg) lamb rib chops, cut 1 to 1½ inches (2.5 to 3.75 cm) thick between the bones (16 to 20 each)

½ cup malt vinegar

¼ cup lemon juice

½ cup minced garlic

2 tablespoons grated ginger

2 tablespoons Garam Masala (page 220)

2 tablespoons toasted cumin

2 teaspoons ground cardamom

1 teaspoon cayenne pepper

½ teaspoon ground mace

½ teaspoon ground nutmeg

¼ cup canola oil

6 tablespoons unsalted butter, melted

1. Drain the yogurt in a cheesecloth-lined strainer or coffee filter until it has thickened slightly, 2 to 3 hours. Alternatively, you may use sour cream or crème fraîche instead of the strained yogurt.

2. Mix all of the remaining ingredients except for the oil and butter in a gallon-sized, ziplock plastic bag. Add the chops and turn to coat in the marinade. Refrigerate the chops overnight.

3. Heat the grill to a medium-high heat (you should be able to hold your hand 5 inches/12 cm above the grate for no more than 3 to 4 seconds).

4. Add the oil to the bag, reseal, and massage the chops to incorporate. Remove the lamb from the marinade, place on the grill, and cook for 3 to 4 minutes on each side, or until the chops look grill-marked. Transfer to a baking sheet and let the lamb rest for 5 minutes. Brush with the melted butter and grill until each side is evenly browned, about 2 more minutes per side, and serve.

Adapted from a recipe by SUVIR SARAN

KOREA

This hearty chicken dish has fresh chestnuts, pumpkin, and garlic cloves. The sweetness of the braising liquid is a perfect complement to the spiced stuffing. To make ginger juice, grate ginger as finely as possible and use the resulting juice and pulp. Monitor the heat: If it is too high, the liquid will evaporate too quickly and the rice will not cook properly. Garnish with toasted sesame seeds and thinly sliced green onions.

BRAISED CHICKEN BREAST WITH RICE AND CHESTNUTS

SERVES 4

Four 7-ounce (200 g) skin-on chicken breasts
½ teaspoon salt
½ teaspoon ground black pepper
1½ tablespoons vegetable oil
1½ quarts (1½ liters) chicken stock

BRAISING SAUCE

¼ cup plus 2 teaspoons soy sauce
2 tablespoons packed brown sugar
2½ tablespoons sugar
1½ tablespoons chopped garlic
¼ cup chopped onions
1½ tablespoons ginger juice
6 tablespoons rice wine
⅔ cup dried whole chiles
2 teaspoons Korean chili powder
2 teaspoons light corn syrup

STUFFING

3½ ounces (100 g) soaked glutinous rice
½ cup ginseng hairs (optional)
4 fresh chestnuts, roughly chopped, or as needed
6 ginkgo nuts, roughly chopped
4 jujube dates
1 cup medium-diced pumpkin
4 cloves garlic, roughly chopped
2 tablespoons soy sauce
1 tablespoon honey

4 bamboo skewers
(3 to 4 inches/7.5 to 10 cm long)

1. Lay each chicken breast skin side up on a cutting board. With a sharp knife parallel to the cutting board, cut a 1-inch (2.5-cm) slit into the side of the chicken breast, taking care not to cut through to the other side. Swivel the knife inside the breast and cut a pocket that extends the length of the inside of the breast. Take care not to cut all the way through the breast and try to make the pocket as large as possible. Rub the inside of each breast with the salt and pepper.

2. Combine all of the ingredients for the braising sauce except the corn syrup and mix.

3. Mix together all of the stuffing ingredients and stuff 4 to 6 tablespoons into each chicken breast pocket. The chicken breast should only be about two-thirds full in order to have room for the rice to expand. Fasten with a bamboo skewer by threading the skewer through the opening of the chicken breast.

4. Heat the vegetable oil in a large sauté pan over high heat. Sauté the chicken breast in the oil until golden brown, 1 to 2 minutes per side. Reduce the heat to medium-low and reserve until needed.

5. Combine the chicken stock and the braising sauce in a large saucepan and bring to a boil over high heat. Add enough liquid to the pan with the chicken so that it comes one-third to halfway up the chicken, cover, and simmer on medium-low until the rice is cooked through, 30 to 40 minutes, adding liquid as needed if the pan starts to go dry. Flip the chicken every 10 minutes and baste frequently while the chicken cooks.

6. Cook until only a small amount of cooking liquid remains (about 1½ cups) and add the corn syrup. Swirl the pan to mix thoroughly. Raise the heat to high and cook until the liquid is almost completely absorbed by the chicken. There should be about ½ cup left. Check that the rice is done and serve.

Adapted from a recipe by DR. HEE SOOK CHO

Curries

One of the most flavorful ways of cooking meat is in curries. In Asia, there are literally thousands of recipes, but the most common styles can be categorized as Thai, Malaysian, or Indian in origin. While it's impossible to pinpoint the exact origin of each, the word "curry," or *kari* in Tamil, is loosely used to denote any stew or gravy-like dish that has been cooked with spices. Most curries in this book are built around a spice paste of some form—the heart and soul of a curry. It can be a moist, stiff paste or a loose, wet paste or a mix of dried, hard spices.

The Thais create wonderful versions with *kaeng*, a moist paste made by pounding a variety of chiles, lemongrass, galangal, and shallots along with shrimp paste and dried spices such as coriander and cumin seeds. Red curry paste is made predominately from dried red chiles; green curry paste is made from fresh green chiles and so on.

Traditionally, home cooks prepare this spice paste by pounding with a mortar and pestle different proportions of spices to form a palette of spicy, salty, pungent, and earthy flavors from which the final dish can be created. For a Thai curry, the cook begins by simmering the paste with coconut cream or milk until it becomes bubbly and fragrant. Once the liquid has evaporated and small bubbles of oil have formed, the protein and vegetables can be added along with the cooking liquid, which could be coconut milk or stock or a combination of the two. For the best flavor, curries should always be simmered over medium to medium-low heat and not allowed to boil aggressively. Thai curries are generally brothy, intensely flavorful, and spicy with a thin layer of oil floating on top.

It's best to make the curry paste from scratch, especially if you're able to get the necessary fresh herbs. To make the process faster, use a food processor. If you cannot find the ingredients, a good compromise would be to use a store-bought version but add fresh chiles and herbs to "lift" and refresh the flavors.

In countries such as Singapore, Malaysia, and Indonesia, a Malay or Nonya spice paste called *rempah* forms the base of many curries. Typically wetter than *kaeng*, it's also made by pounding and grinding dried spices along with fleshy herbs and roots. If you're using a mortar and pestle, it's best to start with the dried spices and the denser ingredients, such as lemongrass and galangal, before adding the more tender ginger and chiles, for example. If you're using a food processor, you can just add all of the ingredients at once.

A dish made with this paste begins with stir-frying the *rempah* in oil. This process must be done patiently and carefully over medium-low heat to ensure that all the fragrances develop and blend together correctly. Too high a heat will scorch the pan and make the aromatics either too caramelized or bitter or both. On the other hand, too low a heat will result in a curry that is subdued and flat. Once the spice paste is properly cooked, add the meat and other main ingredients, along with the liquid, then stir to loosen the paste from the bottom of the pan. Curries made with *rempah* are usually thick in consistency. Devil Chicken Curry (page 138) and Nonya Shrimp Curry (page 157) are examples of Malay-style curries made with *rempah*.

Because of the wide-reaching influence of the Indian empire and its trade routes in ancient times, Indian curries are probably the most common, with cooks in each country adapting and interpreting recipes according to his or her preferences and the availability of ingredients. There are many ways of cooking a curry but one common technique is to first sauté whole spices in oil (such as those in the essential Garam Masala ground mix, page 220—cinnamon, cloves, black pepper, cardamom, cumin, coriander, and red chiles). In southern India, cooks prefer the additional touch of popping and toasting black mustard seeds and legumes with fresh curry leaves and chiles in the oil before adding a similar spice mix. When prepared this way, the curry is intensely flavored and complex, imparting a back-of-mouth type of heat because of the spice-infused oil used to build the dish.

Once the aromatic base is ready, other ingredients such as puréed or finely chopped onions—usually in ample amounts—as well as ginger and garlic are added. This mixture simmers until the onions are quite soft and impart a subtle sweetness. Then, according to the recipe, one can add liquid (either water or coconut milk or yogurt), additional ground spices, and lemon, mango powder, or other souring agents to balance the flavors. The sauce is then ready for the meat and vegetables.

SINGAPORE

this chicken curry recipe gets its fun name from the wicked spiciness of the chiles used in the dish. According to Auntie Belle, the talented Malaysian Portuguese chef from Malacca who shared this recipe, it truly reflects the culinary melting pot of the region, with some versions calling for the addition of English mustard and European-style sausages such as bockwurst.

DEVIL CHICKEN CURRY
NARI AYAM DEVIL

SERVES 8

1 large whole chicken
(3 to 3½ pounds/1.4 to 1.6 kg)
1¼ cups minced onions
6 tablespoons minced garlic
½ cup minced ginger
5 lemongrass stalks, minced
¾ to 1 cup dried chiles, or as needed,
soaked in warm water and puréed
1½ teaspoons ground turmeric
½ cup vegetable oil
1¾ cups sliced onions
3 tablespoons thinly sliced garlic
½ cup thinly sliced ginger
1 tablespoon mustard seeds
4 potatoes, peeled and cut into quarters
½ small head cabbage, cut into eighths
1½ cups water, or as needed
2 tablespoons *kecap manis*
3 tablespoons white vinegar
2½ tablespoons salt, or as needed
1 tablespoon sugar, or as needed
6 fresh red chiles, sliced in half,
plus as needed for garnish

1. Wash the chicken and trim off any excess fat. Debone the chicken and cut into 1-inch (2.5-cm) pieces. Reserve until needed.

2. Combine the minced onions, minced garlic, minced ginger, lemongrass, puréed chiles, and turmeric together in a bowl.

3. Heat the oil in a large saucepan over medium heat. Cook the sliced onions, sliced garlic, sliced ginger, and mustard seeds until fragrant, 4 to 5 minutes. Add the minced items and cook until light brown and fragrant, 3 to 4 minutes.

4. Add the potatoes, cabbage, enough water to cover the potatoes, the *kecap manis*, vinegar, and salt. Bring to a boil and then reduce the heat so that the liquid is at a simmer. Simmer until the cabbage is almost tender, 10 to 15 minutes.

5. Add the chicken and stir well. Simmer until the chicken is cooked through and the liquid has thickened, 5 to 8 minutes.

6. Adjust the seasoning with salt and sugar and add the sliced red chiles before removing from the stove. Garnish with additional halved red chiles, if desired.

Adapted from a recipe by CHRISTIBELLE "AUNTIE BELLE" SAVAGE

Thailand

of all Thai curries, Massamun is one of the least spicy. While its preparation is similar to other curries, the ingredients in the curry paste itself are different, thanks to the addition of hard spices such as cinnamon and nutmeg. As with most Thai curries, it is commonly served with rice.

LAMB SHANK IN MASSAMUN CURRY

SERVES 8

8 lamb shanks

2 tablespoons plus ¾ teaspoon salt, or as needed

¼ teaspoon freshly ground black pepper, or as needed

5 tablespoons canola oil

5 quarts (5 liters) chicken or white beef stock

5 tablespoons Massamun curry paste

Five 14-ounce (400-g) cans coconut milk

3 tablespoons fish sauce, or as needed

5 tablespoons tamarind pulp, dissolved in ½ cup water and strained

1 teaspoon sugar

2 onions, peeled and cut into large pieces

5½ cups large-dice potatoes

1. Preheat the oven to 350°F (180°C).

2. Heat a roasting pan on the stove over medium-high heat. Season the lamb with ¾ teaspoon salt and the pepper. Pour 3 tablespoons of the canola oil into the heated roasting pan. Carefully place the lamb in the roasting pan and sear until golden brown, 3 to 4 minutes. Sear the shanks on all sides and in batches, if necessary.

3. Remove the lamb from the heat and rest on a plate in a cool place. Discard the excess oil from the pan. Add the stock and lamb back to the roasting pan. Bring to a boil over medium heat. Remove from the heat and cover with foil. Place the pan in the oven and braise for 2 hours. Remove the lamb from the pan and drain off the braising liquid. Reserve the pan.

4. Heat the remaining 2 tablespoons of canola oil in a wok or saucepan over low heat and roast the Massamun curry paste for 2 to 3 minutes or until it is fragrant. Add the coconut milk, raise the heat to medium, and bring to a boil. Season the mixture with the fish sauce, tamarind juice, and sugar. Pour into the roasting pan.

5. Return the lamb to the roasting pan along with the onions and potatoes. Cover the pan with foil and place back in the oven. Continue braising for 1 more hour or until the lamb is tender. Adjust the seasoning with salt and pepper and serve.

Adapted from a recipe by IAN CHALERMKITTICHAI

INDIA

biryani is a signature rice dish in Indian cuisine known especially for its scrumptious, festive colorful presentation. Made with basmati rice, it can be created with lamb, chicken, beef, or vegetables and features generous amounts of sweet spices, as well as nuts and raisins. In this recipe, it's best to marinate the lamb in the turmeric-spiced yogurt overnight.

LAMB BIRYANI

SERVES 8

2 pounds 3 ounces (975 g) lamb shoulder, cut into 1-inch (2.5-cm) pieces

1 cup plain yogurt

1 teaspoon powdered turmeric

1 head garlic, cloves peeled

4 green chiles

One 2-inch (5-cm) piece ginger

½ cup cilantro

½ cup mint

2 cinnamon sticks

4 cloves

4 cardamom pods

½ teaspoon aniseed

½ teaspoon ground nutmeg

1 tablespoon poppy seeds

10 almonds

½ cup milk

3 tablespoons ghee or vegetable oil

10 cashew nuts

2 tablespoons golden raisins

1 tablespoon sultanas

2 cups sliced red onions

2 tablespoons salt

1 cup chopped plum tomatoes

2 pounds 3 ounces (975 g) cooked basmati rice

2 tablespoons ghee or butter

¼ cup finely chopped red onions

1. *C*ombine the lamb, yogurt, and turmeric and marinate overnight.

2. *G*rind the garlic, chiles, ginger, cilantro, and mint in a blender or food processor until the mixture achieves a paste, about 2 minutes, scraping the sides. Set aside.

3. *G*rind the cinnamon, cloves, cardamom, aniseed, nutmeg, poppy seeds, and almonds in a blender or spice grinder until the mixture achieves a paste, about 30 seconds. Combine the spice mixture with the milk. Refrigerate until needed.

4. *H*eat 1 tablespoon of the vegetable oil in a small sauté pan over medium-high heat. Cook the cashew nuts for 30 seconds and then add the golden raisins and sultanas and cook until the nuts are toasted and the raisins puff up slightly, about 1 minute. Drain the mixture on a paper towel and set aside.

5. *I*n a heavy saucepan, heat the remaining vegetable oil over high heat. Add the sliced red onions and season with about 1 teaspoon salt. Cook the onions until golden brown, about 6 minutes. Remove the onions from the oil and reserve both.

6. *H*eat the reserved oil over high heat. Add the garlic-herb paste and cook for 2 minutes or until it looks wilted. Add the tomatoes and cook for 2 minutes. Add the onions to the mixture. Add the marinated meat and the remaining salt and mix well. Cover and cook until tender, about 1 hour.

7. *P*lace the pan over high heat and add the spice-milk mixture. Mix well, bring to a simmer, and remove from the heat.

8. *I*n an ovenproof dish, layer half of the meat mixture (about 3 cups), half of the cooked basmati rice (3 cups), the remaining meat mixture, and then the remaining rice. Dot with ghee or butter.

9. *C*over tightly and bake for 30 minutes at 350°F (180°C) or until the mixture is heated through and the flavors have combined. Garnish with the red onion, cashews and raisins, and serve immediately.

Adapted from a recipe by NIMMY PAUL

CHINA

pork belly is a particularly fatty and rich cut of meat and, while it is commonly sliced to make bacon or pancetta, it is often braised and presented whole, as in this recipe. Slow-cooked with familiar Chinese flavors such as star anise, ginger, and soy, this meat dish is a stand-out main course. Serve it with lots of rice and a side dish of vegetables or a salad.

MAO'S BRAISED PORK WITH SOY SAUCE

SERVES 8

3½ pounds (1.6 kg) pork belly, boneless and skin on

2 quarts (2 liters) water

½ cup Shaoxing cooking wine

1 tablespoon salt

¼ cup soy sauce

1 star anise

1 cinnamon stick

½ cup sugar

2 tablespoons cornstarch

1 tablespoon minced ginger

2 green onions, cut into ¼-inch (6-mm) thick slices on the bias

⅓ cup preserved bean curd sauce

1 cup red wine

2 tablespoons sesame oil

1. *C*ut the pork into 1-inch (2.5-cm) cubes. Bring a large pot of water to a boil over high heat and boil the pork until most of the fat has rendered out and it is fairly well done, about 1 hour. Drain the pork and place in a medium saucepan.

2. *P*reheat the oven to 350°F (180°C).

3. *A*dd the remaining ingredients except for the sesame oil to the pork and stir well to combine. Cover and braise for 3½ to 4 hours, or until the pork is darker and is completely tender.

4. *R*emove the pork and keep warm. Reduce the braising liquid over medium heat until it has thickened, 15 to 20 minutes. Add the pork back and simmer until the pork is warmed through.

5. *P*lace the pork on a serving platter with the braising liquid and pour the sesame oil over the pork.

Adapted from a recipe by LIN WANG

Korea

one of the greatest dishes from the Korean kitchen is *galbi,* or short ribs marinated with soy, garlic, and sugar, then grilled over charcoals. The traditional cut is short ribs that have been thinly sliced into a sheet about ¼ inch (6 mm) thick still attached to the bone. You could buy this cut at Asian markets, or buy regular short ribs and cut it into thinner slices as in this recipe, or use other cuts such as tri-tip or sirloin.

KOREAN BARBECUED SHORT RIBS
GALBI

SERVES 8

2 pounds (900 g) beef ribs, bones cut 3 inches (7.5 cm) wide (8 each)

MARINADE
1 Asian pear
6 green onions
½ cup soy sauce
12 peeled cloves garlic
¼ cup sugar
¼ cup sesame oil
½ teaspoon ground black pepper

1. To prepare the ribs, cut the meat into a thin sheet that is still attached to the rib bone. Starting at the outside of the rib and working toward the bone, gently cut the meat into a ¼-inch (6-mm) thick sheet as you rotate the bone. After the meat is cut, make 3 to 4 crisscross shallow scores in the meat so that it will absorb the flavors of the marinade and so that it will not shrink when it is grilled.

2. Soak the ribs in cold water for 30 minutes to 1 hour to remove any impurities. Take the ribs out of the water and dry briefly with a paper towel to remove the water and any residual impurities.

3. For the marinade: Peel and core the pear and cut into medium dice. There should be 1¼ cups.

4. Cut the green onions into 2- or 3-inch (5- or 7.5-cm) lengths.

5. Place all of the ingredients in a food processor and pulse until just combined. If you pulse the mixture too much, it will become too liquid.

6. Add the marinade to the beef ribs and mix well. Make sure the marinade coats all parts of the meat. Marinate the beef overnight.

7. Preheat the grill to high.

8. Grill the ribs until cooked, about 5 minutes on each side.

Adapted from a recipe by MYUNG SOOK LEE

CHAPTER FIVE

Seafood

HEALTHY AND FULL OF FLAVOR

Water, water, everywhere. If it's not oceans, it's rivers and lakes. Asia is blessed with literally thousands of miles of coastlines and a web of river systems teeming with marine life. For much of the region, fish and seafood are the primary source of protein and are eaten often, second only to rice and vegetables.

*F*ish, crustaceans, mollusks, and other seafood are eaten both fresh and preserved in all different ways. In Japan, freshness is key as much of the seafood is consumed raw in sushi and sashimi. The attendance of the Tsjukiji fish market in Tokyo, for example, is one telling sign of this passion for fresh seafood. Each dawn, hundreds of people swarm this wholesale market, one of the largest in the world, to inspect the vast varieties of species, from sea bream and mackerel to octopus and shellfish, before purchasing. In the tuna section, whole, gutted frozen tuna, many weighing several hundred pounds each, are laid out in row after row, waiting to be auctioned off and carted away.

In China, fish is equally prized although their preference leans toward smaller fish with white flesh and mild flavor. At a Guangzhou neighborhood market, freshly butchered fish are smeared with blood to keep them moist and fresh. At restaurants, entryways are lined with tanks filled with live fish, eels, and crustaceans so customers can preview the menu. The Chinese love fresh fish, simply steamed with soy sauce, ginger, and scallions or deep-fried and served with a delicate sauce. Clams and mussels are wok-fried in garlic and black beans and shrimp and squid are dusted in cornstarch, then flash-fried and served with a salt and pepper dip.

In Thailand, freshwater fish is simmered in an aromatic lemongrass hot and sour soup. Whole catfish threaded onto large bamboo skewers are slow-roasted over an open fire or deep-fried until ultra-crispy, then shredded and tossed in a spicy green mango salad. In Vietnam, fish is simmered in a clay pot along with black pepper and caramel sauce (see page 164) or it's pan-fried and served with a spicy ginger-lime sauce (see page 150).

Fish and seafood are also delicious when cooked with spices, tomatoes, and coconut as they're done in Kerala and Goa and other coastal towns in India. In Singapore, fish is pounded with chiles, garlic, and galangal, then wrapped in banana leaves and grilled over charcoals. Crab is a beloved crustacean, and the almost national frenzy surrounding its famous Chili Crab dish (page 163) illustrates the Singaporean love of seafood.

When not eaten fresh, seafood is preserved in various forms to flavor food. Some of these include salted, fermented, or pickled fish and seafood. Dried shrimp, a staple used to give flavor and depth to food such as the ubiquitous Korean *kimchi*, is used in all cuisines in Asia. Another related ingredient, shrimp paste, made from fermented shrimp, is the reason Thai curries are so different from, say, Indian curries. Fish is also the source of an important seasoning ingredient, fish sauce, an extract made from fermented fish that is the quintessential seasoning in Southeast Asian cooking (see page 159).

But perhaps the most useful lessons from the Asian seafood kitchen boil down to a few important ideals. First, delicious seafood dishes can only be had from very fresh ingredients. Purchase seafood from reputable markets that are known for their fresh selections. Shop at Asian markets that specialize in live seafood. Look for fish that smells oceany, not fishy. Check to see that the eyes are clear, the gills are red, and the flesh looks firm and shiny. You can also judge freshness just by looking at the fish counter. Is it clean and properly iced? Good fish comes from a staff that cares and pays attention to details. Also, in today's health-conscious world, good, fresh fish comes frozen as preportioned fillets often referred to as IQF, or individual quick frozen. With consumers eating more seafood for health and wellness reasons, supermarkets are now carrying a wider selection.

Second, the best way to prepare seafood is to go with the "less is more" guideline. Grill, broil, boil, or steam seafood, but serve it in interesting ways with tasty sauces or condiments and sides. If you're adding seafood to soups or curries or stews, make sure the timing is correct and perhaps add the seafood toward the very end. You certainly don't want to overcook it.

With proper purchasing and handling, seafood is truly amazing, healthy and full of great flavors, especially when prepared as in the delicious recipes here.

Vietnam

take one bite of this dish and you'll be amazed by the magic of ginger and pan-fried fish. This classic home-style Vietnamese favorite is equally delicious with salmon, snapper, mahi mahi, or halibut. The cucumber "noodles" add a refreshing note and helps keep the flavor of the sauce on the fish and off the plate.

PAN-SEARED ALASKAN BLACK COD WITH GINGER-LIME SAUCE

SERVES 4

½ hothouse cucumber, unpeeled

1 cup Ginger-Lime Dipping Sauce (page 229), or as needed

¼ cup vegetable oil

Four 6-ounce (170-g) pieces black cod, skinless and boneless, washed and patted dry

4 small cloves garlic, uncut

1. *Using* a Japanese Benriner with the julienne blade, hold the cucumber at an angle and push against the blade to cut into long, thin strips 5 to 6 inches (12 to 15 cm) long and ¹⁄₁₆ inch (1.5 mm) thick. Rotate the cucumber as you cut to avoid the seeds. Alternatively, you can use a knife to cut the cucumbers. Add the cucumber "noodles" to the dipping sauce and set aside.

2. *Heat* the oil in a large nonstick frying pan over moderate heat. Cook the fish fillets until golden and just cooked through, 3 to 4 minutes on each side depending on the thickness. Halfway into the cooking, add the whole garlic cloves and cook until they turn golden. If the fish fillets are thick, cover with a lid and cook a few minutes longer.

3. *Remove* the fish and garlic and drain on paper towels.

4. *Arrange* the fillets on a serving dish. Remove the cucumber noodles from the sauce and arrange them on the fish. Pour half of the sauce on top and serve the remaining sauce on the side. Top each fillet with a garlic clove.

Adapted from a recipe by MAI PHAM

in this Vietnamese homestyle shrimp dish, Charles Phan of the Slanted Door in San Francisco adds his special touch by using "brown candy," which has a deeper, more rounded flavor than regular sugar. Sold as slabs at Asian markets, scrape or break it into pieces and dissolve into the cooking liquid. This recipe calls for head-on shrimp, which gives the dish a wonderful flavor. Use a clay pot for cooking if possible.

CARAMELIZED SHRIMP WITH LEMONGRASS AND THAI CHILES

SERVES 4

1 pound 8 ounces (675 g) shrimp (16/20 count), heads on

¼ teaspoon freshly ground black pepper

2 tablespoons vegetable oil

2 teaspoons minced garlic

1 to 2 Thai halved bird chiles, or as needed

2 teaspoons sate chili paste (found in Asian markets)

¼ cup finely minced lemongrass

3 ounces (85 g) "brown candy" sugar, broken into smaller pieces

3 tablespoons fish sauce, or as needed

¼ cup low-sodium chicken stock

4 to 6 cilantro sprigs

steamed jasmine rice (optional)

1. *Rinse* and devein the shrimp. Remove the middle section of the shell, leaving the head and tail intact. Sprinkle with black pepper. Set aside.

2. *Heat* the vegetable oil in a medium clay pot or saucepan over high heat. Add the garlic and cook until fragrant, about 2 minutes. Add the Thai chiles, sate chili paste, and lemongrass and cook for 1 minute, or until fragrant.

3. *Add* the "brown candy" pieces, fish sauce, and chicken stock to the clay pot and turn the heat to low. Stir frequently to dissolve the candy pieces and create a caramel sauce.

4. *Add* the shrimp to the caramel sauce, turn the heat to medium, and simmer until cooked through, 3 to 4 minutes. Garnish with the cilantro. Serve immediately with steamed jasmine rice, if desired.

Adapted from a recipe by CHARLES PHAN

*I*NDIA

this curry dish hails from the state of Goa, located on the west coast of India. As it is a coastal town, Goa places great emphasis on seafood and is especially known for its many vibrantly flavored versions of fish and seafood curry. This recipe from Floyd Cardoz of Tabla in New York is an example of the richness and complexity of curries from the region. Serve it with basmati rice.

GOAN SHRIMP CURRY

SERVES 6

1½ cups roughly chopped white onions

5 cloves garlic, peeled

1½ cups fresh coconut or frozen fresh coconut

4 to 6 cups shrimp stock or water

1 tablespoon coriander seeds

1½ tablespoons cumin seeds

3 dried red chiles

1 tablespoon paprika

½ teaspoon ground turmeric

1 tablespoon canola oil

1 fresh green chile, mild to moderately hot, 4 to 6 inches (10 to 15 cm) in length, slit

2 pounds 6 ounces (1 kg) extra-large shrimp, peeled, deveined, and heads left on, if desired

2 teaspoons salt, or as needed

2 tablespoons tamarind paste

12 large or 18 medium okra (about 8 ounces/225 g), trimmed and left whole

One 13-ounce (375-g) can coconut milk, well stirred

1. *P*ut the onions, garlic, coconut, and ½ cup water in a blender and purée until smooth, starting at low speed and increasing to high. If necessary, add another ½ cup water to achieve the proper consistency.

2. *G*rind the coriander seeds, cumin seeds, and red chiles together in an electric coffee/ spice grinder until fine. Transfer to a small bowl or plate and combine with the paprika and turmeric.

3. *H*eat the oil in a medium saucepan over medium-high heat until shimmering. Add the spice blend and coconut purée. Put 3 cups stock or water into the blender and pulse to blend any residual purée. Add that mixture to the purée in the pan along with the green chile. Bring the sauce to a boil, stirring occasionally.

4. *C*ook the sauce over medium-high heat, stirring occasionally, until it is the consistency of thick paste, 15 to 20 minutes. Do not let it scorch. While the sauce is cooking down, season the shrimp with salt and let sit for about 20 minutes.

5. *S*tir the remaining stock or water, tamarind paste, and okra into the sauce and bring to a simmer. Simmer the mixture until the okra is barely tender, about 3 minutes. Stir in the coconut milk and bring the sauce to a boil. Add the shrimp and simmer until the shrimp are just cooked through, about 3 minutes. Taste the sauce and adjust the seasoning with salt. Serve immediately.

Adapted from a recipe by FLOYD CARDOZ

although not as common outside of Thailand, this delicious red curry combines the sweetness of the shrimp with the tangy, fruity flavors of pineapple. For a smooth and evenly textured curry, prepare the paste using the ingredients in the order specified. You can also use ready-made paste, but freshly pounded curry paste is hard to beat. For tips on making curry paste, see pages 136–137.

Thai Red Curry with Shrimp and Pineapple
KAENG KUA

SERVES 4

CURRY PASTE
3 dried long red chiles, deseeded, soaked, and drained

½ teaspoon salt, or as needed

½ teaspoon finely sliced galangal

1 tablespoon finely sliced lemongrass stalk, white parts only

1½ tablespoons sliced shallots

1 tablespoon chopped garlic

½ teaspoon toasted shrimp paste

1½ tablespoons grilled smoked fish (optional)

SHRIMP
2 tablespoons tamarind pulp

3 tablespoons warm water

Two 14-ounce (400-g) cans coconut milk, not shaken

1 pound (450 g) shrimp (16/20 count), peeled and deveined

¾ cup pineapple, cut into ½-inch (1-cm) cubes

3 tablespoons palm or regular sugar, or to taste

3 tablespoons fish sauce, or to taste

4 kaffir lime leaves, thinly sliced

1. *For the curry paste:* Using a mortar and pestle, pound each of the ingredients to a smooth paste in the following order: chiles, salt, galangal, lemongrass, shallots, garlic, shrimp paste, and smoked fish, if using. Make sure each ingredient is pounded smooth before adding the next.

2. *For the shrimp:* Combine the tamarind pulp and water and stir until the tamarind is dissolved. Strain and set aside.

3. *Skim* the creamy part of the coconut milk (the coconut cream) from both cans and add to a heavy-bottomed sauté pan. Heat over medium heat and bring to a boil, stirring constantly. Stir in 2 tablespoons of the curry paste, or slightly more if you like, and cook for 2 to 3 minutes until the mixture is fragrant and thoroughly blended.

4. *Add* the shrimp, pineapple, and the remaining coconut milk. Stir in the tamarind juice, palm sugar, and fish sauce. Continue to simmer until the pineapple and shrimp are just cooked, 3 to 4 minutes. Sprinkle the curry with kaffir lime leaves and serve immediately.

Adapted from a recipe by BANSANI NAWISAMPHAN

the movement of different people and cultures throughout Asia has expanded the breadth of local cuisines. For example, "nonya" means grandmother to the Chinese who immigrated to Singapore and Malaysia in the nineteenth century. Since then, "nonya" refers to a regional style of cooking that is rooted in Chinese cuisine but has been adapted to reflect the local Malaysian palate as well as ingredients.

NONYA SHRIMP CURRY

SERVES 8

SPICE MIXTURE
6 macadamia nuts

2 tablespoons thinly sliced galangal

¼ teaspoon ground turmeric

6 fresh red jalapeños, roasted, peeled, and sliced

1½ teaspoons shrimp paste

3 shallots, peeled and thinly sliced

SHRIMP CURRY
1 lemongrass stalk, white part only

3 tablespoons tamarind pulp

4½ cups warm water

¼ cup vegetable oil

1 cup medium-diced pineapple

2 beefsteak tomatoes, cut into eighths

2 teaspoons sugar

½ teaspoon salt

1 pound (450 g) shrimp (16/20 count), peeled and deveined

1. For the spice mixture: Using a mortar and pestle, pound the macadamia nuts, galangal, turmeric, jalapeños, shrimp paste, and shallots in that order. Alternatively, put all of the ingredients except the shallots in a blender and blend to a rough paste. Add the shallots and purée until the shallots are roughly chopped. Set aside.

2. For the shrimp curry: Remove the outer layers from the lemongrass stalk and bruise with the back of a knife.

3. Soak the tamarind in the water and knead well. Strain and reserve the juice, discarding the seeds.

4. Place a wok over high heat until it begins to smoke. Add the oil and, when hot, add the spice mixture. Reduce the heat and stir-fry over medium heat until the spice paste becomes fragrant and the pounded bits turn slightly crinkly, 6 to 8 minutes.

5. Add the tamarind juice, crushed lemongrass, pineapple, tomatoes, sugar, and salt. Bring to a boil over high heat and then reduce to a simmer. Continue to simmer over low heat for 20 minutes, or until the sauce is thickened and fragrant.

6. Add the shrimp and simmer until the shrimp is cooked, about 2 minutes or when they turn pink. Serve immediately with rice, if desired.

Adapted from a recipe by VIOLET OON

Fish Sauce

One of the main reasons why Vietnamese or Thai food tastes quite different from, say, Chinese or Japanese food, is because it relies heavily upon fish sauce. Called *nam pla* in Thailand, *nuoc mam* in Vietnam, *tuk trey* in Cambodia, and *patis* in the Philippines, fish sauce is the quintessential seasoning ingredient. It's used throughout Southeast Asia and particularly in Vietnam and Thailand, where it appears in almost every dish or meal. It adds savoriness and *umami*—the newly discovered fifth taste—to food, giving it the effect similar to what cheese or mushrooms do to pasta and anchovies to Caesar dressing.

Nam pla is used to season food as well as to make marinades and dipping sauces. In Thailand, cooks add this amber-colored liquid to curries, salads, and stir fries. When added directly to food, it tastes one way but if drizzled directly onto the surface of a hot pan, it quickly caramelizes and makes the final dish exceptionally savory with a slight smokiness. This technique is particularly important with Southeast Asian stir fries.

At the Vietnamese table, no meal is complete without a dipping sauce made from fish sauce and pounded garlic, chiles, sugar, and water. One way to fully appreciate this ingredient is in a dipping sauce paired with grilled or steamed meat or seafood.

Regardless of the origin or style, fish sauce is typically made by layering fish (anchovies are preferred because of their high oil content) with salt and allowing them to ferment in earthenware pots in the hot sun. Good fish sauce, which is high in protein and vitamins, is typically aged for at least 12 months or longer, although the fermentation period is shorter in some cases as manufacturers rush to meet increasing global demands. Once the liquid is ready to be extracted, it's filtered and transferred to bottles where it will undergo more fermentation. The first pressing is the most prized—slightly oily and deeply flavored—and is best eaten raw, as in a dipping sauce or salad dressing. Depending on the quality of the anchovies and the processing, the first pressing could be amber-colored, or much lighter and similar to cooking oil. In Vietnam, *nuoc mam* is considered premium if it contains a high percentage of protein, typically anywhere from 30 to 38 percent.

The second and third extractions are made by adding more salted water to the same fish. The process is repeated although the fermentation is typically shorter. These lesser-quality products are not as flavorful and should only be used for cooking and not for dipping sauces.

In recent years, with the growing popularity of Southeast Asian cuisines, fish sauce has become readily available not only at Asian markets but at gourmet retailers and supermarkets. There are two general types: a darker, full-bodied variety used in Thai cooking as well as a similar Filipino product called *patis*, and a lighter variety preferred in Vietnamese cooking and sold as *nuoc mam nhi* (denotes first pressing or premium quality). Good quality fish sauce can be reddish brown or lighter, but it should always be clear with smooth, rounded flavors. Cheaper products tend to be darker (too much coloring and the possibility of some oxidation), salty, and packed in plastic bottles. When purchasing fish sauce, buy the more expensive, premium brands packed in glass bottles with the Vietnamese words "*nuoc mam nhi*," "*nuoc cot*," or "*thuong hang*."

To store an open bottle, first wrap the neck with plastic and keep it in the refrigerator. This way the strong odor will not permeate other foods. Straight fish sauce can be quite pungent but when cooked or diluted with water, its flavor softens dramatically. With its high salt level, fish sauce will keep for a year or even longer. However, if the liquid turns dark brown and salt crystals start to form at the bottom, it's time to replace it.

CHINA

in this lovely, light dish, the mild flavor of flatfish is complemented by fresh ginger, green onions, and ham. The soy sauce and rice wine permeate the fish during steaming so that the final texture is tender and moist. Small whole fish such as flounder and snapper are great for this dish, or any white fish fillets work too. Cook in a steamer lined with bamboo or cabbage leaves, or on a shallow, oval dish that fits in a steamer.

WHOLE STEAMED FISH WITH GINGER

SERVES 4

1 whole fish, 1 pound 8 ounces to 2 pounds
(675 to 900 g)

1 teaspoon salt, or as needed

¾ teaspoon freshly ground black pepper,
or as needed

½ cup light soy sauce

½ cup Shaoxing rice wine

¼ cup dark sesame oil

¼ teaspoon coarsely ground black pepper

4 ounces (115 g) dry cured ham,
cut into julienne

½ ounce (12 g) ginger, peeled and cut into
very fine julienne

4 green onions, cut on the bias into 2-inch
(5-cm) pieces, plus as needed for garnish

1. Wash the fish well. Score the flesh ¼ inch (6 mm) deep at 1-inch (2.5-cm) intervals from head to tail. Sprinkle inside and out with the salt and ½ teaspoon of the black pepper.

2. Combine the soy sauce, rice wine, and sesame oil in a small bowl. Place the fish into a ceramic dish suitable to its size and shape and pour the soy sauce mixture over it.

3. Sprinkle the remaining black pepper, ham, ginger, and green onions over the fish. Cover the dish with plastic wrap and refrigerate until 30 minutes before you are ready to serve.

4. Set a bamboo steamer over a simmering pan of water over medium heat. While the steamer comes up to temperature, remove the fish from the refrigerator and bring to room temperature.

5. Place the fish in the steamer and steam until cooked through, about 12 minutes, depending on the type of fish. The internal temperature of the thick end of the fish should be 140°F (60°C).

6. Remove the green onion pieces and scatter the surface of the cooked fish with thin slices of freshly cut green onions to garnish.

Adapted from a recipe by THE CULINARY INSTITUTE OF AMERICA

Vietnam

if you happen to have Hoisin Peanut Sauce in the refrigerator, you can whip up this recipe with little effort. For best flavor, buy ahi (also called yellowfin) tuna steaks that are at least a half inch thick so they'll stay moist when cooked. Mahi mahi, halibut, or catfish also work and Peanut Satay Sauce (page 222) makes a great sauce substitute or variation. If you don't have a grill, you can also pan-sear the tuna.

GRILLED AHI TUNA WITH GINGER HOISIN PEANUT SAUCE

SERVES 4

2 tablespoons minced lemongrass
½ teaspoon salt
½ teaspoon ground black pepper
2 tablespoons vegetable oil
Four 6-ounce (170-g) fresh ahi tuna steaks

SAUCE

1 teaspoon minced garlic
½ teaspoon ground chili paste
1½ tablespoons minced ginger
1 cup Hoisin Peanut Sauce (page 230)
3 tablespoons water

2 green onions, thinly sliced on the bias
3 tablespoons chopped. roasted peanuts

1. Combine the lemongrass, salt, pepper, and 1 tablespoon of the vegetable oil in a mixing bowl. Add the tuna and toss several times. Cover and refrigerate for 20 minutes to marinate.

2. Meanwhile, heat the remaining oil in a small saucepan over medium heat. Add the garlic, chili paste, and ginger and stir until fragrant, about 20 seconds. Add the Hoisin-Peanut Sauce and water and simmer until the sauce is slightly thickened, 3 to 4 minutes. Remove from the heat and set aside.

3. Preheat your grill to high heat. Grill the tuna steak to medium-rare, 2 to 3 minutes on each side, depending on the thickness. Just before serving, reheat the Hoisin-Peanut Sauce.

4. Transfer the fish to a serving platter. Drizzle half of the sauce on top of the tuna and garnish with green onions and peanuts. Serve the remaining sauce on the side.

Adapted from a recipe by MAI PHAM

probably the most iconic dish of Singapore, chili crab is traditionally made with mud crab. For this recipe, you can use whole Dungeness or blue crab, which are more easily available, or even soft-shelled crab, which should be deep-fried before adding it to the sauce. To truly enjoy this dish, first lick the sauce on the shells and then crack and eat. Serve with a soft bread to soak up every last drop of the sauce.

SINGAPORE CHILI CRAB

SERVES 4

CHILI PASTE

3 tablespoons chopped garlic

1 shallot, peeled and roughly chopped

2 fresh chiles, seeded, stemmed, and roughly chopped

1 tablespoon minced Thai bird chiles, or as needed

3 macadamia nuts, roughly chopped

¼ teaspoon shrimp paste

1½ tablespoons dried shrimp, washed in warm water

1½ tablespoons roughly chopped ginger

1 teaspoon peanut butter

¾ teaspoon ground turmeric

½ cup vegetable oil

½ lemongrass stalk, white parts only, chopped

¾ teaspoon sugar

¾ teaspoon salt, or as needed

1½ tablespoons chili paste

2 pounds 2 ounces (960 g) live crab

1 tablespoon vegetable oil

1 teaspoon chopped garlic

1 cup water

1 to 2 tablespoons sugar, or as needed

1 teaspoon sweet *shiro miso* (soybean paste), optional

1 tablespoon cornstarch

3 tablespoons tomato ketchup

2 eggs

2 tablespoons cilantro leaves

1. *F*or the chili paste: Blend all of the ingredients together until it achieves the consistency of a thin paste. Stir the mixture again thoroughly before using.

2. *C*lean the crab and cut it into 8 pieces.

3. *H*eat up a wok or large saucepan over medium heat and add the oil. Add the chopped garlic and 3 tablespoons of the Chili Paste to the wok and stir-fry briefly. Add the crab and stir-fry until the crab is well coated with the sauce. Add the water and cover the wok for about 1 minute.

4. *A*dd the sugar and soybean paste and cover the wok for another 4 to 5 minutes.

5. *R*emove the cover and lower the heat. Mix the cornstarch with a little water to dissolve it, and add it along with the tomato ketchup. Bring the mixture to a simmer. It should thicken slightly.

6. *R*emove the crab and place it on a serving platter. Reheat the wok and and crack in the eggs. Stir and cook until the eggs are thoroughly set, 3 to 4 minutes. Pour the sauce over the crab, then garnish with the cilantro.

Adapted from a recipe by NG KWOK YIN

it would not be an exaggeration to say almost every Vietnamese family cooks this dish at least once a week. For the best flavor, use a one-quart clay pot or sand pot available at Asian markets. To season a new clay pot, soak it in water for at least four hours, then boil some water in it before using it for the first time. If you don't have a clay pot, a regular pot will do. For delicious variations, substitute shrimp or pork.

CATFISH IN A CLAY POT
CA KHO TO

SERVES 4

1 tablespoon vegetable oil

2 tablespoons coarsely chopped garlic

1 pound (450 g) fresh catfish fillets,
cut in halves or thirds

1 cup water

3 tablespoons fish sauce

2 to 3 tablespoons Caramel Sauce (page 230),
or as needed

1 green onion, cut into paper-thin rings

6 cilantro sprigs, chopped (about ⅓ cup)

½ teaspoon freshly ground black pepper

1 to 2 Thai bird chiles (optional)

1. Heat the oil in a clay pot or regular saucepan over medium heat. Add the garlic and stir until fragrant and golden, about 20 seconds. Add the catfish, skin side up, the water, fish sauce, and caramel sauce. The water should cover the fish.

2. Bring the mixture to a boil, then reduce the heat and simmer for 3 minutes. Turn the fillets over, skin side down, then cover and continue to simmer for another 4 minutes. Uncover and cook until the sauce has reduced and thickened and the catfish is cooked, another 2 to 3 minutes.

3. Remove the clay pot from the heat and garnish with the green onion, cilantro, black pepper, and chiles, if using. Serve immediately right in the clay pot.

Adapted from a recipe by MAI PHAM

Handling Seafood

To bring out the best flavor in seafood, cook it the day that it was purchased. If you need to hold it for a day or so, remove it from the original wrapping and rinse it in cold water. Pat dry, place it on a clean plate, then cover and store it in the coldest part of the refrigerator. For live clams, mussels, and oysters, place them in a bowl and cover with a damp cloth. Crabs and lobsters should be kept in a large paper bag inside a sturdy plastic bag. (This is usually how Asian markets pack them.) Cover with wet newspaper but keep the bag open. As an alternative, fill an ice chest with ice, then store the seafood there until you're ready to cook.

FISH

Whole fish cooks up moist on the inside and nicely crisped on the outside if it's done under a broiler or on a grill. Buy your fish from a reputable fish market or supermarket. Some species that are good to eat whole include striped bass, snapper, sole, black sea bass, and trout. They can be steamed, grilled, pan- or deep-fried, or braised. To avoid grease splattering in the kitchen, consider deep-frying or pan-frying outdoors.

If you prefer larger fish such as tuna, salmon, and mahi mahi, fillets are a better choice and readily available. Check for signs of freshness and try to purchase seasonal catches. For example, wild salmon is at its peak from June to late September. The fish should have only an ocean (not fishy) smell and the flesh should be moist and plump with no discolorations. Fillets cook quite fast and usually take just minutes. As a general rule, the proteins in seafood react to heat at a lower temperature than in meat. Fish cooked to medium-rare is just above 120°F (48°C) while meat will be closer to 140°F (60°C). For this reason, it's best to always cook fish over moderate heat so the outer layers do not overcook and become dry and the inside is just cooked. More often than not, a perfect fish fillet is one pulled from the heat about a minute or two before it's actually done cooking. The residual heat will continue to cook the fish through.

For sushi and sashimi, it's best to only buy from a reputable fish market or grocery store that specializes in fish meant to be eaten raw. Seafood intended for this use should be handled under the strictest sanitation standards.

SHRIMP

Shrimp can be either farm-raised or wild, the latter being generally more flavorful. It's sold by type, such as brown or black tiger, and by size, such as 21-25, meaning there are that many in a pound. Almost all shrimp are sold as thawed, frozen shrimp. Buy the freshest looking ones with the shells on. Properly thawed shrimp is moist and the shells a bit shiny. Whenever possible, cook them unpeeled since most of the flavor comes from just underneath the shells. To eat, do what Asians do: pick up the shrimp with chopsticks or fingers and first nibble any seasonings that are stuck to the shells. Then peel and eat. If you're using a larger size shrimp and want to devein them, use scissors to slit open the shells along the back and remove the dark vein. Then you can eat the shrimp using a fork and knife to loosen the shells from the meat.

SCALLOPS/SQUID

Fresh sea scallops are one of the best tasting seafoods, with a sweet, ocean flavor and creamy texture. Look for plump scallops with opaque, ivory-colored flesh. Avoid those sitting in milky white liquid, a sign that they were not handled correctly and probably were soaked in a preservative. Scallops are delicious pan-seared and served with a dipping sauce or lightly simmered in an Indian or Thai curry. Don't over-cook as they will get chewy and dry.

Fresh or frozen squid can be prepared the same way although they're also delicious grilled. One of the best ways to prepare squid is cut them into ½-inch rounds, blanch for no more than 5 seconds, then toss in a spicy lime dressing.

CRAB/LOBSTER

The best crab and lobster are whole and live, simply steamed, and eaten with a dip of roasted salt, pepper, and lime. But they're also delicious in other preparations such as stir-fries with ginger, chiles, and garlic. If you don't have access to live crab, the precooked variety also works well, especially if it was fresh to begin with. At Chinese restaurants, whole crabs are often cut into smaller chunks and flash-dried and then added to a stir-fry. You can emulate this technique at home by buying precooked crab, or if you buy live ones and boil them first before cooking.

To boil the crab or lobster, fill a very large pot with water. Add about 3 to 4 tablespoons of salt for every gallon of water. This technique is designed to create balance between the density of the crab (or lobster) and the cooking liquid so that the sweet juices of the crab will not be drawn out. Wait for the water to boil vigorously, then add the crabs. Depending on the size of the pot, you may need to do this in batches.

Bring the water to a boil again and cook for about 12 minutes for a 1½- to 2-pound (675–900 g) crab and about 18 minutes for a 2½-pound (1-kg) or bigger crab. Lobsters cook faster, about 8 minutes for the first pound (450 g) and 3 to 4 minutes for each additional pound. When in doubt, cook a little less in the initial parboil phase and, if necessary, adjust the time during the second phase of cooking.

MUSSELS/CLAMS/OYSTERS

The majority of oysters harvested are consumed raw on the half shell, although they're also delicious barbecued. When buying mussels and clams, make sure they are heavy to the touch, a sign that they're still fresh. Check open ones to see if they're alive by squeezing the shells together. If they are, they will close up; otherwise, discard them. In Southeast Asia, mussels and clams are often just steamed with lemongrass and sometimes with guava leaves, then served with a spicy fish sauce dip with lime, garlic, and chiles.

there are many recipes for pad thai, but this version from Chai Siriyarn of Marnee Thai in San Francisco has earned prestigious awards both in the United States and Thailand. Sweet radish and tamarind juice add a complex and savory note. Tamarind purée can be found at Asian markets. If you can't find it, double the vinegar and lime juice, or dissolve 2 tablespoons tamarind pulp in ¼ cup water and strain.

PAD THAI

SERVES 4

SAUCE

2 tablepoons palm sugar, chopped until soft
and crumbly and packed

1 tablespoon tamarind purée

2 to 3 tablespoons fish sauce, or as needed

1 tablespoon lime juice

2 tablespoons white vinegar

1 teaspoon paprika

½ teaspoon chili powder, or as needed

1 teaspoon salt, or as needed

8 ounces (225 g) dried rice stick noodles
(*banh pho*)

¼ cup vegetable oil

1½ teaspoons minced garlic

1 tablespoon minced shallots

1 tablespoon minced sweet radish

¼ cup julienned firm tofu

2 eggs

8 shrimp (26/30 count), peeled and deveined

¼ cup chicken stock or water

3 green onions,
cut into 1½-inch (4-cm) lengths

1 cup bean sprouts

⅓ cup chopped, roasted peanuts

1 lime, cut into wedges

1. For the sauce: Combine all of the ingredients in a bowl and stir well. Set aside.

2. Soak the rice noodles in warm water for 15 minutes and drain. Set aside.

3. Heat the oil in a wok or large pan over high heat. When the wok is very hot, add the garlic, shallots, radish, and tofu and toss gently. Crack the eggs into the wok. Using a spatula or a wooden spoon, stir until set, about 20 seconds.

4. Add the noodles and shrimp and stir together briefly with the other ingredients.

5. Add the chicken stock and cook until the noodles begin to soften, 2 to 3 minutes.

6. Drizzle in the sauce and toss to evenly coat the noodles. Reduce the heat to medium and continue to cook until the noodles absorb most of the sauce and become dry, 5 to 6 minutes.

7. Stir in the green onions, bean sprouts, and half of the chopped peanuts. Toss a few times and transfer to a plate. Sprinkle with the remaining peanuts and serve with lime wedges on the side.

Adapted from a recipe by CHAI SIRIYARN

INDIA

this fish stew comes from Kerala, India, an area known for its delightful coconut milk–enriched dishes. This recipe is mildly spiced with nuts and raisins to sweeten and add texture. Traditionally, one makes the coconut cream and milk from scratch as described on page 245, but canned coconut milk is fine too. For an authentic touch, serve this with Palappam (page 241) or bread and sliced tomatoes.

KERALA FISH STEW

SERVES 8

1 pound 2 ounces (510 g) halibut,
cut into large dice or bite-sized pieces

3 tablespoons vegetable oil

4 teaspoons salt

½ teaspoon ground white pepper

20 cashew nuts

20 golden raisins

2 red onions, peeled and thinly sliced

8 green chiles, stemmed, seeded,
and thinly sliced, or as needed

One 1-inch (2.5-cm) piece ginger,
peeled and thinly sliced

4 cloves garlic, peeled and thinly sliced

2 sprigs curry leaves

2 cups thin coconut milk

4 plum tomatoes,
sliced ¼ to ½ inch (⅛ to ½ cm) thick

1 cup thick coconut milk

1. Season the fish with 1 tablespoon of the vegetable oil, 1 teaspoon salt, and white pepper and set aside.

2. Heat 1 tablespoon of the oil over medium heat in a medium sauté pan. Cook the nuts for 1 minute and add the raisins. Cook, stirring occasionally, until the nuts are toasted and the raisins plump, about 1 more minute. Set aside.

3. Heat the remaining oil over medium-high heat and add the onions, chiles, ginger, and garlic and sauté for 2 minutes, or until the mixture softens.

4. Remove the curry leaves from the stem and add them to the pan. Pour in the thin coconut milk and bring to a boil.

5. Move the gravy to the sides and place the fish pieces in the center of the pan. After cooking for a minute, turn the fish over, and pull the gravy mix over the fish.

6. Reduce the heat to low (if the sauce boils vigorously, the coconut milk will curdle), add the tomatoes and the remaining salt and simmer just until the fish is cooked, about 5 minutes.

7. Pour in the thick coconut milk and remove from the heat immediately. Take care not to let the stew boil after adding the thick milk.

8. Garnish with the nuts and raisins and serve hot.

Adapted from a recipe by NIMMY PAUL

VIETNAM

in Hanoi, this popular dish is typically cooked on a charcoal brazier right at the table with diners assembling their own bowls throughout the meal. In this adapted version, the catfish is first fried and then served on a bed of rice noodles with sautéed green onions and dill. Halibut or mahi mahi is also delicious in this recipe.

HANOI FISH WITH DILL

SERVES 8

VIETNAMESE DIPPING SAUCE
8 Thai bird chiles
1 tablespoon minced garlic
¼ cup sugar
¾ cup warm water
3 tablespoons lime juice
7 tablespoons fish sauce
3 tablespoons finely shredded carrots, rinsed and patted dry

FISH
12 ounces (340 g) rice noodle vermicelli
1½ tablespoons peanut oil
1 cup julienned green onions
¼ cup Thai basil leaves, halved lengthwise
6 tablespoons cilantro leaves
1 cup dill sprigs, stemmed
¾ cup rice flour
1½ teaspoons turmeric
2 teaspoons salt
6 cups vegetable oil
2 pounds 4 ounces (1 kg) catfish fillets, cut into 2-inch (5-cm) squares
¼ cup roasted peanuts

1. *For the dipping sauce:* Slice 6 of the chiles into paper-thin rings and set aside for garnish. Mince the remaining chiles and transfer them to a medium bowl.

2. *Add* the garlic, sugar, water, lime juice, and fish sauce. Whisk to dissolve the sugar, 1 to 2 minutes. Add the carrots. Let the sauce rest for 10 minutes.

3. *For the fish:* Bring a pot of water to a rolling boil. Add the rice noodles and cook until they turn white and are soft, about 5 minutes, depending on the thickness. While cooking, stir to loosen the noodles and prevent them from sticking to the bottom of the pot. Once they're cooked, drain and rinse thoroughly. Set aside at room temperature.

4. *Heat* the peanut oil in a large sauté pan and stir-fry the green onions for 5 seconds or until they are just sweated. Add the basil, cilantro, and dill and stir-fry just until the herbs wilt, 30 to 45 seconds. Remove immediately and cool to room temperature.

5. *Combine* the rice flour, turmeric, and salt in a large bowl.

6. *Heat* the vegetable oil to 375°F (190°C) in a 3-quart (3-liter) pot.

7. *Toss* the fish in the flour mixture, shake off any excess, and immediately deep-fry until golden and crispy, about 4 minutes. Drain on paper towels and keep warm.

8. *Serve* 3 pieces of the fish on a bed of about ¾ cup of the noodles. Top with ¼ cup of the herb mixture. Garnish with 1½ teaspoons of the roasted peanuts and ¼ teaspoon of the chile rings. Repeat with the remaining fish and serve with the Vietnamese Dipping Sauce.

Adapted from a recipe by THE CULINARY INSTITUTE OF AMERICA

sambal is a simple Southeast Asian sauce made from chiles and basic seasonings such as salt or sugar and shrimp paste. It's used both as a condiment as well as a spice mixture to add to food during cooking. Here it complements cockles but it's great with any shellfish.

SAMBAL COCKLES
KAMPONG SAMBAL KERANG

SERVES 6

15 fresh red chiles, cut into thick slices, or as needed

1 teaspoon shrimp paste

5 shallots, peeled

1 pound 8 ounces (675 g) fresh cockles, clams, or mussels

5 tablespoons lard or vegetable oil

1 large onion, peeled and thinly sliced

½ teaspoon salt

1 teaspoon sugar

1 teaspoon lime juice, *calamansi* if possible

1. *Pound* or grind the chiles, shrimp paste, and shallots until fine.

2. *Wash* the cockles, clams, or mussels and soak in water for a few minutes to let the shellfish open and exude sand. Discard the water.

3. *Heat* a wok over medium heat, add the oil, and when it is hot, add the sliced onion. Stir-fry briefly and then add the chile paste and stir-fry until the oil from the paste and the mixture is fragrant, 1 to 2 minutes.

4. *Add* the shellfish and cover with a lid. Cook until the shells open, 4 to 5 minutes. Add the salt, sugar, and lime juice and serve.

Adapted from a recipe by LOUIS TAY

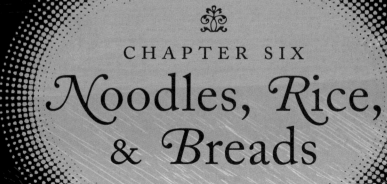

CHAPTER SIX

Noodles, Rice, & Breads

A DIVERSE FOOD GROUP

It's the last place one would expect to run into fresh noodles. Here, in an open lot near a freeway exit in Guangzhou, China, against the backdrop of traffic noise and concrete posts, Chen Ji Guo stands out with his chef's whites and toque, his arms and hands flying as he kneads and pulls *la mien*, a traditional handmade noodle. Behind him is a makeshift café with wobbly long tables where dozens of hungry construction workers gather to watch while eating their lunch.

A specialty noodle that originated and is eaten mostly in the northern provinces, *la mien*, with its theatrical technique, is becoming popular throughout China and Asia. Guo learned it from his father and grandfather while growing up in a village near Lanzhou, but recently moved here in hopes of making a better living. Every day he shows up at the café, slapping dough, stretching, braiding, and pulling it. Every 5, 10 minutes, he holds up long, beautiful, uniform strands and tosses them into boiling water. His sister, with a wire basket in hand, waits for them to rise to the top before pulling them out of the pot and assembling a bowl of noodles. Knowing when to pluck them from the water is critical. A minute too soon and the noodles will be tough and doughy; a little too late turns them into mush. Even in this casual setting, one can have some of the best noodles in the world, all made in front of your eyes.

In Japan, at a fancier garden-style restaurant tucked on a narrow street on the east side of Tokyo, the dining room echoes with faint hissing and slurping sounds. The family who runs this establishment has been making soba noodles for over a hundred years using buckwheat grown in a particular region. At one table, a diner slurps a bowl garnished with shrimp, *kombu*, egg, and shaved scallions. His lunch mate is chewing soba from a bed of cracked ice in a lacquer box. He picks up the noodles, dips them in an accompanying sauce, and quickly swallows them.

The art of noodles may have its genesis in China but they're made and eaten everywhere in Asia. If there's one unifying factor, it's that noodles—be they wheat, buckwheat, rice flour, sweet potato, or mung bean—are an essential food, beloved and enjoyed at all meals.

They show up in soups, salads, stir-fries, and snacks and as accompaniments to dishes such as curries and braises. Bread, especially flatbread, is not typically iconic of Asian cuisine, but it's a staple in northern China where wheat is grown, as well as in the Indian subcontinent and the Muslim-concentrated cities of Southeast Asia. In Beijing, markets are filled with flatbreads cooking over smoky griddles and vendors kneading and shaping dough to make buns and dumplings. In India and Singapore, it's hard not to see *roti prata* or *naan* of some kind served with curries or *dal*.

But for much of Southeast Asia, rice is the most essential starch—the building block of most meals. Deeply ingrained in Asian cultures for millennia, it's used in countless ways and forms—as a staple grain and as a flour in cakes, dumplings, rice sheets, noodles, breads, and desserts. It's also used to make alcoholic drinks such as rice wine and liquor, as well as other products such as ground rice, which is integral in making fermented fish products.

Rice is the symbol of life and the phrase "let's eat rice'" or even just the single word "rice" is an endearing phrase used to call friends and family to the table to eat. Traditionally, in an agrarian society, life evolves around the planting and harvesting of rice, and a family's wealth is often measured by the sacks of rice it owns. Fortunately for today's home cooks, the choice for rice is plentiful, from Indian basmati to Thai jasmine to Japanese short grain and to specialty varieties such as red or black rice and the many subvarieties within each group. This chapter will take you on a whirlwind tour of rice and noodle techniques as well as share with you enticing recipes that capture the very diverse nature of this food group.

this recipe is one of the many *bun* (rice vermicelli) dishes eaten all over Vietnam, both as a snack or a meal-in-a-bowl. It characterizes Vietnamese cooking on many levels—the layering of fresh greens and herbs, the room temperature noodles, and the hot grilled meat topping. Except for the hot topping, everything can be prepared in advance and assembled just before serving. Try it also with beef, chicken, or tofu.

VIETNAMESE RICE NOODLES WITH GRILLED PORK
BUN THIT NUONG

SERVES 4

PORK
2 tablespoons minced lemongrass

2 tablespoons sesame seeds,
lightly toasted (optional)

½ teaspoon shrimp sauce
or 1 tablespoon oyster sauce (optional)

1 tablespoon fish sauce

1½ teaspoons Caramel Sauce (page 230)
or 1 teaspoon light brown sugar

2 shallots, minced

1 clove garlic, minced

2 tablespoons vegetable oil

1 pound (450 g) pork shoulder, untrimmed,
partially frozen, cut along the grain into thin slices
(about 2 inches/5 cm wide by 4 inches/10 cm
long and ⅛ inch/3 mm thick)

12 bamboo skewers, soaked in water
for 15 minutes

NOODLE SALAD
10 ounces (280 g) dried (vermicelli-style)
rice sticks

2 cups shredded red or green leaf lettuce

1½ cups bean sprouts

⅓ cucumber, seeded, cut into thin matchsticks

⅓ cup mint leaves, cut into thirds

⅓ cup Asian basil and/or *rau ram* (Vietnamese
coriander) leaves, cut into thirds

2 tablespoons sliced shallots,
deep-fried until crispy

¼ cup chopped, roasted peanuts

1½ cups Vietnamese Dipping Sauce
(page 229)

1. **For the pork:** Combine the lemongrass, sesame seeds, if using, shrimp or oyster sauce, if using, fish sauce, Caramel Sauce, shallots, garlic, and oil in a bowl and stir well to blend. Add the pork and let it marinate for 20 minutes. Thread the meat onto the skewers and set aside.

2. **For the noodle salad:** Bring a large pot of water to a rolling boil over high heat. Add the rice sticks and stir gently to loosen them. Cook until they are white and soft, 4 to 5 minutes or more, depending on thickness. Drain and rinse under cold running water. Set them aside for at least 30 minutes. The noodles should be dry and "bouncy" before serving.

3. **Just** before serving, gently toss together the lettuce, bean sprouts, cucumber, mint, and basil. Divide the salad mixture among 4 large bowls. Top each with one-quarter of the rice noodles and set them aside.

4. **Preheat** a grill or broiler to high heat. (You can also cook in a pan.) Oil the grill, then grill the pork until the meat is done and the edges are nicely charred, 3 to 4 minutes total.

5. **To serve,** remove the pork from the skewers and divide among the four noodle bowls. Garnish each bowl with ½ tablespoon fried shallots, 1 tablespoon peanuts, and 3 to 4 tablespoons Vietnamese Dipping Sauce. Toss gently before eating.

Adapted from a recipe by MAI PHAM

CHINA

this dish is named after the capital city of the southwestern Chinese province of Sichuan. One of China's largest cities, Chengdu is known for its spicy food, which is built around chili oil, peppercorns, and chili powder. In this traditional cold noodle dish, the crisp and cool ingredients are contrasted by the chili oil and chili powder.

CHENGDU NOODLES

SERVES 8

1 pound (450 g) soba noodles

2¼ teaspoons canola or vegetable oil

3 cups mung bean sprouts

½ cup chiffonade iceberg lettuce head

2½ tablespoons chopped green onions

2 teaspoons salt

2 tablespoons thinly sliced garlic

2 tablespoons thinly sliced ginger

2 tablespoons peanut butter

2 tablespoons toasted sesame seeds

¼ cup chili oil

2¼ teaspoons crushed Sichuan peppercorns

¼ cup light soy sauce

6 tablespoons dark Chinkiang rice vinegar

¼ cup brown sugar

3 tablespoons Korean chili powder

2¼ teaspoons sesame oil

1. *B*ring 2 quarts of water to a boil in a 3-quart (3-liter) stockpot over high heat. Cook the noodles in the boiling water for 5 to 6 minutes, or until they are cooked through, then shock in cold water, and drain. Sprinkle the oil over the noodles and mix well.

2. *B*ring 6 cups of water to a boil over high heat. Blanch the bean sprouts until just cooked, 1 to 2 minutes, and drain. Shock the bean sprouts in ice water to stop the cooking. Drain the bean sprouts and toss with the iceberg lettuce and green onions.

3. *C*ombine the remaining ingredients thoroughly to make the sauce.

4. *T*oss the noodles in the sauce and divide among 8 bowls (about ¾ cup per bowl). Place ¼ cup of the bean sprout mixture on top of the noodles and serve.

Adapted from a recipe by SHIRLEY CHENG

Korea

a classic Korean noodle dish, *jap chae* is made with glass noodles or bean thread noodles. Made from mung bean or sweet potato starch, these dried noodles are clear and come in several thicknesses, from fine (about $\frac{1}{32}$) to medium ($\frac{1}{8}$). Choose a Korean brand as the noodles cook up plump and velvety. For an authentic meal, serve this with *Bulgogi* (page 122) or *Galbi* (page 145). It also makes a great salad by itself.

Stir-Fried Glass Noodles with Beef and Vegetables

JAP CHAE

SERVES 4

MARINADE

3 tablespoons soy sauce, or as needed

2 tablespoons sugar

1½ teaspoons corn syrup

1 tablespoon chopped garlic

2 tablespoons chopped green onions

1 tablespoon sesame oil, or as needed

½ teaspoon black pepper, or as needed

⅓ cup toasted sesame seeds, or as needed

1 tablespoon sesame oil, or as needed

2 tablespoons vegetable oil

½ teaspoon freshly ground black pepper

8 ounces (225 g) beef rib eye roll or strip steak, cut into a fine julienne

7 ounces (200 g) dried glass noodles

1 cup oyster mushrooms

1 cup julienned shiitake mushrooms

3 eggs

1½ tablespoons plus 2 teaspoons vegetable oil

1 teaspoon salt

1 cup julienned zucchini

¾ cup julienned carrots

1 cup julienned onions

1 julienned red bell pepper

Salt and freshly ground black pepper

1 tablespoon soy sauce

1 teaspoon sugar

1 tablespoon toasted pine nuts

1. *For the marinade:* Combine all of the ingredients for the marinade. Toss evenly to coat with the beef and marinate for 1 hour.

2. *Place* the glass noodles into warm water for 30 to 40 minutes.

3. *Meanwhile,* fill a large pot with water and bring to a boil over high heat. Add the oyster mushrooms and blanch until just barely cooked, about 2 minutes. Remove the mushrooms from the water and let cool.

4. *Bring* the water to a boil again. Blanch the shiitake mushrooms until just barely cooked, about 1 minute. Strain the shiitake mushrooms and set aside.

5. *Cut* the oyster mushrooms into half or thirds, depending on the size of the mushrooms.

6. *Separate* the egg yolks from the whites and lightly beat the whites. Heat 1 teaspoon of oil in a small sauté pan over medium-high heat. Add the egg whites and swirl the pan to create a crepe. Cook until the egg whites are set, about 2 minutes per side. Cool completely and cut into ⅛-inch (3-mm) julienne. Repeat with the egg yolks and another teaspoon of oil. Cool completely and cut the yolks into ⅛-inch (3-mm) julienne.

7. *Salt* the julienned zucchini with ½ teaspoon salt for 10 minutes to draw out the moisture and soften, then rinse off the salt and squeeze dry with a paper towel. Repeat this process with the carrot and the remaining salt.

8. *Add* 1 tablespoon of the oil to a large sauté pan and heat over medium heat. Sauté the mushrooms, zucchini, carrot, onion, and red bell pepper until just softened, 2 to 3 minutes. Season the vegetables with salt and pepper. Remove the vegetables from the pan and lay in a single layer on a baking sheet or plate.

9. *Heat* the remaining oil in the sauté pan over medium-high heat. Sauté the marinated beef until cooked through, 2 to 3 minutes. Remove the pan from the heat and set aside.

10. **Bring** a large pot of water to a boil and add the glass noodles. Cook until the glass noodles become tender and are cooked through, about 3 minutes. Drain and wash the glass noodles in cold water. Mix the soy sauce and sugar together and toss the noodles in the mixture.

11. **Place** the vegetables, beef, and noodles in a large bowl. Adjust the seasonings with soy sauce, sesame seeds, sugar, black pepper, and sesame oil. Mix all of the ingredients and then divide the noodle mixture among each of 4 bowls. Garnish with the egg strips in a crisscross pattern. Sprinkle 3 to 4 pine nuts on each portion and serve.

Adapted from a recipe by Dr. Hee Sook Cho

JAPAN

these little gems show what noodles can be when you apply Japanese aesthetics and sensibilities. Elizabeth Andoh of A Taste of Culture Cooking School in Tokyo prepares a noodle sushi by bundling the noodles before boiling and rolling them. Practice the tying technique a few times—once you get the hang of it, this dish is a great make-ahead. A single roll feeds one person as a light lunch or two as an appetizer.

BUCKWHEAT NOODLE ROLL

MAKES 4 ROLLS
(Serves 8 as an appetizer)

1 pound 4 ounces (560 g) dried soba noodles

2 cucumbers with edible peels
(about 6 ounces/175 g)

2 bunches radish sprouts (about 4 ounces/
115 g), rinsed and trimmed

4 full-sized sheets toasted nori

1 teaspoon wasabi paste

2 tablespoons white sesame seeds,
dry-roasted and cracked or ground

¼ cup Seasoned Soy Concentrate (page 232)

¼ cup Dashi Stock (page 60)

1. *If* your soba noodles come divided into bundles of about 3½ ounces, leave the bundles intact. Otherwise, divide the noodles into 4 bundles. Cut 8 pieces of kitchen string about 6 inches (15 cm) long. Lay 1 length of string on a dry cutting board and place 1 bundle of noodles on top, perpendicular to it. Wind the string twice around one end of the bundle and secure with an ordinary knot. Pull tightly to make sure the string is snug. Stand the noodles up to make sure they are perfectly flush to the board and that the string is as close to the bottom edge as possible without having it slip off. If your noodles were prebundled, tie them as above and carefully slip the band off the opposite end of the bundle. Repeat with all 4 bundles of noodles.

2. *Bring* several quarts of water to a rolling boil in a deep, wide pot. Holding single bundles by the twine, swish the noodles in the boiling water to separate out individual strands, then gently release the bundle into the water. Use long cooking chopsticks to gently poke the bundles and separate the strands.

3. *When* the water returns to a boil, adjust the heat to keep a steady but not vigorous boil and begin to time the noodles as per the package directions. If no time is listed, start with 4 minutes. Test the end of a strand; it should be firm and cooked through.

4. *When* the noodles are done, carefully lift them out of the water with a strainer and transfer them to a bowl of ice water. Reserve the cooking water.

5. *Gently* "comb out" the tangles from the noodles and lift them from the bowl of cold water, allowing excess water to drip off. Cover the noodles in plastic wrap if you will not be rolling them for several hours or more. Cook the remaining bundles using the reserved cooking water.

6. *Cut* the cucumbers on the diagonal into very thin slices. Stack the slices and cut them lengthwise into long shreds, each tipped with a dark green peel. Divide the cucumbers into 4 equal piles.

7. *Divide* the radish sprouts into 4 equal piles, leaving the stems aligned.

8. *Lay* a *sudare* (bamboo mat) on your work surface so that the slats run horizontally.

If there are string tassels on your mat, they should be away from you. Place a full sheet of nori, rough side up, and with shorter sides at the top and bottom, on the mat.

9. **Each** roll uses 2 bundles of noodles. Place one bundle of noodles on the nori with the open, fanned-out end aligned to the right and the tied end hanging over the end of the mat. Next, place the second bundle in the same manner but with the tied end to the right. The noodles should be spread out in an even layer with just a bit of overlap in the center, and with an uncovered border of nori on top to ensure complete coverage of the contents once the roll is formed. Trim away the tied ends of the noodles.

10. **Paint** a horizontal stripe of wasabi across the center of the noodles and sprinkle half the sesame seeds over it. Scatter one pile of cucumber over the sesame seeds and then top with 2 clusters of sprouts, their stems at the center of the roll.

11. **Place** your thumbs under the slatted mat near the corners. Lift up the edges of the mat and flip the nori over the noodles and the fillings, aiming to make contact just beyond the sloped noodles. An inch or so of uncovered nori should be clearly visible after flipping.

12. **With** one hand, hold this nori in place while tugging back slightly on the rolled portion of the mat. This will ensure that your fillings are enclosed. Continue to roll, lifting up from the top of the mat and gently pushing the noodle sushi away from you at the same time.

13. **Let** the finished roll sit, seam side down, on a cutting board while you make the other 3 rolls.

14. **Cleaning** your blade between each cut, slice each roll into 6 slices. Use the edge of the mat as a guide for cutting.

15. **Arrange** the slices on a platter. Mix the Seasoned Soy Concentrate and Dashi Stock and serve as a dipping sauce.

Reprinted with permission from Washoku *by* ELIZABETH ANDOH. *Copyright 2005 by Elizabeth Andoh, Ten Speed Press, Berkeley, CA. www.tenspeed.com*

Noodles

Buying the right kind of Asian noodle can be a daunting task, especially if you're at a well-stocked Asian market and staring at dozens of brands. For example, dried Vietnamese *bun* and *banh pho* noodles are different in terms of appearance, flavor, and usage and yet both are often labeled "rice sticks." Rice noodles called for in a Thai dish may be quite different from those used in a Singaporean recipe and so it's important to purchase the correct kind and size. The following list includes the most common noodles called for in this book.

RICE VERMICELLI

There are two common types of dried rice vermicelli. One is sold as Vietnamese *bun*, which turns white, soft, and bouncy when cooked, and is available in three sizes: small (similar to capellini), medium, and large (similar to spaghetti). The smaller varieties are used in Vietnamese noodle salads and salad rolls and with Thai curries. The thicker ones are used for noodle soups. Depending on the thickness, *bun* noodles need to be boiled in ample water and for a longer period than one would expect. For best results, taste-test several times during cooking—the medium to large noodles can take almost 15 minutes. Recently fresh vermicelli has been showing up at many Asian markets.

The second type of dried rice vermicelli is the thin, slightly wiry noodles, sometimes labeled "rice sticks." More firm and dense than *bun*, they cook up beige, and are used in Chinese stir-fries and Thai noodle soups.

RICE STICKS

Often called by their Vietnamese name *banh pho* or the Thai name *jantaboon*, these dried, flat, linguine-style rice noodles are typically used for pad thai and other stir-fries as well as noodle soups such as *pho*. They're available in three sizes: small, medium, and large ($\frac{1}{16}$, $\frac{1}{8}$, and $\frac{1}{2}$ inch thick, respectively). The thin ones are best for soups and the wide for stir-fries. To parcook these noodles, drop them in boiling water and stir vigorously just until they're soft but still firm in the center, anywhere from 10 seconds for the small, 2 minutes for the medium, and 4 to 5 minutes for the large. Rinse in cold water and drain completely before using to prevent sticking. For soups, re-dunk in hot water before assembling the dish. If you need to portion the noodles, do it immediately after rinsing while they're still easy to handle. For stir-fries, add directly to the pan. Fresh rice sticks used for Vietnamese *pho* are now available at many Asian markets. Packed in 1-pound or 10-pound plastic bags, the noodles are off white and stiff. Once blanched in boiling water for 30 seconds, the noodles soften and are ready to be bathed in a good noodle broth.

EGG, WHEAT, AND SOBA

Both fresh and dried egg noodles are readily available. The most common fresh ones are the round, spaghetti-like noodles often used for *chow mein*, the thin ones (also called "wonton noodles") used for soups, and the thick, linguine style also referred to as "Shanghai noodles." As a general rule, thin noodles are best for soups and thicker ones for stir-fries. Dried egg noodles—available as regular or instant—come in many flavors, such as shrimp and chicken, and are sold as single-portion packs or as bags of nests. These are great for noodle soups and stir-fries.

In the dried wheat noodle category, the thin, straight wheat noodle sold as *somen* in Japanese cooking is great for noodle salads and soups and is a good substitute for rice vermicelli. Make sure to boil them in plenty of water and rinse them vigorously before using. *Udon*, also made from wheat, is sold fresh, dried, and semidried (these are cooked but sold in individual packages), and is used in hot soups and cold dishes.

Another great Japanese noodle is *soba*, made from buckwheat and sometimes a small amount of wheat or yam flour for added pliability. Depending on the type, soba cook to an earthy color with whole-grain flavor and are delicious in soups and salads.

CELLOPHANE/SWEET POTATO NOODLES

Also known as "glass noodles" or "mung bean threads," cellophane noodles are made from mung bean starch. These clear, thin, wiry noodles are typically sold in bundles of 1-pound packages. Popular in all Asian cuisines, they're used in braises, soups, stir-fries, and salads. The greenish variety preferred in Korean cooking is made from sweet potato starch and comes in several thicknesses. Despite their delicate form, these noodles are resilient and should be soaked in water for about 30 minutes before using. Be sure to drain them completely before using in a stir fry. They absorb a lot of water during cooking so add more stock or water at the end for a moist dish.

*S*INGAPORE

this very popular Singaporean noodle dish is a cousin of the classic Cantonese *chow fun*, only adapted to include local ingredients such as cockles and chili paste. Traditionally the noodles are made with lard and pork cracklings, but vegetable oil works equally well. For the best flavor, cook this in two batches and make sure the pan is very hot so the noodles don't stick. If you're using a wok, get it smoking hot.

SINGAPORE STIR-FRIED NOODLES
CHAR KWAY TEOW

SERVES 4

1 to 2 Chinese sausages

5 tablespoons water

½ teaspoon salt

1 pound (450 g) fresh rice noodles (chow fun noodles) or 8 ounces (225 g) dried large-sized rice noodles

½ cup vegetable oil

2 teaspoons finely minced garlic

2 cups bean sprouts, roots removed, washed and drained to dry

1 tablespoon black sweet soy sauce (*kecap manis*), plus 1 to 1 ½ tablespoons for garnish

3 eggs, lightly beaten

½ to 1 tablespoon chili paste, or as needed

1 bunch chives, cut into 2-inch (5-cm) lengths

½ cup cooked cockles or mussels, meat only (optional)

1. *B*ring a medium saucepan of water to a boil over high heat. Lightly blanch the sausages, about 1 minute. Drain the sausages and cool at room temperature until they can easily be handled. Peel the skin off the sausages and cut each one into ⅛-inch (3-mm) thick slices.

2. *C*ombine the water and salt and set aside.

3. *B*ring a large pot of water to a boil. If using dried rice noodles, boil the noodles until they are halfway cooked, 2 to 3 minutes. Drain and set aside.

4. *H*eat a wok over high heat and, when it starts to smoke, add 3 to 4 tablespoons of oil. Add the garlic and stir-fry until lightly browned, about 10 seconds.

5. *A*dd the bean sprouts and rice noodles and stir-fry vigorously for a few seconds before sprinkling 2 to 3 tablespoons of the water and salt mixture over the top, stir-frying the entire time. Add the black soy sauce and continue stir-frying for a few seconds or until the noodles look coated.

6. *P*ush the noodle mixture to one side of the wok, add another 2 to 3 tablespoons of oil and, when it is hot, add the eggs. Stir-fry the eggs until they just start to cook, about 30 seconds. Stir well with the noodle mixture.

7. *P*ush the noodles to the side of the wok again and add 1 more tablespoon of oil. Add the chili paste and Chinese sausages. Stir-fry well for about 5 seconds, or until the sausages look wilted and slightly darker, then stir into the noodle mixture.

8. *A*dd the chives, additional sweet soy sauce, and cockles, if using. Stir-fry briefly and then serve.

Adapted from a recipe by VIOLET OON

although cellophane noodles originated in China, they are used throughout Asia. Their mild flavor and transparent color make them a perfect backdrop for all sorts of soups, salads, and stir fries. This simple recipe from Charles Phan of the Slanted Door in San Francisco epitomizes his passion for using very fresh ingredients and allowing their flavors to shine through. Get your wok or pan really hot before cooking.

STIR-FRIED CELLOPHANE NOODLES WITH DUNGENESS CRAB

SERVES 4

4 ounces/115 g (2 packages) thin cellophane (mung bean thread) noodles

2 tablespoons canola oil

1 tablespoon minced garlic

3 green onions, sliced ¼ inch (½ cm) thick

4 ounces (115 g) Dungeness crabmeat, picked through

1½ tablespoons fish sauce, or as needed

1 tablespoon soy sauce

1 to 2 tablespoons oyster sauce, or as needed

1 tablespoon sesame oil

8 fresh cilantro sprigs

1. Soak the noodles in hot water (about 180°F/80°C) for about 10 minutes or until they soften. Drain and set aside.

2. Heat a wok or large sauté pan over high heat. This will dry out any moisture and help to prevent food from sticking to the cooking surface.

3. Add the oil to the pan. Heat until it begins to smoke.

4. Add the garlic, green onions, and noodles. Cook, tossing and stirring, to mix the ingredients together, about 20 seconds.

5. Add the crab and stir gently to mix all of the ingredients together.

6. Add the fish, soy, and oyster sauces. Continue to toss and stir.

7. Drizzle in the sesame oil and combine it well with the other ingredients.

8. Serve immediately and garnish with cilantro.

Adapted from a recipe by CHARLES PHAN

CHINA

this dish from Beijing calls for a sauce made with soybean paste and aromatics. The noodles topped with a pork and yellow soybean paste evokes images of the classic pasta and meat sauce. The yellow soybean paste imparts a salty, savory flavor. If this is not available, you can substitute hoisin sauce.

BEIJING NOODLES WITH PORK

SERVES 4

PASTE
2 tablespoons vegetable oil
10 ounces (280 g) minced pork loin
2 tablespoons minced leek
1 teaspoon minced ginger
1 clove garlic, minced
3 to 4 tablespoons Chinese yellow soybean paste, or to taste
1 tablespoon Chinese yellow rice wine
1 tablespoon dark Chinese soy sauce
1½ teaspoons sugar
1 tablespoon chicken powder or chicken bouillon (optional)

2 pounds (900 g) fresh wheat noodles or 1 pound (450 g) dried wheat noodles

1. *For the paste:* Heat the oil over medium-high heat in a wok or large sauté pan. Add the pork and sauté briefly until it is just barely cooked, 1 to 2 minutes. Remove the pork from the pan and set aside.

2. *Add* the leek, ginger, and garlic to the pan and sauté until their aroma is released, about 30 seconds. Add the soybean paste, rice wine, soy sauce, and sugar. Sauté briefly until the paste is slightly darkened, about 1 minute. Add the pork back to the pan with its juices and mix thoroughly with the paste. Keep warm, covered.

3. *Bring* a large pot of water to a boil over high heat. Add the noodles and cook until tender, 5 to 6 minutes.

4. *Add* ½ cup of the pasta water to the sauce and rewarm over medium-low heat.

5. *Divide* the noodles among 4 bowls and top with the meat sauce. Serve immediately.

Adapted from a recipe by QIANG JIN

Rice

In the West, rice is often regarded as a side dish meant to accompany a savory entrée. In Asia, however, it's almost the reverse—rice is the main dish and meat and other savory foods are served in smaller portions to complement the rice. According to Chinese beliefs, a nutritious meal should have proper harmony between *fan,* or grains and rice, and *t'sai,* or vegetables and meat. How one cooks and eats rice is of great importance.

There are thousands of varieties and subvarieties of rice although, today, most of the world production comes from a much smaller pool. For practical purposes, rice is typically identified and grouped by the size of the grain: long, medium, and short. Long grain means the milled grain is three times as long as it is wide; medium grain is twice to less than three times as long as it is wide; and short grain is less than twice as long.

For rice lovers, the good news is that there are plenty of choices. The most common Asian rices available today are the aromatic long-grain Thai jasmine variety, which cooks to a soft, slightly clingy texture, and the Indian basmati, which is slender with needle-shaped ends and stays separate when cooked. The Japanese medium- and short-grain rices are soft, shiny, and slightly sticky when cooked. There are also many other good quality medium- and long-grain varieties grown in the United States that are readily available.

Another important type of rice is glutinous rice, also referred to as "sticky rice" or "sweet rice," and it can be long, medium, or short grain. In some countries such as Thailand and Laos, sticky rice is a staple and eaten in lieu of rice. More dense and filling than regular rice, sticky rice needs less water and is often soaked overnight before steaming. When soaked for at least 4 hours, the rice cooks quickly but still maintains its soft, fluffy texture.

In recent years, different brown rice varieties as well as specialty grains, such as red and black rice, are showing up on the shelves. These varieties often have a more intense, nutty, whole-grain flavor with a firmer texture. Thai black rice, which is a long-grain sticky rice, is commonly used to make desserts and sweet puddings. Dishes made from a blend of both black and white sticky rice turn into a beautiful purple-black color.

When buying short-grain rice, make sure it's fresh and preferably from a "new crop" lot. If you don't eat much rice, buy a small amount because the sweet fragrance of rice does dissipate over time. To minimize this, store it for up to 1 month in a tight-lidded container in a dry place or use ziplock plastic bags.

WASHING AND SOAKING

These days, with all the modern technology surrounding the milling, cleaning, and polishing of rice, one does not actually *need* to wash rice before using. But in Asia, practically every cook washes rice in several changes of water. Washing removes all surface starch from the raw kernels, making the rice less sticky and more translucent when cooked. This makes the rice

smell and taste pure, aromatic, and nutty as opposed to being "muddied" by the excess surface starch.

To wash, measure the rice into a large bowl and cover with cold water. Swish vigorously (but not so much that it breaks the grains) until the water becomes starchy. Drain and repeat until the water runs clear, which should take 3 to 4 washes. Drain the rice in a fine-mesh strainer after the final rinsing.

COOKING RICE

Good rice is fresh rice, period. You can start with the best batch of grains, but if it's been cooked even half an hour in advance, the taste and texture will be less than optimal. Try to time the rice so it's done just minutes before you eat.

There are several ways to cook rice but the best ways are the absorption method with the exact amount of rice and water and, for sticky rice and specialty rice, the steaming method. For the former, place the rice and cold water in a rice-cooker insert pan, or in a heavy-bottomed pot with a tight-fitting lid. As a general rule, use 1 part rice to 1⅓ parts water. If you washed the rice, make sure it's completely drained before cooking. If the rice has turned somewhat opaque, reduce the water slightly. If the rice is from a "new crop," meaning it came from a recent harvest with higher moisture than normal, it'd be wise to reduce the water to 1¼ parts. Also, if you prefer a firmer texture, reduce the water slightly.

Let the water come to a boil in the pot, then give it one stir and cover with a lid. Reduce the heat to medium and cook for 5 minutes. Then reduce the heat again, this time to the lowest possible setting and allow the rice to finish cooking for another 15 minutes. Remove from the heat, but do not open the lid. Let the rice sit for at least 5 minutes before serving.

If you're using a rice cooker, simply go with the same rice-to-water proportion and hit the "cook" button. The cooker will automatically set the appropriate temperature and time. An automatic cooker not only simplifies the cooking but allows you to cook the rice closer to serving time. If you do not already have one, invest in an insulated rice cooker. This feature is useful because it will keep the rice warm for several hours.

The steam method is often used to cook glutinous or sticky rice, which benefits from soaking overnight or for at least 4 hours. The kernels should be completely swollen before steaming. You can use a three-tiered Chinese steamer by placing water on the bottom pan and lining the trays above with wet cheesecloth. Or, you can use a Thai or Lao rice-steaming bamboo basket that sits on the narrow opening of a rounded, no-handle, potbellied pot. This produces sticky rice that stays separate and firm when cooked. Soak the basket for at least 30 minutes before using to prevent the rice from sticking.

The Chinese tiered steamer can also be used for steaming regular rice in small, individual bowls. For this method, place the washed rice with just enough water to cover it in a bowl and steam for about 20 minutes. This method is particularly useful and attractive when other ingredients like small dices of vegetables are added. A beautiful no-handle teacup with a lid makes a great container for this purpose.

For tips on how to prepare perfect rice in the Japanese tradition, see page 195. This technique applies to medium- or long-grain rice.

in asking the question, "how do you cook rice," one should be prepared for many different answers as there are many ways of cooking rice. On the one hand, it's a simple dish but on the other, it's a dish that requires a lot of skill as well as art. In this recipe, Kunio Tokuoka shares his method for obtaining the perfect moist and fluffy bowl of rice.

PERFECT RICE, THE JAPANESE WAY
KOME NO TAKIKATA

SERVES 8

3 cups polished, short-grain rice
or medium-grain rice
3 cups plus 3 tablespoons water

1. Fill a large bowl with cold tap water. Place the dry rice in a finely meshed strainer. Have a tall and narrow, heavy-bottomed cooking pot with a tight-fitting lid ready. It should be about 8 inches (20 cm) in diameter and 5½ inches (14 cm) tall.

2. Submerge the rice in the strainer in the cold water and give several large, quick stirs with your hand. The starch and rice bran residue from the rice milling process turns the water immediately milky in color. Quickly remove the strainer from the water so that the rice does not absorb unpleasant odors and flavor from the cloudy water and discard the water.

3. Fill the bowl again with fresh cold tap water and resubmerge the rice in the strainer in the bowl. Give several quick and large stirs to the rice with your hand. Remove the strainer, discarding the water. Refill the bowl again with cold tap water.

4. Form one of your hands into a fist. Place it gently against the rice in the strainer and move it back and forth over the rice about 10 times. Then submerge the strainer into the water and give several quick stirs. Repeat the process—rubbing the rice and rinsing it in water—three additional times. Drain the rice in the strainer, cover it with a moist kitchen towel, and leave it for half an hour. Covering the rice with the moist towel prevents the surface of the rice grains from cracking when they dry. At the same time this helps each grain of rice to hold moisture down to the center of the grain.

5. Transfer the rice to the pot, add the measured water, and let it stand for 1 hour.

6. Place the pot, covered with the tight-fitting lid, over high heat and bring it to a boil. Once it boils, carefully remove the lid and give a couple of large and deep stirs to the rice, maintaining the high heat. Return the lid immediately. This process helps the temperature of each grain of rice in the pot stay equal, and it also prevents the rice from sticking to the bottom of the pot.

7. After returning the lid to the pot, bring the mixture almost to another boil. Then turn the heat to low and cook for an additional 13 minutes. Remove the lid from the pot and serve the rice immediately in individual rice bowls. There is no need to stir the rice before serving.

Adapted from a recipe by KUNIO TOKUOKA

typically an autumn dish, this rice recipe features the earthy and comforting combination of sweet potato and gingko nuts. During other times of the year, different vegetables may be used. A pot of rice can be enhanced by adding fresh peas, lotus root, or mushrooms.

RICE WITH SWEET POTATO AND GINGKO NUTS

SATSUMAIMO, GIN'NAN GOHAN

SERVES 8

3 cups short-grain, polished white rice

6½ cups water

¼ teaspoon salt

7 ounces (200 g) sweet potato, cut into medium cubes

12 gingko nuts

1. *H*ave a tall and narrow, heavy-bottomed cooking pot with a tight-fitting lid at hand. It should be about 8 inches (20 cm) in diameter and 5½ inches (14 cm) high.

2. *R*inse the rice following the instructions on page 195 through Step 4. Drain the rice and leave it in the strainer for 20 minutes. Transfer the rice to a bowl and add 3 cups of water. Let the rice stand for 20 minutes. In another bowl combine the remaining water with the salt and stir to dissolve.

3. *D*rain the rice and transfer it to the pot. Add the salt water to the pot and level the surface of the rice. Arrange the sweet potato cubes evenly over the rice. Cover the pot with the lid, place it over high heat, and bring the ingredients to a boil. Boil for 7 to 10 minutes. Carefully remove the lid and add the gingko nuts. Return the lid immediately and cook until it boils again, 1½ to 2 minutes. After coming to a full boil, quickly reduce the heat and cook over medium-low heat for 5 minutes. Turn the heat to low and cook an additional 5 minutes.

4. *L*et the rice stand, covered, for 10 minutes. Remove the lid and stir the rice gently and briefly so that the potato and nuts are evenly mixed with the rice. Serve the rice in individual rice bowls while hot.

Adapted from a recipe by YOSHIHIRO TAKAHASHI

one of Singapore's most iconic street foods, this simple dish is particularly delicious if the chicken is the full-flavor organic type. The essence of this dish is in the sweet, natural flavor of the chicken and the delicate gelatinous juices between the meat and bones. Traditionally, the leftover broth is served as a soup and garnished with thin slices of cabbage as well as deep-fried shallots.

SINGAPORE HAINAN CHICKEN RICE

SERVES 4

CHICKEN

2 quarts (2 liters) chicken stock

2 quarts (2 liters) water

2 teaspoons sea salt

1 chicken (about 2 pounds 8 ounces/1 kg)

2 to 3 scallions, washed and cleaned

4 to 5 ginger slices

RICE

6 tablespoons vegetable oil

1½ tablespoons chopped garlic

1 tablespoon minced galangal or ginger

3 cups long-grain uncooked rice, washed, and drained

4 pandan leaves, lightly bruised, tied into a knot

1 teaspoon salt, or as needed

½ cup Ginger Sauce (page 228), or as needed

½ cup Chile-Garlic Sauce (page 228), or as needed

1. *F*or the chicken: Combine the chicken stock, water, and salt in a large stockpot and bring to a boil over high heat. Meanwhile, stuff the cavity of the chicken with the scallions and ginger.

2. *W*hen the water comes to a rolling boil, add the chicken, breast side down. Lower the heat to a simmer (just under the boiling point) and cook, covered, until done, 35 to 40 minutes. Check for doneness by piercing the leg; the juices should run clear.

3. *T*ransfer the chicken to an ice-water bath and leave it there for 5 to 6 minutes. This stops the cooking and firms the chicken skin. Remove the scallions and ginger from the chicken and return them to the pot with the stock. Debone the chicken, cut the meat into bite-sized pieces, and set aside. Keep the chicken stock hot.

4. *F*or the rice: Heat the oil in a large stockpot over high heat. Add the garlic and galangal and stir-fry until fragrant. Add the uncooked rice grains and stir-fry for 1 to 2 minutes, then transfer to a rice cooker or pot. Add 3 to 3¼ cups of the hot chicken stock (the liquid should be about ½ inch/1 cm above the rice level), the pandan leaves, and salt. Stir, then allow the rice to cook until done, about 25 minutes. Serve immediately with the chicken and Ginger and Chile-Garlic sauces. Serve the remaining stock as soup on the side.

Adapted from a recipe by VIOLET OON

Korea

bibimbap, a popular Korean rice dish, is very versatile and can be topped with just about any meat or vegetable. What makes it special and festive is the stone pot it's traditionally served in, the beautiful arrangement of the vegetable toppings, and the accompanying sauce. This lighter version calls for tuna and tofu as well as many vegetables.

KOREAN RICE BOWL WITH TUNA AND VEGETABLES
BIBIMBAP

SERVES 4

VEGETABLE SAUCE
1 teaspoon minced garlic
1 tablespoon chopped green onions
¼ cup sesame oil
1½ tablespoons salt
1 tablespoon honey
½ teaspoon cracked black peppercorns

1½ cups soybean sprouts
½ cup julienned celery root
½ cup julienned cucumbers
¼ cup julienned carrots
¾ cup julienned Pyogo or shiitake mushrooms
8 ounces (225 g) tuna, cut into thin strips
¼ cup julienned tofu
1½ teaspoons sesame seeds
½ teaspoon salt
2 cups cooked white rice
1 tablespoon red pepper paste
1 tablespoon vegetable oil
4 large eggs
1 tablespoon pine nuts

1. *For the vegetable sauce:* Mix all of the ingredients together. Set aside.

2. *Bring* a medium pot of salted water to a boil. Blanch the soy bean sprouts in the water until cooked, soft, and transparent, 1 to 2 minutes. Remove the sprouts and rinse in cold water to stop the cooking. Mix the sprouts with ½ teaspoon vegetable sauce and set aside.

3. *Bring* the water back to a boil and blanch the celery root until cooked, about 15 seconds. Remove the celery root and rinse in cold water to stop the cooking. Mix the celery root with ½ teaspoon vegetable sauce and set aside.

4. *Soak* the cucumbers for about 10 minutes in the salted water, or until they soften slightly. Drain. Heat a small sauté pan over low heat, add ½ teaspoon of the vegetable sauce to the pan, and sauté the cucumbers until cooked, 1 to 2 minutes. Repeat with the carrot and Pyogo mushrooms, cooking the carrots for 2 to 3 minutes in 1 teaspoon vegetable sauce, and cooking the mushrooms for 1 to 2 minutes, setting them aside separately.

5. *Mix* the tuna with ½ teaspoon vegetable sauce. Mix the tofu with 1 teaspoon vegetable sauce.

6. *Combine* the sesame seeds and salt to make sesame salt.

7. *Mix* the cooked rice with the red pepper paste, 1½ teaspoons of sesame salt, the remaining vegetable sauce, and half of the reserved vegetables.

8. *Place* the mixed rice and vegetables in a serving bowl. In an attractive circular pattern, neatly arrange the remaining vegetables and tuna on top of the rice (see photo at right).

9. *Heat* a small sauté pan over medium heat. Add the vegetable oil and eggs to the pan and fry until the whites are cooked but the yolks are still runny, 2 to 3 minutes. Place an egg in the center of each bowl and garnish with the pine nuts. Serve immediately.

Adapted from a recipe by MYUNG SOOK LEE

according to sushi expert Hiroko Shimbo, sushi rice—called *sumeshi* (vinegar-flavored) or *shari* in Japanese—should not be eaten immediately after cooking but allowed to set for an hour. Transfer the rice to a plastic container, lay a moist paper towel on top, and cover with a lid. Float in a bowl of warm water, changing it as it gets cool. The best tasting rice is about 98°F (36°C) when used. Never refrigerate the rice.

Sushi Rice

MAKES 6 CUPS RICE
(Enough for 6 thick rolls)

2¼ cups dry raw Japonica or medium-grain
California rice

2¼ cups water

5 tablespoons rice vinegar

1½ teaspoons sea salt

2 tablespoons sugar

1. Pour the rice into a large fine-mesh strainer and have on hand a larger bowl into which the strainer can fit. Fill the bowl with cold water and lower the strainer into the bowl so that the water covers the rice.

2. With both hands, gently rub, turn, and toss the rice. Do not press the grains too hard against the strainer or against one another, or the fragile grains may break, especially if you are using a lower grade of rice. The water will instantly turn milky white, so remove the strainer from the large bowl, discard the water, and refill the bowl with fresh cold water. Repeat two or three times until the water is almost clear. Drain the rice and let it sit in the strainer for 10 minutes.

3. Transfer the rice to a heavy-bottomed pot that is deeper than it is wide and has a heavy, tight-fitting lid. During cooking, rice swells to as much as two and a half times its original volume, so your pot should be at least three times deeper than the level of rice and water. Add the water and let sit for 20 minutes.

4. Set the rice over medium heat and cook, uncovered, until the water is nearly absorbed by the rice, about 10 minutes. Quickly reduce the heat to very low, cover the pot with the lid, and cook until the rice is plump and cooked through, another 10 minutes.

5. After a total of 20 minutes cooking, take a quick look: the rice should be completely transparent. If you see any dry, very white-looking grains, sprinkle a little warm water over the dry spots and cook another couple of minutes over very low heat. During cooking, never stir the rice.

6. After confirming that all the rice grains are transparent, immediately put the lid back on before the built-up steam can escape. Turn off the heat and let the rice stand for 5 minutes.

7. While the rice is cooking, place the vinegar, salt, and sugar in a bowl and stir with a whisk until the sugar and salt are almost dissolved.

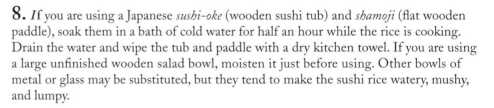

8. *If* you are using a Japanese *sushi-oke* (wooden sushi tub) and *shamoji* (flat wooden paddle), soak them in a bath of cold water for half an hour while the rice is cooking. Drain the water and wipe the tub and paddle with a dry kitchen towel. If you are using a large unfinished wooden salad bowl, moisten it just before using. Other bowls of metal or glass may be substituted, but they tend to make the sushi rice watery, mushy, and lumpy.

9. *Transfer* the steaming hot rice all at once to the sushi tub or salad bowl. Quickly and gently break up the rice, crisscrossing it with the side of your paddle.

10. *Pour* the prepared vinegar dressing evenly over it and, with the paddle, break up the lumpy clumps and turn the rice over, working one area at a time. Repeat once or twice until you can tell by looking that the vinegar dressing is evenly distributed. Push the rice toward one side of the tub.

11. *Now* hold the paddle horizontally and insert the paddle into the rice in one area, then rapidly move it back and forth with many small strokes. By cutting the rice this way, you are breaking up the clumps and pushing a portion of the rice toward the opposite side of the tub. Work on the remaining areas of the rice in the same way until you have moved all the rice to the other side of the tub. Rotate the tub 180 degrees and repeat the process. The whole procedure should take about 2 minutes.

12. *Fan* the rice for about 30 seconds. This quick fanning gelatinizes the surface of the rice to give it a glossy appearance and also cools it, helping the vinegar dressing to settle inside each grain.

13. *If* the rice is still very hot, cover with a moist kitchen towel and allow to cool to about 98°F (36°C) until using.

CHINA

chinese sausage, which is a firm, dry sausage, gets its distinctive flavor from cured pork and spices. It's often used to give rice dishes, such as this one, a savory smoky flavor. This may need to be done in 2 batches if the pan is too small. Do not use overcooked rice.

FRIED RICE WITH CHINESE SAUSAGE

SERVES 4

¼ cup medium diced carrots

¼ cup vegetable oil

2 ounces (50 g) Chinese sausage, medium dice (¼ cup)

¼ cup minced onions

¾ cup medium diced shiitake mushrooms

¾ cup roughly chopped napa cabbage

2½ cups cooked long-grain rice, chilled

1 teaspoon salt, or as needed

¼ teaspoon freshly ground black pepper

1 cup snow peas, cut in half

8 ounces (225 g) shrimp (16/20 count), peeled and deveined

2 eggs, beaten

1 tablespoon mushroom soy sauce, or as needed (optional)

1. **B**ring 2 quarts (2 liters) of water to a boil over high heat in a medium saucepan. Blanch the carrots until they are just cooked, about 2 minutes.

2. **H**eat 1 tablespoon of the oil in a wok or large sauté pan over medium heat. Add the sausage and cook until the fat is rendered, 2 to 3 minutes.

3. **Increase** the heat to medium-high and add the onions. Stir-fry until they are aromatic and beginning to brown, about 1 minute.

4. **A**dd the carrots and cook until they begin to brown, about 2 minutes. Add 1½ teaspoons of the oil and allow it to heat up. Add the mushrooms and cook until they begin to brown, about 2 minutes. Add the cabbage and cook until it begins to brown, about 2 minutes.

5. **A**dd the rice, salt, and pepper and stir-fry until the rice is hot and begins to brown, about 3 minutes.

6. **A**dd the snow peas and shrimp and cook until the snow peas are bright green and the shrimp is almost cooked through, about 3 minutes.

7. **A**dd the remaining oil to the sides of the wok and drizzle the eggs around the top of the rice. As the egg cooks, fold it into the rice.

8. **A**djust the seasoning with salt, pepper, and soy sauce, if using. Serve immediately.

Adapted from a recipe by THE CULINARY INSTITUTE OF AMERICA

INDIA

bread is an integral part of Indian cuisine. Made with wheat flour, yeast, and yogurt, this flatbread is a great side dish or appetizer served with chutney. When baked in a clay tandoori oven, the extremely hot chamber creates crisp bubbles on the outside of the bread and makes it fluffy and toasty. But naan can also be baked in a regular oven and filled with meat, cheese, raisins, nuts, or simply brushed with butter as in this recipe.

NAAN

SERVES 8

1 pound 8 ounces (675 g) all-purpose flour

1½ teaspoons salt

1½ teaspoons sugar

1 egg

¼ cup milk

¼ cup plain yogurt

2 tablespoons melted butter or vegetable oil,
plus as needed for garnish

¾ teaspoon yeast

1 to 1¼ cups warm water, or as needed

1. Mix all of the ingredients except for the water together in a bowl.

2. Gradually add the water and knead until a smooth, soft dough is achieved, about 10 minutes.

3. Set aside for about 6 hours in a warm place.

4. Make tennis ball–sized pieces of dough, and place the balls in a warm place until they rise again, about 1 hour.

5. Preheat the oven to 475°F (240°C).

6. Flatten each dough ball and spread it with a rolling pin or by hand by tossing and slapping with both hands. Gently stretch each piece of dough into a round 7 inches (18 cm) in diameter, so that the center is ¼ inch (6 mm) thick and there is a border ½ inch (1 cm) wide all around. Pull one edge out to elongate each round slightly, creating a teardrop shape.

7. Place the bread onto a parchment paper–lined sheet pan and brush with a little butter.

8. Bake the naans in the oven until golden brown and puffed, 4 to 5 minutes. Cool completely on racks.

9. Garnish with a little butter, if desired.

Adapted from a recipe by ROHIT SINGH

one of the most popular street foods in Vietnam, this light, eggless crepe is traditionally made with sliced pork belly and shell-on shrimp, then served with mustard leaves and fresh herbs. The key to this recipe is to make sure the pan is very hot before the batter goes in (this helps set it quickly) and to use Asian rice flour. Consider serving this dish for your next barbecue.

SIZZLING SAIGON CREPES

SERVES 4

BATTER
2 cups rice flour
⅓ cup unsweetened coconut milk
2⅓ cups water
1 teaspoon ground turmeric
1 teaspoon sugar
1 teaspoon salt
½ teaspoon curry powder
3 green onions, cut into thin rings

5 tablespoons vegetable oil
2 cups sliced shiitake mushrooms
1 teaspoon salt
½ teaspoon freshly ground black pepper
½ cup thinly sliced yellow onions
4 ounces (115 g) pork shoulder or chicken breast, thinly sliced
12 shrimp (16/20 count), peeled and deveined
4 cups bean sprouts

1 cup Vietnamese Dipping Sauce (page 229)
Table Salad (page 114)

1. For the batter: Place all of the ingredients in a bowl and stir well to blend. Set aside.

2. For the filling: Heat 1 tablespoon of the vegetable oil in a large sauté pan over medium-high heat. Lightly sauté the shiitakes until they have just wilted slightly, 4 to 5 minutes. Season with ½ teaspoon salt and ¼ teaspoon pepper while cooking. Remove the mushrooms from the pan and set aside. Drain off any excess liquid from the mushrooms before using.

3. Heat 1 tablespoon of the oil in a large (preferably 12-inch/30-cm) nonstick sauté pan over high heat. Add 2 tablespoons of the onion, 1 ounce (25 g) of the pork, and 3 shrimp to the pan and stir until fragrant, about 15 seconds. Season the mixture with about one-quarter of the remaining salt and pepper.

4. Whisk the batter well and ladle about ⅔ cup into the pan. Swirl the pan so the batter completely covers the surface. Neatly place 1 cup of the bean sprouts and ½ cup of the sautéed mushrooms on one side of the crepe, closer to the center than the edge.

5. Reduce the heat slightly, cover, and cook until the edges pull away from the sides of the pan, about 5 minutes. Reduce the heat to very low. Uncover and cook until the crepe is crisp and the pork and shrimp are done, another 2 to 3 minutes. Slip a spatula under the crepe to check the bottom. If it's not brown, cook another 1 to 2 minutes.

6. Slip the spatula under the part of the crepe without the bean sprouts and fold it over. Gently slide the crepe onto a large plate and keep warm. Wipe the pan clean and make the remaining 3 crepes the same way. Be sure to oil the pan before each crepe.

7. Serve the crepes with the Vietnamese Dipping Sauce and Table Salad. To eat, tear a piece of the crepe and wrap with lettuce or mustard leaves and herbs. Roll into a packet, dip into the sauce, and eat.

Adapted from a recipe by MAI PHAM

*S*INGAPORE

evolved from the Indian bread *paratha*, *roti prata* is a type of Singaporean flatbread made with wheat flour and ghee, or clarified butter. The dough gets stretched, pulled, and folded before being grilled on a flat griddle. *Roti prata* is commonly served with curries, although it can also be made into a savory snack stuffed with meat, or a dessert with condensed milk and powdered sugar or banana and honey.

Roti Prata Tekka Market

SERVES 8

8½ tablespoons water, or as needed

2¼ teaspoons fine sugar

½ teaspoon fine salt

6 tablespoons melted ghee or butter

1½ tablespoons evaporated milk

8¾ ounces (245 g) all-purpose flour, sifted into a large bowl

2 tablespoons vegetable oil

1. *M*ix ½ cup water with the sugar and salt. Stir in 1½ tablespoons of ghee or butter and the evaporated milk.

2. *A*dd the mixture to the flour and knead until the dough is soft, smooth, and firm, 8 to 10 minutes. Add more butter if needed. If the dough is too hard and floury, add the extra 1½ teaspoons water. Rest the dough for 30 minutes.

3. *S*hape into 2-inch (5-cm) balls and coat each with butter to prevent sticking. Repeat with the remaining dough. Stack the balls in a bowl and cover. Leave for 3 to 4 hours, or until they are soft and pliable.

4. *H*eat a griddle on medium heat and add a little oil. Flatten each piece of dough on a greased marble surface by stretching outward and then toss in the air to get a paper-thin dough. If you are not able to master the technique of throwing the dough in the air, just roll each ball into a paper-thin piece with a lightly floured rolling pin on a floured tabletop.

5. *F*old the sides inward to form a square. Put on the hot griddle, folded side down, and fry until golden brown, 4 to 5 minutes. Turn over and fry until browned, 3 to 4 minutes. Repeat with the remaining pieces of dough. For a lighter texture, once the *roti* is done, lay it on a counter to cool slightly, then clap it between your hands. This creates folds in the bread and makes it fluffy.

Adapted from a recipe by Zulkifli Bin Packeer Bawa

CHAPTER SEVEN

Chutneys, Pastes, & Sauces

THE SOUL OF A CUISINE

It's lunchtime at the Ben Thanh Market in Saigon and like most days, Kim Luong
is fanning her tiny charcoal grill, flipping lemongrass pork while assembling bowls.
Her customers, some of whom are seated at the counter while others are waiting
for an empty spot, are eagerly waiting for their *bun thit nuong*, or rice noodles
with grilled pork. Business is always brisk here.

*I*t's not that you can't find this dish elsewhere in the market; it's just that Kim's version is clearly different and unique. According to her, the secret is not the main ingredients but the condiments. Her counter is adorned and stacked with big glass jars of "secret" ingredients, including fish dipping sauce, fried shallots, scallion oil, pickled daikon radish and carrots, roasted peanuts, and chili sauce, all the condiments that turn a good dish into a phenomenal dish.

Certainly one of the greatest flavor treasures of Asia lies in its wealth of condiments. Often overlooked, it's really a category to pay attention to if you want to master any cuisine in the region. The Indian subcontinent boasts an incredibly vast collection of delicious chutneys, which are thick in consistency and made of puréed vegetables and fruits and often blended with spices, as well as yogurt-based raitas and pickles. The Thais have their *nam priks* and curry pastes, with the former being used as dipping sauces and the latter as bases for curries, soups, and salads. The Vietnamese have their many variations of *nuoc cham*, or fish sauce–based dipping sauces, and the Singaporeans, with their multicultural heritage, enjoy a wide repertoire, from Indian chutneys to Malay and Indonesian *sambals.* The Korean kitchen relies heavily on their distinctive *gochujang* chili paste as well as pickled vegetables. The Chinese enjoy oil-based dips made with fermented soybeans, chili, and garlic as well as other soybean and soy sauce–based sauces with their foods and, of course, the Japanese are known for their affinity for soy sauce– and miso-based dipping sauces.

An important thing to remember about condiments— be they dipping sauces, pastes, or more seasoned mixtures such as chutneys—is that not only do they add flavor, texture, and contrast to the foods they accompany but they help lift and multiply the existing flavors of a given dish. Extremely versatile, they can be paired with any food, from curries, stews, and grilled foods to vegetables and rice. Another great advantage is that they can be made in advance. If you're planning a dinner party of grilled foods, for example, all the condiments—which in some cases could dictate the overall theme and flavor of the meal—can be made beforehand and brought out just before serving. The only cooking necessary is to grill the meat once the guests have arrived.

Having a jar or two of chutney or dipping sauce can also make meal planning easy. Don't know what to make for dinner but you have some leftover coconut chutney? Broil some fish and serve it on top. Or dress up a store-bought roasted chicken with a spicy green mango chutney or a ginger-lime sauce. Most condiments are quick and easy to make and can be used to add sparkle to any dish including non-Asian ones. For example, for the cooler months, consider serving lamb or other meats with a chutney. During the summer, when herbs are plentiful and outdoor cooking beckons, grill some fish and serve it with the lighter dipping sauces made either with fish sauce or soy sauce.

On many levels, condiments—regardless of the format or culture that inspired them—are the extended soul of a cuisine. Experiment with the recipes in this chapter and serve them as they've been recommended. As you become more familiar with their preparations and tastes, try them with other foods and learn how they can literally transform a dish.

coconut chutney is a classic component of South Indian vegetarian cooking. This chutney is a slight variation—the almonds have all the richness of coconut but with an intense nutty flavor. It's great with breads, rice pancakes, or light dishes to balance its rich, buttery flavor.

ALMOND CHUTNEY

MAKES 3 CUPS

2 cups blanched almonds

8 dried red chile peppers

1 tablespoon salt, or as needed

1 cup curry leaves

SEASONING

1 tablespoon canola oil

½ teaspoon black or brown mustard seeds

½ teaspoon ground *urad dal*

1 dried red chile pepper, stemmed, halved

6 curry leaves

1. *Soak* the almonds in warm water for 30 minutes and drain. In a blender, grind the almonds, chile peppers, salt, curry leaves, and just enough water to make a thick, smooth purée. You may prepare this chutney without curry leaves, but it will lack the fragrance of these aromatic leaves.

2. *For the seasoning:* In a small sauté pan, heat the oil over medium heat and add the mustard seeds. When the mustard seeds start sputtering, after about 2 minutes, add the *urad dal*, red chile pepper, and curry leaves and fry until the *dal* turns golden, about 2 minutes.

3. *Add* the ground almond purée to the sauté pan and stir. Remove from the stove and transfer to a serving bowl. Serve at room temperature.

Adapted from a recipe by AMMINI RAMACHANDRAN. *From Grains, Greens, and Grated Coconuts by Ammini Ramachandran Copyright © 2007, 2008 by Ammini Ramachandran. Reprinted by permission of iUniverse, Inc. All right reserved.*

if you have homegrown tomatoes in the summer or have access to them, this is a definite must-make chutney. In this essential Indian condiment, the ripe tomatoes are combined with toasted spices, resulting in a vibrant, red chutney with complex sweet, sour, and spicy flavors. It makes a good dip for *dosas* and is a great accompaniment to roasted meats as well as scrambled eggs and tofu.

TOMATO CHUTNEY

MAKES 3 CUPS

1 pound 2 ounces (510 g) plum tomatoes (about 8)

½ teaspoon fenugreek seeds

½ cup white vinegar

2 tablespoons black mustard seeds

2 tablespoons cumin seeds

¼ cup chili powder

1 head garlic, cloves peeled and roughly chopped (10 tablespoons)

One 2-inch (5-cm) piece ginger, peeled and roughly chopped

½ cup sesame oil

2 teaspoons salt

½ cup sugar

1. Bring a medium saucepan of water to a boil over high heat. Remove the cores from the tomatoes and score an "X" at the bottom of each tomato. Place the tomatoes in the water and boil until the skins have loosened slightly, about 30 seconds. Remove from the boiling water and plunge into ice water immediately. Once cooled, remove the skin from the tomatoes and coarsely chop. Set aside.

2. Roast the fenugreek seeds in a small sauté pan over medium-high heat until toasted, about 2 minutes. Grind the fenugreek to a powder in a spice grinder.

3. Grind the fenugreek, white vinegar, mustard seeds, cumin seeds, chili powder, garlic, and ginger in a blender until it achieves a pastelike consistency, about 1 minute, scraping the sides after 30 seconds.

4. Heat the oil in a small sauté pan over low heat and add the paste. Sauté for 20 minutes or so or until the mixture dries out.

5. Add the chopped tomatoes and cook for a further 30 minutes, or until the moisture evaporates.

6. Add the salt and sugar and cook until they dissolve. Adjust the seasoning as needed. Refrigerate for 24 hours before serving.

Adapted from a recipe by NIMMY PAUL

this South Indian chutney is finished with an aromatic tempering oil and is delicious with grilled meats and fried appetizers, such as *pakoras*. For this recipe, fresh coconut is best but store-bought dried coconut flakes also work.

when peeling a mango, peel until you only see white flesh and there are no green veins. While typically served with *pakoras*, this popular and spicy chutney goes well with everything from seafood to potatoes.

COCONUT CHUTNEY
NAALIKERA CHUTNEY

GREEN CHUTNEY
HAREE CHUTNEY

MAKES 2½ CUPS

2 cups freshly grated coconut

4 green chiles, less for a milder taste (Serrano or Thai bird)

4 teaspoons grated ginger

1½ teaspoons salt

¼ cup plain yogurt

2 tablespoons canola oil

1 teaspoon mustard seeds

1 teaspoon *urad dal*

2 dried red chile peppers, halved

16 curry leaves

MAKES 3 CUPS

1 cup chopped cilantro

1 cup chopped mint

1½ cups roughly chopped green mango

3 jalapeños, seeded, veined, and roughly chopped

3 tablespoons roughly chopped gingerroot, peeled and cut into chunks

½ red onion, quartered

2 tablespoons lemon juice

1 tablespoon sugar

2 teaspoons kosher salt, or as needed

¼ cup water

1. *In* a blender, grind the coconut, green chiles, ginger, and salt with the yogurt and just enough water to make a smooth, thick purée.

2. *In* a sauté pan, heat the oil over medium heat and add the mustard seeds. When the mustard seeds start sputtering, add the *urad dal*, red chile peppers, and curry leaves and fry until the *dal* turns golden. Remove it from the stove and stir it into the coconut purée. Serve at room temperature.

Adapted from a recipe by AMMINI RAMACHANDRAN. *From* Grains, Greens, and Grated Coconuts *by Ammini Ramachandran Copyright © 2007, 2008 by Ammini Ramachandran. Reprinted by permission of iUniverse, Inc. All right reserved.*

1. *Place* all of the ingredients in a blender or food processor and blend until smooth, scraping down the sides of the bowl as needed. If the chutney doesn't blend easily, add a little water to facilitate the process (this will make the chutney milder). Or combine the water and lemon juice and slowly drizzle it into the processor.

2. *Taste* and adjust the seasoning with salt, transfer to a covered plastic container, and refrigerate for up to 5 days.

Adapted from a recipe by SUVIR SARAN

this chutney is very hot and should be served by the teaspoon, with a sweet chutney for contrast. It's great with grilled meats as well as *naans* and *roti*. If you want to make it less spicy, use the larger dried red chiles and remove the seeds.

RED CHILE CHUTNEY
LAL MIRCHI KI CHATNI

MAKES 1 CUP

2 teaspoons coriander seeds
2 teaspoons cumin seeds
12 large cloves garlic
14 dried red chiles, soaked in hot water until pliable
1 tablespoon ground cayenne pepper
½ teaspoon salt
1 tablespoon fresh lemon juice

1. *Toast* the coriander and cumin seeds in a dry skillet over medium-high heat until they brown lightly, about 1 minute.

2. *Place* the seeds, garlic, chiles, and cayenne in a blender. Add ¼ cup of water or more as necessary (no more than ½ cup total) and blend the mixture into a smooth paste. If there is too much liquid in the blender at this point, the resulting purée will not be smooth enough.

3. *Add* the salt, lemon juice, and about ¼ cup more water and blend to make a sauce with the consistency of heavy cream.

Adapted from a recipe by THE CULINARY INSTITUTE OF AMERICA

tamarind comes from the flesh of the tamarind pod, which is sold fresh or dried, or as compressed blocks and liquid concentrates. For the best flavor, use the dried whole pods or blocks. This chutney is an important component of *chaats* in India.

TAMARIND CHUTNEY

MAKES 2½ CUPS

⅔ cup roughly chopped tamarind pulp, packed
2½ cups water
2 tablespoons canola oil
2 teaspoons cumin seeds
2 teaspoons ground ginger
1 teaspoon cayenne pepper
1 teaspoon fennel seeds
1 teaspoon asafetida (optional)
1 teaspoon Garam Masala (page 220)
2½ cups sugar

1. *Soak* the tamarind pulp in the warm water for 1 hour. Pass through a wire strainer and discard all seeds and fibers.

2. *Heat* the oil over medium-high heat in a medium saucepan. Add the spices and the asafetida, if using, and cook, stirring, until toasted and aromatic, about 1 minute.

3. *Add* the strained tamarind and sugar. Bring to a boil, turn the heat down, and simmer until it turns chocolaty brown and is thick enough to coat the back of the spoon, 25 to 30 minutes. Store the chutney in the refrigerator in a tightly closed container for up to 2 weeks.

Adapted from a recipe by SUVIR SARAN

Chutneys

Chutneys, which can be fiery hot or wonderfully sweet and sour or somewhere in between, are astonishingly versatile and can instantly add unexpected spark to any dish. They're made and eaten all over India, though they vary from region to region and from cook to cook.

There are three basic varieties: fresh, cooked, and dry chutneys, with the first two being most popular outside of India. For the uncooked version, they can be a blend of fresh ingredients such as puréed herbs, spices, coconut, or tamarind seasoned with cumin and coriander seeds as well as fresh aromatics such as ginger and chiles. The Green Chutney (page 216) is an example of a simple chutney that requires no cooking, only that the ingredients be blended in a food processor. For most fresh chutneys, simply place the fleshy ingredients in a food processor and mince to a wet paste. Add a little water to facilitate the grinding. If your recipe calls for a tempering oil, prepare that in a pan. Put the chutney mixture into a bowl, then top it with the tempering oil. Chutneys prepared this way have a distinctively sharp and complex flavor. Even though traditionally chutneys were made by hand-grinding in a mortar and pestle, they can be successfully made with a food processor or blender. Use the grind and pulse feature and be careful to not overheat the mixture, which can affect the flavor.

In Kerala and the southern part of India, there's a wonderful tradition with coconut chutneys that are made from freshly grated coconut and spices. Depending on the ingredients used, they can be white if made mostly with coconut and green chiles, green if made with herbs, and red if they contain dried red chiles. The consistency also varies. Those meant to be served with rice are thicker and those intended as a dip have more liquid.

Chutneys can also be made by cooking vegetables or fruits until they're soft and pulpy (as in a jam) and sometimes finished with a tempering oil that includes mustard seeds, *dal*, chiles, and curry leaves. In India, a chutney is often made to be eaten fresh, using whatever ingredients that are local and traditional or available and whatever peaks the cook's interest at the time. Some are made with seasonal fruits, in which case they are meant to be stored and eaten throughout the year.

Another very important condiment at the northern Indian table is *raita*, a flavorful mixture made with yogurt as a base and seasoned with spices, herbs, and vegetables. Like chutneys, they're very simple to prepare and the variations are endless. Traditionally *raitas* are served with *pulaos*, *biryani*, or *roti* as a cooling contrast.

When making chutneys and condiments, make sure the ingredients used are extremely fresh as the dish is meant to accent and lift the flavor of other dishes. For example, the Green Chutney (page 216) should be made with the correct crunchy, green variety meant-to-be-eaten green, not the unripe version of a sweet mango, and the chiles and herbs must be of utmost freshness. And for the Coconut Chutney (page 216) to really sparkle and help flavor the dish it accompanies, it should be made with fresh coconut, the kind you grate yourself.

another star condiment from the Indian kitchen, this is very similar to salsa cruda. Its salty, sour, and spicy flavors enhance grilled meats and curries as well as rice dishes. The heat can be reduced by using fewer chiles or by removing the seeds.

to make this spice mix, simply toast the spices in a pan and grind into a powder. *Garam masala* adds its unique and bold flavor in countless Indian recipes from soups and marinades to meats and sauces.

ONION AND CUCUMBER KACHUMBER

MAKES 4 CUPS

2 small onions, cut into ⅓-inch dice
1 European cucumber, cut into ⅓-inch dice
1½ cups seeded and chopped plum tomatoes
3 to 4 Thai bird chiles, chopped with the seeds, or as needed
Juice of 3 lemons
⅓ teaspoon salt, or as needed
½ cup chopped cilantro

1. Gently mix all of the ingredients in a bowl except the cilantro.

2. Ten minutes before serving, add the cilantro and check the seasoning. Make sure that you mix the ingredients together gently.

Adapted from a recipe by THE CULINARY INSTITUTE OF AMERICA

GARAM MASALA

MAKES ¾ CUP

1 cinnamon stick, broken into pieces
2 bay leaves
¼ cup cumin seeds
⅓ cup coriander seeds
1 tablespoon green cardamom pods
1 tablespoon black peppercorns
2 teaspoons whole cloves
1 dried red chile
⅛ teaspoon ground mace

1. Combine the cinnamon, bay leaves, cumin, coriander, cardamom, peppercorns, cloves, and red chile in a frying pan and toast over medium heat, stirring constantly, until the cumin turns uniformly brown, 4 to 5 minutes.

2. Put into a spice grinder and grind to a powder. Stir in the mace and store in an airtight container.

Adapted from a recipe by SUVIR SARAN

raitas can be made with just about any fruits and vegetables along with yogurt, spices, and herbs. *Raitas* are served chilled or at room temperature and are typically used as an accompaniment to spicy dishes, although some are quite spicy all on their own. They can be smooth or chunky, like this one, which has both chopped and julienned ginger to boost its fresh, spicy flavor.

SEARED GINGER RAITA

MAKES 2 CUPS

1½ cups plain yogurt
¼ cup finely chopped ginger
1 teaspoon salt, or as needed
1 tablespoon vegetable oil
1 to 2 fresh green or dried chiles
6 to 10 curry leaves
¼ cup finely julienned ginger
½ teaspoon brown mustard seeds
¼ cup cilantro leaves

1. Combine the yogurt, chopped ginger, and salt in a mixing or serving bowl.

2. Heat the oil in a small frying pan over medium-high heat. Add the chiles and let them sizzle for a moment. Follow with the curry leaves and when they begin to change color, after about 30 seconds, add the ginger and toss until it begins to brown and caramelize, about 1 minute. Quickly add the mustard seeds. The moment they begin to pop, 1 to 2 minutes, tip the entire contents of the pan into the yogurt-ginger mixture. Stir well.

3. Let stand for at least half an hour before serving. Taste the sauce and adjust the seasoning with salt.

4. Garnish with cilantro leaves. Serve at room temperature.

Adapted from a recipe by NILOUFER ICHAPORIA KING. *Excerpted from* My Bombay Kitchen *by Niloufer Ichaporia King, © 2007. Used by permission of the University of California Press.*

*T*HAILAND

every country has its own version of peanut sauce—some are sweet and mild, others are boldy flavored with chiles and tamarind and hard spices. This version from Thailand is a nice balance and quite easy to make. Serve this with Chicken Satay (page 40) or any grilled meats or tofu or vegetables. A little roasted Chile Jam (see opposite) really enhances the flavor of this condiment.

PEANUT SATAY SAUCE
NAM JIM SATAY

MAKES 1 CUP

1 cup coconut milk

1 tablespoon red curry paste

1 tablespoon roasted Chile Jam (page 223)

2 tablespoons creamy peanut butter

¼ cup chicken stock or water

1 tablespoon chili oil

1 tablespoon toasted white sesame seeds

1 tablespoon roasted, ground peanuts

1½ teaspoons sugar

1½ teaspoons palm sugar or brown sugar

Fish sauce or salt, as needed

1. Place half of the coconut milk in a nonstick saucepan and warm it over medium heat. Stir until the oil from the coconut milk surfaces. Add the curry paste and Chile Jam. Keep stirring for 2 to 3 minutes.

2. Add the peanut butter and the remaining coconut milk, the chicken stock, chili oil, sesame seeds, peanuts, sugar, palm sugar, and fish sauce. Reduce the heat to low.

3. Stir constantly for a few minutes until the sauce thickens, then bring to a boil. Transfer to a metal bowl or container. Skim off some of the excess oil, leaving only what's needed for a shiny appearance.

Adapted from a recipe by CHAI SIRIYARN

chile jam is the base seasoning for many Thai soups and salads. It's made by pounding twice-cooked fried shallots and garlic along with dried shrimp, chiles, and galangal. When the tamarind and sugar are added, the mixture transforms into a thick, flavorful jam. Use this as a seasoning as well as an accompaniment to meat and fish dishes.

CHILE JAM
NAM PRIK PAO

MAKES 2 CUPS

¼ cup vegetable oil

2 cups sliced shallots

1 cup sliced garlic

1 cup dried shrimp

½ cup dried long red chiles, deseeded and chopped

5 thin slices galangal

1½ teaspoons shrimp paste, roasted

¼ cup palm sugar

2 tablespoons tamarind paste

1½ tablespoons fish sauce

½ teaspoon salt, or as needed

1. *H*eat the oil in a pan and working with one ingredient at a time, fry them according to the following times, or until golden: about 4 minutes for the shallots, 2 minutes for the garlic, 30 seconds for the dried shrimp, and 30 seconds to 1 minute for the chiles. Using a slotted spoon, transfer to a plate as they finish.

2. *U*sing a mortar and pestle or a blender, grind the cooked ingredients with the galangal and shrimp paste.

3. *B*ring the mixture to a simmer over medium heat in a saucepan with the palm sugar, tamarind paste, and fish sauce. Simmer until quite thick, 3 to 5 minutes, stirring. Taste the sauce and adjust the seasoning with salt. The resulting "jam" should taste sweet, sour, and salty.

Adapted from a recipe by ASSISTANT PROFESSOR KOBKAEW NAIPINIJ

THAILAND

although *massaman* curry paste shares similar ingredients with Thai Red Curry Paste, it's quite distinctive because of the Muslim influence with the addition of cinnamon, cloves, and nutmeg. Thai cooks make curry pastes in a mortar and pestle, which produces very intense flavors. However, a blender may also be used. *Massaman* is often paired with beef and lamb although it's also delicious with chicken and duck.

MASSAMAN CURRY PASTE
NAM PRIK KAENG MASSAMAN

MAKES 2 CUPS

8 dried large red chile peppers, destemmed and cut into 2- to 3-inch (5- to 7-cm) pieces

¼ cup warm water

3 tablespoons thinly sliced shallots

2 tablespoons thinly sliced garlic

1 tablespoon thinly sliced lemongrass

1 tablespoon coriander seeds

1 teaspoon cumin seeds

1 teaspoon thinly sliced galangal

1 teaspoon white peppercorns

2 cloves

¼ teaspoon vegetable oil

1 tablespoon paprika

1 teaspoon Thai shrimp paste

1 teaspoon salt

½ teaspoon freshly grated nutmeg

½ teaspoon ground cinnamon

1. Place the dried chile peppers in a small, microwave-safe bowl and cover with the warm water. Cover with plastic wrap and microwave for 2 to 3 minutes to soften the chiles. Drain the chiles and set aside.

2. Combine the shallots, garlic, lemongrass, coriander, cumin, galangal, peppercorns, and cloves in a nonstick pan. Add the oil and place the pan over medium heat. Stir the mixture until fragrant, 4 to 5 minutes.

3. Transfer to a blender and add the soaked chiles (and soaking liquid), paprika, shrimp paste, salt, nutmeg and cinnamon. Process the mixture until a smooth paste forms, 4 to 5 minutes.

Adapted from a recipe by CHAI SIRIYARN

this sauce is simple to put together and makes a great accompaniment to Chinese steamed dumplings (*sui mai*), fried snacks, and fritters, as well as steamed vegetables and fried rice.

there are countless versions of this dipping sauce, including simmering mirin, sake, and rice vinegar with dried bonito flakes and kombu and finishing it with *yuzu* juice. This simpler version is a great dip for sashimi, sushi, and braised seafood.

SESAME SOY DIPPING SAUCE

PONZU SAUCE

MAKES 1¼ CUPS

3 tablespoons minced ginger
¼ cup light soy sauce
½ cup rice vinegar
¼ cup water
1 tablespoon sesame oil
2 tablespoons sugar, or as needed

MAKES 1 CUP

½ cup soy sauce
¼ cup dashi (page 60)
4 teaspoons sake
4 teaspoons fresh lemon juice
2 teaspoons mirin
4 teaspoons pickled ginger juice (optional)

Whisk together all of the ingredients in a stainless-steel bowl until the sugar is dissolved. This sauce will keep for 2 to 3 days in the refrigerator. If making in advance, add the ginger at the last minute to give it more flavor.

Adapted from a recipe by THE CULINARY INSTITUTE OF AMERICA

Mix all of the ingredients including the ginger juice, if using, thoroughly. Refrigerate overnight before using.

Adapted from a recipe by THE CULINARY INSTITUTE OF AMERICA

Mortar & Pestle

The workhorse of the Asian kitchen, the mortar and pestle is truly an indispensable tool. In Vietnam and Thailand, it's particularly important because it's used to make essential dipping sauces and bases. While a food processor may be used for small amounts of chili pastes, it's easier to pound a few chiles and garlic cloves in a mortar than to try and process them in a blender.

A mortar can be of any size and made from a number of materials, from the heavy, dense granite, marble, and brass to the more porous clay and wood. Most commonly available are the 4½-inch (11-cm) size, which is perfect for grinding small amounts of chiles and spices, and the 6½-inch (16-cm) size, which is a great all-purpose tool. The clay and wood varieties have deeper bowls and longer pestles, perfect for pounding fleshy ingredients and, if you cover the top of the mortar with your hands, you will not have juices squirting into your eyes. (This is important when pounding chiles and garlic.) Pounding imparts a more intense flavor than chopping and mincing. In the case of the Green Papaya Salad (page 109), pounding bruises the flesh and releases the sap flavor, thereby making the dish quite distinctive. A mortar and pestle is also handy for grinding roasted peanuts, sesame seeds, and rice paper as well as making chewy fish cakes, meatballs, and meat patés.

When using a stone mortar, hold the pestle and freely pound in an up-and-down motion.

Many novice users make the mistake of pressing (as opposed to pounding) the pestle into the mortar, which makes the job much harder and longer. Once in a while, run the pestle in a circular motion against the sides to push the ingredients back into the center of the mortar. If you're working with a long pestle and want to grind, hold the pestle with two hands. Firmly hold the top of the pestle with one hand and use the second to rotate the bottom of the pestle. If you're grinding hard spices, use this circular motion technique since it will give you a more fine, even texture.

For best consistency, work with one ingredient at a time and start with the hardiest first. If you're using hard spices, pound them first into a powder, then remove from the mortar and move on to other tough or fibrous ingredients. Fresh ingredients such as lemongrass and ginger should be chopped into small pieces before pounding, and dried chiles should be soaked in warm water until they become pliable, then torn into small pieces. To make the pounding go faster and easier, and to pull the flavors of the ingredients together, add coarse salt or sugar, within the parameters of the recipe, to the mortar. This also helps to keep any juices from squirting into your eyes.

Softer and wetter ingredients such as garlic and shallots can be placed in the mortar whole as they mash up relatively easily. When all the ingredients have been reduced to a powder or paste, put them back into the mortar and pound them together until they are well blended, or combine them in a larger bowl. Every cuisine has its version of a mortar and pestle and the guidelines for using it depends on the cuisine, the tool, and the ingredients that need to be ground. For example, the Japanese ceramic mortar called *suribachi* works quite differently. A shallow bowl with a wide opening, it has an unglazed interior with rough, narrow groove patterns to facilitate grinding. This tool is especially great for sesame seeds that benefit from the gentler, circular motion grinding. In southern Indian cooking, a large, flat, and rectangular grinding stone, *arrakallu,* is used to grind herbs and spices.

If you're planning to cook Asian food regularly, you can start by investing in a small granite or stone mortar designated for spices and a larger one for all other ingredients. To clean, wash your mortar and pestle with soapy water and wipe dry.

this simple, basic chile sauce from Singapore makes a great accompaniment to steamed chicken and seafood but it can be used on any food. If you can't find red Serrano, use any red chiles. For interesting variations, add ginger or cilantro.

look for very fresh knobs of ginger that have thin, shiny skin with juicy flesh. This sauce is traditionally served with Hainan chicken, but it's also delicious with steamed shrimp. For a delicious variation, add the Green Onion Oil on page 231.

CHILE-GARLIC SAUCE

GINGER SAUCE

MAKES ½ CUP

5 red serrano chiles
6 cloves garlic, peeled
½ teaspoon sea salt, or to taste
¼ cup boiling chicken stock
2 to 3 tablespoons lime juice

MAKES ½ CUP

Two 2-inch (5-cm) knobs fresh ginger, peeled
¼ cup boiling chicken stock
½ teaspoon sea salt, or to taste
½ teaspoon sugar

1. Bring a small pot of water to a boil. Add the chiles and blanch for 20 seconds. Remove and drain. Remove the stems and, if preferred, remove some of the seeds to reduce the spiciness. Grind the chiles and garlic in a mortar and pestle or food processor to a rough paste.

2. Transfer to a bowl and combine with the salt, stock, and lime juice. Reserve until ready to use.

Adapted from a recipe by VIOLET OON

1. Cut the ginger into thin slices, then pound in a mortar and pestle or use a food processor to grind it into a fine paste. If using a processor, add the stock to facilitate the grinding.

2. Transfer the ginger to a small bowl and add the remaining ingredients. Stir well. Set aside for an hour for the flavors to develop. Keep refrigerated until ready to serve.

Adapted from a recipe by VIOLET OON

this versatile sauce enhances almost everything it touches—from grilled meats to fried fish. If you need to double the recipe to save for later use (you'll want to once you've tasted it), reduce the ginger in the sauce and add it back just before serving.

Vietnamese *nuoc cham* varies with proportions of fish sauce, lime juice, and sugar. This recipe is great for spring rolls and for drizzling on noodles and rice. Reduce the water for a more salty, limey, spicy sauce—perfect for grilled meat or fish.

GINGER-LIME DIPPING SAUCE

VIETNAMESE DIPPING SAUCE

NUOC CHAM

MAKES 1 CUP

1 to 2 cloves garlic

2 Thai bird chiles or 1 serrano chile, chopped

3 tablespoons minced ginger

3 tablespoons sugar

¼ cup fish sauce

3 tablespoons lime juice

2 tablespoons water

MAKES 2 CUPS

6 Thai bird chiles or 2 serrano chiles, or as needed

2 cloves garlic, thinly sliced

6 tablespoons sugar

1⅓ cups warm water

3 tablespoons lime juice

½ cup plus 2 tablespoons fish sauce

¼ cup finely shredded carrots, for garnish (optional)

1. Place the garlic, chiles, ginger, and sugar in a mortar and pound into a paste.

2. Transfer to a small mixing bowl and stir in the fish sauce, lime juice, and water. Let it sit for 15 minutes before serving.

Adapted from a recipe by MAI PHAM

1. Cut the chiles into thin rings. Reserve one-third of the chiles for garnish.

2. Place the remaining chiles, garlic, and sugar in a mortar and pound into a coarse, wet paste.

3. Transfer to a small bowl and add the water, lime juice, and fish sauce. Stir well to dissolve. Add the reserved chiles and carrots, if using.

4. Set aside for 10 minutes before serving to allow the flavors to blend.

Adapted from a recipe by MAI PHAM

called *tuong* in Vietnamese, this dipping sauce is served with salad rolls or any food designed to be wrapped with rice paper or lettuce. Traditionally, it's made with a yellow soybean sauce, but this version calls for hoisin sauce, which is more readily available.

the "secret" ingredient of the Vietnamese kitchen, this is a simple caramel sauce cooked until it becomes almost black. A few drops impart a sweet, savory flavor to clay pot dishes and braises. It also works miracles in grilled dishes.

Hoisin Peanut Sauce

MAKES 1½ CUPS

1 tablespoon vegetable oil
1½ teaspoons minced garlic
⅓ cup finely minced yellow onions
1 cup hoisin sauce
½ cup water
¼ cup rice vinegar
1 tablespoon ground chili paste, or as needed
2 tablespoons roasted, chopped peanuts

1. Heat the oil in a small saucepan over medium heat. Add the garlic and stir until fragrant, about 15 seconds. Add the yellow onion and stir for another 2 to 3 minutes or until translucent.

2. Add the hoisin sauce, water, and rice vinegar and allow to simmer until thickened, 5 to 7 minutes. Add a little water if the sauce is too thick. Set aside to cool. Transfer the mixture to a sauce dish and garnish with the chili paste and chopped peanuts.

Adapted from a recipe by Mai Pham

Caramel Sauce

MAKES 1 CUP

1 cup water
⅔ cup sugar

1. Bring the water to a boil.

2. Place the sugar in a small, heavy-bottomed saucepan over medium heat. The sugar will melt and start to caramelize in 2 to 3 minutes. Stir a few times (the edges will start to brown fast) and let the mixture bubble until it turns dark chocolate, about another minute or so.

3. Carefully move the pan away from the heat and slowly pour in two-thirds of the boiling water. Stand back as the mixture will splatter. If the sauce appears too thick, add more water. Set aside to cool. If stored in a tight-lidded jar, this sauce will keep for up to a month.

Adapted from a recipe by Mai Pham

in Vietnamese cooking, this topping is quite common, appearing on many rice, noodle, and grilled meat dishes. For the minimal amount of work that this requires, it surprisingly adds a lot of flavor, aroma, and richness to food.

GREEN ONION OIL

MAKES ½ CUP

1 bunch green onions (5 or 6), cleaned and patted dry
½ cup vegetable oil
½ teaspoon salt

1. Remove the white part of the green onions and save them for another use. Cut the remaining green sections of the green onions into thin rings.

2. Heat the oil in a small pan over medium heat. Stir in the green onions and salt. Cook the green onions only until they turn bright green, 20 to 30 seconds. Immediately transfer the mixture (oil included) to a bowl and place in the rcfrigerator. (If the green onions are not chilled immediatcly, they will turn a pale olive color.) This oil will keep for two to three days.

Adapted from a recipe by MAI PHAM

this is the vegetarian version of the chili-lime fish sauce that's so popular in Vietnamese and Thai cuisines. Here, soy sauce is transformed with pounded ginger and cilantro. Use for dipping meats and tofu and for drizzling on noodle and rice dishes.

CILANTRO-LIME SOY SAUCE

MAKES ⅔ CUP

1 clove garlic
2 Thai bird chiles
1 teaspoon ground chili paste
One 1-inch (2.5-cm) piece fresh ginger, peeled and thinly sliced
3 tablespoons finely chopped cilantro leaves and stems
¼ cup soy sauce
2 tablespoons fresh lime juice with pulp
3 tablespoons water
2 tablespoons sugar

1. Place the garlic, chiles, chili paste, and ginger in a mortar and pestle and pound into a paste. (You can also chop by hand.)

2. Transfer the paste into a glass jar with a tight-fitting lid and add the remaining ingredients. Mix well until the sugar is dissolved. This sauce will keep for one week if refrigerated.

Adapted from a recipe by MAI PHAM

this multipurpose soy concentrate can be used as a dipping sauce, marinade, or as an addition to other sauces. Diluted with water, it can also be used as a broth for noodles.

SEASONED SOY CONCENTRATE

MAKES ABOUT ⅔ CUP

5 to 6 large *iriko*, trimmed

8 to 10 square inches (20 to 25 square cm) *kombu*, preferably *rausu kombu, rishiri kombu,* or *ma kombu*

1 dried shiitake mushroom or stems from 3 or 4 mushrooms

¼ cup *atsu kezuri* or ½ cup tightly packed *katsuobushi*

⅔ cup soy sauce

⅓ cup sake

3 tablespoons sugar

3 tablespoons water

2 tablespoons mirin

1. Place the *iriko, kombu,* shiitake, *atsu kezuri,* soy sauce, and sake in a small, deep saucepan and leave to infuse for 1 hour or up to 12 hours. (If you are using ordinary *katsuobushi,* add the flakes later, as directed in step 3.)

2. Add the sugar, water, and mirin to the pan and place over low heat. When the liquid begins to simmer, adjust the heat to keep it from boiling vigorously. As the sauce simmers, it becomes quite foamy, rising up in the saucepan. Watch to make sure it does not overflow. Continue to simmer, until the volume has been reduced by about one-quarter and the sauce is a bit syrupy.

3. Remove from the heat. (If you are using ordinary *katsuobushi,* scatter the *kastuobushi* flakes over the surface of the liquid. Let stand for 2 to 3 minutes, until the flakes have settled to the bottom.) Pour the mixture through a coffee filter–lined strainer into a glass jar with a tight-fitting lid. Reserve the solids to make broth, if desired. If not using immediately, let cool, cover, and chill before using. Refrigerate for up to one month.

Reprinted with permission from Washoku *by* ELIZABETH ANDOH. *Copyright 2005 by Elizabeth Andoh, Ten Speed Press, Berkeley, CA. www.tenspeed.com*

this is the sauce that gives *ssam*—the Korean lettuce wrap dishes—
their distinctive flavor. Using fermented chili paste and fermented soybean paste
as a base, *ssamjang* can be made in countless ways. This quick, delicious version
calls for just the addition of sesame oil, but it can also be enhanced with chopped
fresh chiles, garlic, and sesame seeds.

SPICY BEAN PASTE
SSAMJANG

MAKES 1¼ CUPS

½ cup *dwenjang* or fermented soybean paste
½ cup *gochujang* or fermented chili paste
¼ cup sesame oil

Combine all of the ingredients thoroughly and refrigerate until needed.

Adapted from a recipe by THE CULINARY INSTITUTE OF AMERICA

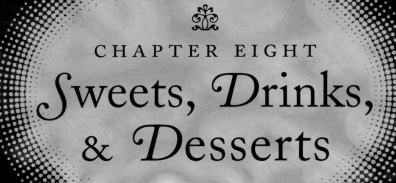

CHAPTER EIGHT

Sweets, Drinks, & Desserts

SWEET FLAVORS

By dusk, the glow from the bare lightbulbs dangling from the food carts along Nakornchaisri Road in Bangkok is becoming brighter and brighter by the minute. Soon wearied office workers and shoppers alike will descend on the sidewalks, some searching for sweets and desserts while others look for savory foods. As they do every night, the vendors here are hurriedly setting up, arranging ingredients, stacking bowls and plates, and pulling out small chairs. This is the calm before the storm.

*A*t one cart, the one where a crowd of anxious customers are already waiting in line, a mother and daughter team is busy making *khanom krok*, or grilled coconut pancakes. Working with two large dimpled griddles (which resemble large apple-skiver pans but with shallow molds), the mother quickly pours the rice flour batter into the molds. Then she gently shakes the pan so the batter sloshes around, creating a crisp, feathery edge. Her daughter follows with a small kettle filled with fresh coconut milk and pours in just enough to fill the mold. This coconut milk helps thin out the bottom rice flour layer, leading to a light and airy cake. She adds a sprinkling of thin scallion rings, then covers the pan with a lid. In less than a minute the cakes are done. The outside is warm and toasty, the silky coconut custard inside oozes in your mouth and the scallions are an unexpected savory finish.

Khanom krok is just one example of many sweet snacks eaten throughout Asia. Unlike the Western style of pastries and cakes that require leavening, dairy products, and oven baking, many traditional Asian sweets are simply cooked on the stove or steamed. These include cakes made from rice or glutinous flour, simmered in sweet soup or wrapped in banana leaves and steamed. Or they could be dumplings filled with mashed mung beans or other legumes, then cooked in a sweet coconut milk sauce. Other sweet soups include those made from dried fruits and nuts, hot and cold puddings, and a vast variety of sweet drinks filled with things to chew on while drinking. For example, walk into any dessert stand in a hawker's center in Singapore and you'll be dazzled by the colorful mounds of julienned grass jellies, mung bean paste, black-eyed peas, white beans, or red beans simmered in syrup, as well as coconut shreds and pandanus noodles. Point here and there and you might get a small bowl of

tapioca or sago pudding laced with fresh and dried fruit, or a tall glass filled with layers of legumes, seeds, and *agar agar* (a jello made from seaweed) topped with shaved ice and coconut sauce. To enjoy this refreshing dessert, poke through the layers with a long spoon and nibble away at the unexpected flavors and textures. These sweets are eaten throughout Southeast Asia, from Vietnam to Thailand to Singapore, Malaysia, and Indonesia.

In India, sweets are an integral part of religious, cultural, and social activities and the repertoire here is rather extensive. Thanks to Persian, Moghul, and Western influences, the Indian treasures range from colorful, beautiful confections such as *mithai* sold in sweet shops near temples and other busy centers to dumplings in syrup such as *jalebi*, the crisp-fried coils of sourdough bathed in a warm, sugary saffron syrup, and the beloved *kheer* or rice puddings perfumed with spices. Milk- and yogurt-based drinks and coolers as well as spiced beverages such as chai are delightful especially after a spicy meal or as an afternoon pick-me-up.

But if there's one common thread that runs through Asian sweets, drinks, and desserts, it's that many of these sweet snacks are eaten throughout the day whenever hunger pangs hit or whenever one craves something sweet as opposed to only indulging in them after a meal.

The recipes in this chapter offer a wide range of choices. For the summer, freshly cut fruit chilled on cracked ice may be a good, easy choice as is freshly made ice cream such as Ginger-Peanut Ice Cream (page 254). For the cooler months, you can't go wrong with any of the luscious pudding-style desserts. Serve them in pretty, small individual bowls with long-handled spoons—either warm or at room temperature. Don't forget the garnishes because, like other dishes across the meal, Asian desserts are as much about sweet flavors as they're about colors and textures.

this dessert, one of Thailand's most popular, is actually simple to prepare. Make sure the mangoes are ripe and sweet and the sticky rice slightly warm or at room temperature. The mung beans add a delightful contrast to the soft rice and fruit. Pandanus leaf is a flavoring used throughout Southeast Asia in both sweet and savory dishes. The leaves are slightly bruised and tied into a knot to intensify the flavor.

STICKY RICE WITH MANGOES
KAO NIAW MA MUANG

SERVES 4

STICKY RICE
2 cups sticky rice, soaked for at least
4 to 6 hours or overnight
⅓ cup coconut milk
½ cup sugar
1½ teaspoons salt, or as needed
2 pandanus leaves, tied in a knot

COCONUT TOPPING
1 cup coconut milk
1½ tablespoons sugar, or to taste
¼ teaspoon salt
1½ teaspoons rice flour
2 tablespoons mung beans, soaked
in hot water for 1 hour
2 mangoes, thinly sliced, or as needed

1. For the sticky rice: Drain the soaked rice and place in a steamer lined with cheesecloth. Steam until the grains are soft, 20 to 25 minutes (20 minutes if the rice was soaked overnight).

2. While the rice is steaming, combine the coconut milk, sugar, salt, and pandanus leaves in a bowl and mix well. Microwave or heat for 2 minutes to dissolve the salt and sugar; strain and set aside.

3. When the sticky rice is done, transfer from the steamer to a bowl. While the rice is still hot, add the coconut milk mixture. Using a rubber spatula, stir to coat the grains quickly and evenly. Cover with plastic wrap and set aside for 15 minutes to allow the rice to absorb the sauce.

4. For the coconut topping: Combine the coconut milk, sugar, and salt in a small saucepan. Bring to a boil and reduce the heat. In a bowl, blend the rice flour with 1 tablespoon of water and mix well to dissolve the rice flour. While the coconut sauce is simmering, slowly drizzle in the rice flour slurry and stir constantly. Return to a boil, immediately remove from the heat, and set aside.

5. Drain and pat dry the mung beans. Toast in a nonstick saucepan over medium heat, stirring constantly, until they are light brown and crispy, 1 to 2 minutes. Set aside.

6. To serve, place a small amount of sticky rice onto a plate with the mango slices arranged on the side. Pour 1 to 2 tablespoons of the coconut topping over the sticky rice and sprinkle with the toasted mung beans.

Adapted from a recipe by KANNIKA SIRIYARN

INDIA

this unique rice flour pancake comes from Kerala. It's typically served with meat or vegetable stews at breakfast but is also delicious as a sweet snack with coconut sauce. An *appam* pan, which is similar to a mini wok and available at Indian markets, works best because the pancakes come out slightly thicker in the center and the edges are thin and crispy. But don't worry, a small sauté pan is also fine.

PALAPPAM

SERVES 8 TO 12

1 cup water
2 tablespoons semolina flour
2 cups fine rice flour
1 teaspoon dry yeast
2 cups coconut milk, or as needed
¼ cup sugar
½ teaspoon salt
½ cup sesame oil

1. *Bring* the water to a simmer over medium-high heat in a small saucepan. Add the semolina to the water, stirring constantly. Simmer until the mixture achieves a porridge-like consistency, 1 to 2 minutes. Cool to room temperature.

2. *Combine* the semolina with the remaining ingredients except the salt and sesame oil. Mix lightly until just combined.

3. *Set* aside, covered, in a warm area until the dough has doubled in size, 4 to 5 hours.

4. *Add* the salt and mix thoroughly. The batter should be the consistency of heavy cream.

5. *Heat* an *appam* or medium sauté pan over low heat and brush lightly with the sesame oil. Make sure that the pan is not too cold or the *palappam* will not form the lace properly and also that it is not too hot or the *palappam* will not hold its shape.

6. *Ladle* about ¼ cup batter into the center of the pan. Twirl the pan just once to stir the batter and spread it so as to form a lace.

7. *Cover* and cook over low heat for a couple of minutes or until the *palappam* is cooked and light golden brown. Traditionally, *palappam* is cooked only on one side. Take care not to overheat the pan. And be careful not to break the crisp lace around the *palappam* when removing it from the pan. Repeat with the remaining batter and serve.

Adapted from a recipe by NIMMY PAUL

Vietnam

this dessert combines two complementary ingredients, coconut milk and bananas, which become very fragrant when cooked. It's typically made with the more starchy finger or baby bananas but if you can't find them, the regular variety works. If possible, buy the tapioca pearls from Asian markets. They're slightly larger than the regular kind and are shiny, transparent, and beautiful sitting in a pool of white creamy coconut sauce.

WARM BANANAS WITH TAPIOCA PEARLS

SERVES 6 TO 8

3½ cups water
⅓ cup small tapioca pearls (1⁄16 inch/2 mm wide)
1 cup unsweetened coconut milk
⅓ cup sugar, or to taste
Pinch of salt
3 ripe but firm bananas
¼ cup chopped, roasted peanuts

1. Bring the water to a rolling boil in a saucepan over high heat. Add the tapioca pearls and stir to separate them. Reduce the heat to medium and simmer until the tapioca becomes translucent, about 20 minutes. Add the coconut milk, sugar, and salt and stir well.

2. Peel the bananas and cut each into six equal rounds. Add them to the pan and cook until just soft, 3 to 4 minutes. At this point the tapioca should be almost clear and cooked.

3. Remove from the heat and transfer to individual dessert bowls, making sure there's an equal amount of sauce and bananas. Garnish with the peanuts and serve warm or at room temperature. The dessert will thicken as it cools.

Adapted from a recipe by MAI PHAM

Coconut

The coconut palm is one of the most useful and versatile tree crops. In the old days, a family who owned even a couple of coconut palms in the backyard was guaranteed not only a steady supply of staples such as coconut milk, cooking oil, and firewood but enough raw materials to make dozens of items from mats, baskets, brooms, and other household items.

The taste of fresh coconut milk is quite special and its luscious, complex nutty flavor is far superior to a canned product. If you've never experienced it fresh, you should make it from scratch at least once to taste the difference.

When purchasing a coconut, choose one that looks fresh. Although most are sold without the husks, the brown fibrous exterior should be dry with no signs of mildew and the eyes intact and mold-free. Make sure it's the mature, dark brown coconut used for grating and not the beige, young coconut (often carved into a point at the top) with soft, jelly-like flesh meant to be eaten fresh. Select the heaviest of the bunch, then shake to see if the liquid inside sloshes around. Avoid a light one as it's a probable sign that the juice might have seeped out and the meat has gone rancid.

The traditional way of cracking a coconut is to use the blunt back side of a heavy cleaver. Working over a bowl or a kitchen sink, hold it so you can tap it crosswise in the middle. (Some coconuts sold in the United States have a groove marking the middle.) Hold it firmly (keep your fingers completely out of the way and only on the bottom side) and whack it a few times, rotating the nut as you go. This might seem strange, but it really does work. There's a natural fault line and the nut should begin to crack. Insert the pointed end of the knife to drain the liquid (drink it or use it as a cooking liquid), then pry it into two pieces.

Another method is to first pierce the eyes of the coconut and drain the liquid. Lay it on a kitchen towel on a hard surface (like the floor) and give the nut a few whacks. The coconut should break apart. If you want to make long shreds of coconut, use a special tool with a round, serrated end to grate the meat while it's still in the shells. To mince or chop it fine, use a paring knife to first separate the meat from the shell, then remove the brown skin with a vegetable peeler. For toasted coconut, such as called for in Thai salads or dessert toppings, this is the time to slice it. For Indian chutneys, chop the meat into small chunks, then grind it in a food processor or blender.

To make coconut milk, follow this simple 1-2-3 guideline. One coconut makes roughly 1 cup of cream and 2 cups of coconut milk for a total of 3 cups. After the coconut meat has been removed from the shell and peeled, cut it into small chunks and grind it fine in a food processor. (You may have to do this in several batches.) Transfer to a mixing bowl, then add 1 cup of very hot water. When the mixture is cool enough to handle, transfer to a fine sieve lined with cheesecloth over a bowl.

Squeeze the coconut pulp, twisting the cloth, extracting as much liquid as possible. This first pressing is the coconut cream. Set this aside in a separate container if your recipe calls for it. To continue making coconut milk, add 1 to 2 more cups of boiling water to the shredded coconut and repeat the process. Fresh coconut milk should be used immediately for the best flavor or refrigerated and used within 2 days.

If you're pressed for time and would rather not make fresh coconut milk, there are several alternatives. For curries and desserts, canned coconut milk works well, although frozen coconut milk is better. Dessicated coconut and coconut powder can also be used to make coconut milk, but the flavor is not as good. In recent years, frozen chopped coconut has become readily available and is a good substitute for fresh coconut.

burfi is a popular sweet eaten all over India. It's usually made with condensed milk or coconut milk and, because of its tender texture, is sometimes known as "Indian cheesecake." This version of *burfi* has intense coconut flavor from both the coconut meat and milk. Traditionally, a *thali*—a shallow metal platter—is used for this recipe but a regular cake pan also works.

COCONUT FUDGE BURFI

SERVES 8

2 teaspoons melted ghee or butter

1 pound (450 g) fresh or frozen coconut, defrosted

One 12-ounce (350-g) can coconut milk

1 cup sugar

¼ cup water

½ cup ghee or clarified butter

1 teaspoon green cardamom seeds, crushed to a powder

1. Butter an 8-inch (20-cm) steel *thali* or cake pan with high edges with the melted ghee or butter and set aside.

2. Put the defrosted coconut and coconut milk in a kitchen blender and purée to a fine paste. It will be slightly grainy in texture but should be emulsified well.

3. Combine the sugar and water in a medium-sized saucepan and place over medium heat. Melt the sugar and cook until it turns a light golden brown, 8 to 10 minutes. Cover the pan if the sugar start to crystallize.

4. Add a quarter of the coconut paste to the pan, mix well, and add the rest. Be careful not to touch the hot coconut mixture. Cover the pan with the lid and let the mixture cook over medium heat for about 3 minutes. Turn off the heat and wait for a few seconds before you remove the lid. Stir well, place the lid back on the pan, and place over medium heat. Cook the mixture covered until it boils vigorously for 10 to 15 minutes, stirring occasionally.

5. Once the mixture subsides a little, remove the lid and cook for a couple of minutes. Start adding the melted ghee or butter 1 tablespoon at a time. Stir the fudge using a spatula to keep it from sticking to the bottom.

6. Cook the mixture until the ghee or butter starts to separate from the edges slightly. Add the green cardamom seeds powder and mix well.

7. Pour the mixture into the buttered *thali* and leave to cool. Once cool, refrigerate it for at least 4 hours. Turn the mixture out on a chopping board and cut into the desired shape and size. Serve immediately or store in an airtight container in the refrigerator. This will keep well for 2 weeks.

Adapted from a recipe by SURBHI SAHNI

while panna cotta is traditionally known as an Italian dessert, its mild, milky base makes it the perfect host for a range of different flavorings. Here, chef Surbhi Sahni blends it with Indian chai spices such as cardamom and cinnamon to give this classic dessert a refreshing twist. Note that the panna cotta needs to be frozen overnight and thawed for 6 hours before serving.

CHAI PANNA COTTA

SERVES 8

2 gelatin sheets
2 cups heavy cream
½ cup sugar
3 bay leaves
4 crushed green cardamom pods
2 crushed black cardamom pods
1 teaspoon lightly crushed black peppercorns
2 cloves
1 cinnamon stick
2 tablespoons assam tea leaves
2 tablespoons Earl Grey tea leaves

1. **Soak** the gelatin sheets in cold water until they rehydrate, about 15 minutes. Squeeze any excess water from the gelatin sheets and set aside in a bowl.

2. **In** a heavy-bottomed pan, bring the heavy cream, sugar, and all of the spices to a rolling boil over high heat. Immediately remove the pan from the stove and add the assam and Earl Grey tea leaves. Stir the mixture gently with a spoon. Steep for 5 minutes and strain. This is the base chai liquid for the panna cotta.

3. **Add** ½ cup of chai base to the rehydrated gelatin sheets and stir with a spoon until well blended. Pour this back into the remaining chai base and stir well.

4. **Cover** with plastic wrap and perforate with a knife to allow the steam to escape and to prevent a skin from forming. Allow to cool at room temperature. Pour the cooled mixture into eight 3-ounce (75-g) molds and freeze overnight.

5. **At** least 6 hours before serving, allow the frozen panna cotta to thaw in the refrigerator.

Adapted from a recipe by SURBHI SAHNI

in Thailand the "pearls" in this dessert are also made with pandanus juice and taro, which give the tiny dumplings beautiful bright green and purple colors. They're designed to resemble lotus seeds, considered the sacred flower of Buddhism. For extra texture, add sliced young coconut meat to the sauce. This dish is best served warm.

KABOCHA PEARLS IN COCONUT SAUCE
KHANOM BUA LOY

SERVES 6

RICE FLOUR BALLS
1 cup glutinous rice flour

⅓ cup mashed, cooked kabocha squash

1 tablespoon coconut cream, skimmed from top of can

⅓ cup water

SAUCE
2 cups coconut milk

1 cup water

¾ cup granulated sugar

2 tablespoons palm sugar or light brown sugar

¼ teaspoon salt, or to taste

2 pandanus leaves, lightly bruised and folded and tied into a knot

1. *For the rice flour balls:* Combine the rice flour, kabocha squash, and coconut cream in a mixing bowl. Add the water, 1 to 2 tablespoons at a time, and knead until the dough is soft enough to work with, 2 to 3 minutes. Add more water if needed, but not so much that the dough sticks to your hands.

2. *Roll* into several logs, each about ½ inch (1 cm) thick. Pinch off small pieces of dough and use your fingers to roll into lotus seed–sized balls about ½ inch (1 cm) in diameter. Set them aside. Continue until all of the dough is used up.

3. *Fill* a medium pot with water and bring it to a boil over medium heat. Add the rice flour balls and boil until they float to the surface, about 2 minutes. Remove with a slotted spoon and drop them in cold water.

4. *For the sauce:* In another saucepan, combine all of the ingredients for the sauce. While stirring, bring the liquid to a gentle boil over low heat.

5. *Drain* the cooked rice flour balls and add to the pot. Remove the pot from the heat and set aside to cool for 10 minutes before serving.

6. *Ladle* the coconut sauce and dumplings into 6 individual bowls and serve warm.

Adapted from a recipe by KANNIKA SIRIYARN

this wonderful flaky roti prata is typically served as a bread accompaniment to curries and savory foods as well as a late-night snack. This sweet version, however, makes a great treat for any time of day. For a fun dessert idea, turn these into smaller packets and serve with vanilla ice cream. Any seasonal fruit, including fresh peaches or nectarines or sautéed apples and pears, can be substituted for the bananas.

Roti Prata
with Bananas and Honey

SERVES 8

1 recipe Roti Prata Dough (page 209)
8 bananas, thinly sliced
1 cup honey
3½ ounces (85 g) butter or margarine

1. Prepare the *roti prata* dough through Step 3.

2. Flatten each piece of dough on a greased marble surface by stretching outward and then toss in the air to get a paper-thin dough. If you are not able to master the technique of throwing the dough in the air, just roll each ball into a paper-thin piece with a lightly floured rolling pin on a floured tabletop. Divide the bananas among the pieces of dough, drizzle with honey, and enclose the filling by folding over the dough to form a packet.

3. Heat a griddle on medium heat and add a little butter. Place the packets on the hot griddle, folded side down, and fry until golden brown, 4 to 5 minutes. Turn over and fry until browned, 3 to 4 minutes. Repeat with the remaining butter and packets of dough.

Adapted from a recipe by VIOLET OON

Pandanus Leaf

Pandanus leaf, also called "pandan," "screwpine," and "Asian vanilla," is a beloved aromatic used extensively throughout Southeast Asia to perfume puddings, cakes, drinks such as warm soy milk, and even savory dishes. The long, narrow, dark green leaves resemble those of day lilies and impart a nutty, vanilla-like fragrance only upon being heated. The leaves, often sold by their Thai name, *bai toey*, are 14 to 16 inches (35–40 cm) long and are typically tied together in a knot before being added to food. For exquisitely aromatic rice, tuck a leaf or two into the pot.

Take coconut sauce to the next level by simmering it with pandanus. Rice soup is utterly delicious and complex with just a few pieces added to the pot halfway into the cooking. Grilled meats wrapped with pandanus have a unique savory but sweet, nutty flavor. Regular iced tea becomes truly special with some of its aromatic juice.

In Thailand, desserts made with coconut milk or served with coconut sauce are almost always flavored with *bai toey*. When steaming sticky rice, Thai cooks like to throw a bundle into the water pan so the fragrant steam permeates the sticky rice. In addition to its distinctive floral aroma, the leaves are also pulverized and juiced and used as a bright green dye. Green pandanus noodles make a refreshing drink with crushed ice and coconut milk syrup. Egg noodles are also made with this aromatic ingredient although most of their spinach green color comes from food coloring.

In Malaysia and Singapore, dessert vendors often display colorful sweet offerings, including cakes, pancakes, jellies, and confections, all made from pandanus leaves.

To make pandanus extract, cut the leaves into 6-inch (15-cm) lengths, then tie into a knot. Using the back of a knife or a wooden pestle, tap the leaves several times. Add to a pot of boiling water and simmer for about 10 minutes. Turn off the heat and let the leaves steep for another 20 minutes. If you cook the liquid longer, the subtle fragrance will subside. If you like, you can also sweeten the extract with sugar. Use this fragrant liquid to flavor iced teas or desserts.

In Asia, fresh pandanus is sold everywhere from market stalls to floral stands. In the West, however, it's available frozen and usually found where frozen banana leaves are stored. If you're lucky to find it fresh, buy extra and freeze for later use. Cut the leaves into shorter lengths and portion them into single-use amounts and store in ziplock bags. Pandanus extract is a poor substitute, so if you can't find the real thing it's best to either omit it from the recipe or substitute vanilla beans.

VIETNAM

this dessert showcases two important staples in Asia—ginger and peanuts—while embracing the technique of layering flavors and textures, even in ice cream! The fresh ginger adds a citrusy bite while the candied ginger and roasted peanuts provide contrasting textures. Ginger lovers, beware, as this may be quite addicting.

GINGER-PEANUT ICE CREAM

MAKES ABOUT 1½ QUARTS/LITERS)

1¼ cups unsalted, roasted peanuts
⅓ cup chopped candied ginger
1 cup whole milk
2 cups heavy cream
¼ cup light brown sugar
⅓ cup sugar
¼ teaspoon salt
2 large eggs
2 tablespoons freshly minced ginger

1. *To* make the peanuts more fragrant and nutty, dry roast them in a frying pan over medium heat for 3 to 5 minutes. Do not brown them as they will become bitter. Remove from the heat. When cool, coarsely chop the peanuts and set aside.

2. *Place* the candied ginger in a small bowl and add just enough water to barely cover and set aside.

3. *In* a saucepan over medium heat, add the milk, heavy cream, the sugars, and salt and bring to a soft boil. Meanwhile, whisk the eggs in a large metal bowl.

4. *Add* the hot cream mixture to the egg mixture in a slow stream, whisking constantly. Pour the tempered mixture back into the saucepan.

5. *While* stirring constantly with a wooden spoon, simmer over medium-low heat until the custard is just thick enough to coat the back of a spoon and registers 170° to 175°F (75° to 80°C) on the thermometer. Do not let it boil.

6. *Pour* the custard through a fine-mesh sieve into a metal bowl. Cool to room temperature, then stir in the candied ginger. Cover and refrigerate until cold, at least 3 hours.

7. *Add* the fresh ginger and ½ cup chopped peanuts to the custard and stir to blend. Freeze the custard in an ice-cream maker according to the manufacturer's instructions. Transfer to an airtight container and put in the freezer to harden.

8. *To* serve, scoop ice cream into dessert bowls and garnish with the remaining chopped peanuts.

Adapted from a recipe by MAI PHAM

CHINA

mango pudding is a favorite in Hong Kong and can be found on *dimsum* carts all over the world. In some places, the pudding is chilled in elaborate molds in the shape of animals or flowers. Mango pudding can also be accompanied by fresh fruit such as ripe berries or additional mango pieces.

CHILLED MANGO PUDDING

SERVES 8

2 tablespoons unflavored powdered gelatin

1½ cups warm water

1 cup sugar

3 extremely ripe mangoes (about 1 pound 2 ounces/510 g), freshly mashed by hand

4½ cups ice cubes

⅔ cup heavy cream

1. *P*our the gelatin into the warm water in a small saucepan. Bring to a boil over low heat, then add the sugar and stir well. Remove from the heat and let cool.

2. *P*lace the gelatin and sugar mixture, mashed mangoes, and ice in a mixing bowl; stir until all of the ice has melted.

3. *S*tir in the heavy cream.

4. *D*ivide the mixture among 8 molds or glasses. Refrigerate until set.

Adapted from a recipe by CHOR KEUNG LAU *from The Grand Hyatt Hotel in Hong Kong*

India

this rice pudding is sweetened with *jaggery*, a brown sugar derived from the sap of a date palm tree, traditionally unrefined and found throughout much of Asia. Added to the rice once it has cooked, the *jaggery* is melted with ghee until soft and bubbling. The finished pudding is garnished with sautéed coconut, ghee-plumped raisins, and toasted cashews.

RICE PUDDING WITH BROWN SUGAR AND GHEE
NEYPAAYASAM

SERVES 6

2 cups medium- or long-grain rice
2½ cups *jaggery*
1 cup ghee, freshly made if possible
½ cup unsalted cashew nuts, broken into pieces
½ cup thinly sliced fresh coconut
½ cup seedless raisins
2 teaspoons crushed cardamom seeds

1. Rinse the rice in several changes of water until the water runs clear. In a saucepan, bring 1 quart of water to a boil and stir in the rice. Cook it over medium heat for 15 to 18 minutes, until the rice is well cooked and almost all of the water has evaporated. If necessary add a few more tablespoons of water. Once the *jaggery* is added, the rice will stop cooking.

2. Place a heavy sauté pan over medium heat, and melt the *jaggery* along with 6 tablespoons of water. When the *jaggery* has liquefied and started bubbling, transfer it to the rice pot along with ¼ cup of the ghee, and keep stirring gently.

3. Reserving 6 tablespoons of ghee for frying the garnishes, keep adding the remaining ghee to the rice, a couple of tablespoons at a time, stirring until the rice absorbs all of it. Cook for 15 to 20 minutes. When well cooked, the rice pudding will start leaving the sides of the pot as you stir. Remove the pot from the stove.

4. Heat the remaining ghee in a small sauté pan over medium heat and add the cashew nuts. When they start turning golden brown, about 2 minutes, add the coconut and raisins and keep stirring. The coconut will turn golden brown, and the raisins will become plump as they soak up the ghee, 1 to 2 minutes. Garnish the rice pudding with the toasted nuts, coconut, raisins, and ghee. Sprinkle it with the crushed cardamom and stir gently.

Adapted from a recipe by AMMINI RAMACHANDRAN. *From* Grains, Greens, and Grated Coconuts *by Ammini Ramachandran Copyright © 2007, 2008 by Ammini Ramachandran. Reprinted by permission of iUniverse, Inc. All right reserved.*

this sweet and refreshing drink is enjoyed throughout India and Southeast Asia. It's usually served on its own as a cool treat or alongside spicy foods. Although faluda is traditionally perfumed with rosewater syrup, it can be flavored with saffron, figs, chocolate, or mangoes. Buy the basil seeds used for desserts sold at Indian and Asian markets, not those used for planting. Or substitute fresh chopped basil.

FALUDA

SERVES 6 TO 8

1 tablespoon basil seeds
2 cups water
2 cups whole milk or half-and-half
½ to ¾ cup rose syrup
½ to ¾ cup vanilla ice cream or ice milk

1. Soak the seeds in water for at least 1 hour. They will swell considerably.

2. When ready to serve, line up 8 glasses with all components within easy reach.

3. For small (approximately 8 ounce/225 g) glasses, put 2 teaspoons of the seeds in the bottom of each glass. Pour in some milk to within an inch or so of the top of the glass. Top the milk with 2 teaspoons or more of the rose syrup. The syrup will sink below the milk. Finish with a tiny scoop of ice cream or ice milk in each glass.

Excerpted from My Bombay Kitchen, *by* NILOUFER ICHAPORIA KING, © 2007 *The Regents of the University of California. Published by The University of California Press.*

glossary

GLOSSARY OF SELECT INGREDIENTS AND PREPARATIONS

Banana leaves: Used to wrap fish or other foods before steaming or grilling in Thai, Vietnamese, and Singaporean cooking, the leaf is not eaten but flavors the filling. Available fresh and primarily frozen. Cut away the thick spine and dip the leaf briefly in boiling water to make it pliable.

Basil, Asian or Thai: An anise-flavored basil with purplish stems and flowers traditionally served with *pho*, Vietnamese beef noodle soup, and used liberally in Thai cooking.

Basmati rice: This fine aromatic, long-grain rice grows in the foothills of the Himalaya mountains. If unavailable, any fine long-grain rice may be substituted. Basmati rice should be carefully picked over and washed in several changes of water before being cooked.

Black pepper (*Kurumulaku*): Before Portuguese traders introduced chile peppers from the New World, black pepper was the primary hot ingredient in Indian food. Whether the peppercorns are crushed, coarsely ground, or powdered greatly changes the effect they have on the curry, so take note of the form used in each recipe.

Black salt (*Kala Namak*): This salt, which is highly sulphuric, is pink in its powdered form but turns black when it touches liquid. It is more flavorful, but not as salty, as ordinary salt and there is no substitute. If it is not available, simply omit it and increase regular salt slightly.

Black vinegar: This dark, aged, smoky vinegar may be made from rice or other grains. Chinese cooks use it with cold noodles, with stir-fried greens or eggplant, in twice-fried string beans, and with rich pork dishes.

Cardamom (*Elaichi*): This aromatic spice is generally sold in its pod and native to the hills of eastern Kerala. The green-colored pods are more aromatic than the plumper, bleached, whitish ones. Some Indian grocers sell the seeds separately, a great convenience when grinding spice combinations such as *garam masala*. Many recipes call for whole cardamom pods, which are used as a flavoring and are not meant to be eaten. If a recipe calls for a small amount of ground cardamom seeds, pulverize them in a mortar.

Cardamom, large black (*Bari Elaichi*): They look like black beetles and have an earthier, deeper flavor than green cardamom. Use them only when the recipe calls for them. They can be ground whole, skin and all.

Cellophane noodles (bean threads, glass noodles): These clear, threadlike noodles are made from mung bean starch. Soaking them briefly in hot water makes them pliable and clear, ready for use in soups, salads, and stir-fries. They can also be deep-fried in hot oil, which makes them puff up and turn crisp, producing a crunchy foundation for a stir-fry.

Chana dal: This is very much like the yellow split pea although it is smaller in size and sweeter in flavor. It is used as a spice in South India. Make sure you buy the skinned, split variety.

Chickpea flour: In Indian shops it is known as "gram flour" or "*besan*." It is also available in Britain in health food shops and in the United States in specialty stores where it is known as "*farine de pois chiches.*"

Chiles, fresh hot green: These fresh chiles used in India are 2 to 4 inches (5 to 10 cm) long and quite slim. They are generally green but sometimes ripen to a red color and may be used just as easily. If other varieties of chiles are substituted, adjustments should be made as they could be very mild in flavor, such as Italian hot peppers, or wildly hot, such as the Mexican *jalapeño*. See also Thai bird chiles.

Chiles, whole dried hot red: These chiles are generally 1½ to 2½ inches (3.5 to 6 cm) long and quite slim. Some cooks break the chiles open before adding them to the oil, thereby releasing the seeds and making the dish hotter. They are sold under different names, but look for chiles that are 2 to 3 inches (5 to 7.5 cm) long, deep red, and unbroken.

Chili powder, red/cayenne pepper: This is the dried powdered form of ripe capsicums otherwise known as red chile peppers. Indians refer to ground dried red chiles as "red chilli powder." Indian red chili powder and cayenne pepper may be used interchangeably.

Chinese chili sauce: A thick but not pasty sauce of red chiles, vinegar, and salt, typically thickened with soybeans, black beans, or Asian sweet potatoes. Unlike hot bean sauce, which is thicker and chunkier, Chinese chili sauce is usually a smooth purée.

Cilantro (fresh coriander) root: Thai and Malaysian cooks use not only the leaves but the roots of fresh coriander. You can find fresh coriander with the roots attached in many Asian and farmers' markets.

Coconut milk: In Southeast Asia, coconut milk plays many of the roles that cow's milk does in the West. It adds body to soups, stews, sauces, and curries; it's the foundation of numerous desserts; and it sometimes replaces water as the cooking medium for rice. If a recipe calls for coconut cream and coconut milk from a canned product, scoop the top creamy layer and hold it separately from the thin coconut milk. For more information on making fresh coconut milk, see page 245.

Coriander, fresh green /Chinese parsley/cilantro: This aromatic, floral herb is used extensively throughout Asia, both as a seasoning and a garnish. To store fresh green coriander, put it, unwashed, roots and all, into a container filled with water, almost as if you're putting flowers in a vase. The leafy section of the plant should not be in water. Pull a plastic bag over the coriander and the container and refrigerate the whole thing. It should last for weeks.

Cumin seeds, black: Used in Indian and many other Asian cuisines, this caraway-like seed has a flavor that is more refined and complex than that of the ordinary cumin. As it is expensive, it is used in small quantities. If you cannot find it, use regular cumin seeds as a substitute.

Curry leaves (kari leaves), fresh and dried: These highly aromatic curry leaves are shaped rather like bay leaves and are sold as whole sprigs with leaves attached to their stems. Dried leaves are available in most Western cities, but use the fresh leaves whenever possible. Fresh leaves can be stored in the freezer for months, which is slightly better than using the dried leaves which have less flavor.

Daikon (*Raphanus sativus*): Daikon radish is a large, cylindrical root sold fresh in Asian markets. It varies in size, but the most common variety is 2 to 4 inches (5 to 10 cm) wide and about 12 inches (30 cm) long. It is sold by the piece and is used both cooked and raw, grated as a garnish, or added to sauces.

Dals/dhal (dried split peas and beans): Technically, a *dal* is really a dried split pea though the word is used rather loosely at times for all legumes. Most split peas are sold in India in two forms, skinned and unskinned. It is the skinned variety, also known as "washed," or "white," which are primarily used. *Dal* can be cooked with seasonings, or soaked and ground into batters for pancakes, dumplings, and fritters; sometimes a small handful is fried in hot oil—like a spice—to add crunchiness to a vegetable or rice dish.

Dashi: Dashi is the basic Japanese soup and cooking stock made from *kombu* (kelp) and pre-flaked *katsuobushi* (dried bonito). An instant version requiring only the addition of water is available, packaged, in Japanese markets.

Dried shrimp: Asian markets carry dried shrimp in a range of sizes, all valued for the concentrated fish flavor and saltiness they contribute to dishes. They are usually rehydrated before using, although some recipes call for pounding the dried shrimp to a powder.

Fennel seeds (*Sonf*): These seeds look and taste like anise seeds, only they are larger and plumper. They may be roasted and used after meals as a mouth freshener and digestive.

Fenugreek seeds (*Methi*): Yellow, square, and flattish, these seeds are meant to soothe the intestinal tract. They add a slightly bitter flavor and should not be allowed to burn.

Fish sauce: Considered the quintessential ingredient in Vietnamese, Thai and other Southeast Asian cuisines, this fermented fish sauce provides the salty element in many Southeast Asian dishes and a characteristic pungent flavor. Typically, it's made with anchovies that are brined and fermented for months until they yield an aromatic liquid. See page 159 for more information.

Five-spice powder: Not always limited to five ingredients, this fragrant brown powder typically contains star anise, fennel, Szechwan peppercorns, cloves, and cinnamon. It's used as a seasoning for roasted and braised meats and poultry.

Galangal/galangal: A rhizome related to ginger, galangal is fundamental to Thai cooking. Its rootlike shape resembles ginger, but it is paler, thinner-skinned, and firmer, with a sharper, mustard-like bite and a camphor-like smell. It is typically peeled and thinly sliced for flavoring soups or ground for curries.

Garam masala: A highly aromatic mixture that is often sprinkled over the top of dishes that have almost finished cooking, the name of this ground spice mixture means "hot spices" in Hindi. It is an important ingredient in North Indian cooking, and there are many recipes for it.

Ghee: This is butter that has been so well clarified that you can deep-fry in it. Because it is totally free of all milk solids, it does not need refrigeration. *Ghee* has a very special, nutty taste. If you have access to Indian shops, buy ready-made *ghee*.

Ginger, fresh: Known sometimes as "gingerroot," this is really a rhizome with a refreshing pungent flavor. When buying ginger, look for pieces that are not too wrinkled and have a taut fresh skin. Its potato-like skin needs to be peeled before it can be chopped or grated.

Ginkgo: These nuts are available in Asian markets and specialty food stores, cooked, bottled, or canned.

Goma: Sesame seeds, both black and white, are used throughout Asia as a garnish, seasoning ingredient in sauce and dips, or part of a filling for sweet or savory cakes.

Hoisin sauce: A fermented soybean sauce with other seasonings added—typically garlic, sugar, and five spice. Vietnamese cooks use hoisin sauce as a dip or barbecue sauce for grilled meats.

Jaggery: *Jaggery*, sold by weight in Indian markets, is solidified molasses. It has a caramel flavor important to chutneys. If necessary, substitute ¼ cup brown sugar for every 2 ounces (50 g) of *jaggery*.

Kabocha: A Japanese pumpkin, kabocha squash is revered for its bright orange flesh with creamy texture and sweet flavor. Any winter squash or West Indian pumpkin available in Caribbean markets is the best substitute.

Kaffir lime: The grated zest of this knobby lime is used in Thai curry pastes and fish cakes. The glossy green leaves, finely julienned, figure in Thai soups, salads, stir-fries, and curries. If you can't find the fresh item, look for dried or frozen leaves and dried lime rind.

Karhai: This Indian wok may be made out of cast iron or stainless steel. It is excellent for stir-frying and its rounded bottom makes it very economical for deep-frying.

Katsuobushi: Dried bonito fillet, used for dashi (soup stock) and as a garnish. Looks like a piece of wood.

Kgemono: Deep-fried foods, including tempura.

Kinome: Japanese pepper leaf, used as a garnish.

Kinugoshi tofu: This silky bean curd is a custard-like cake made from white soybeans, sold fresh from the refrigerator section of Japanese markets. Kept refrigerated in water, which is changed daily, this will keep for several days. This is the most delicate of all the forms of bean curd.

Kombu: Also called "tangle" and "Japanese kelp," kelp is a large marine plant that plays an important role in the Japanese kitchen. The leathery fronds of the seaweed are sold dried in packaged sheets in Japanese markets. The seaweed is also sold flaked and shredded.

Lemongrass: A plant that resembles a woody scallion, with a slender, multilayered base and branching leaves. When sliced, chopped, or crushed, it releases a lemony scent and flavor. Discard the branching leaves and the fibrous outer layers of the base.

Lotus: This buff-skinned vegetable looks like a plump link sausage; sliced, it resembles potato but with "piercings" from hollow spaces that run the length of the rhizome. Lightly blanched slices of lotus root add crisp texture and eye appeal to Chinese soups and stir-fries.

Mango: When ripe, mangoes should be very slightly soft to the touch and should begin to smell. You may ripen them yourself at home by wrapping them individually in newspaper and then storing them either in hay or in a basket. There should, however, be no black spots on them. Once they are ripe they can be refrigerated. For Thai desserts, the best varieties are Kent and Alphonso, which have great flavor and practically no fiber.

Mint: The mint favored by Vietnamese cooks is a round-leafed tropical variety. It is an essential element in the salad platter that accompanies many cooked dishes. Thai cooks also make frequent use of cooling tropical mint in seafood and minced meat salads.

Mirin: An essential condiment in Japanese cuisine, sweet rice wine is similar to sake but with a lower alcoholic level. Mirin imparts a delicate, soft, aromatic fragrance to food, similar to how rice wine and sherry accent food.

Miso: An important staple in the Japanese kitchen, this paste is made from fermented, cooked soybeans and is used as a base for soups, braises, and dipping sauce. See page 62 for more information.

Mitsuba: Trefoil, an herb with a distinctive flavor, is used in soups and as a garnish.

Mustard seeds, whole black: These tiny dark round seeds, sometimes quite black, sometimes reddish-brown, are used throughout India for pickling and for seasoning everything from yogurt to beans. When popped in hot oil, they impart an earthy sweetness. However, when they are ground, they turn pungent and slightly bitter.

Mustard seeds, whole yellow: These are commonly available and may be substituted for black mustard seeds should the latter prove elusive. They are less bitter and milder in flavor.

Oyster Sauce: A dark brown, concentrated condiment made from oysters, salt, and cornstarch, oyster sauce adds depth to stir-fries. Asian markets carry brands that differ considerably in quality and price; less expensive products may be made with oyster flavoring, not real oysters.

Palm Sugar: Some species of palm yield a sap that can be boiled down until it crystallizes into a dark sweetener with a taste reminiscent of maple sugar. Palm sugar may be soft and sticky or as hard as an open box of brown sugar. Coconut sugar, made from the sap of the coconut palm, can be used in any recipe calling for palm sugar.

Pandanus leaf (screw pine leaf, Asian vanilla): The long, slim leaves look like finely ridged daylily leaves. They are valued in Thailand and throughout Southeast Asia as a flavoring, primarily for desserts but also for savory foods. Typically, the leaves are steeped in sugar syrup to extract their flavor and green color, and then the syrup is strained for use in sweets. The leaves can also be used to flavor plain rice. See page 252 for more information.

Pappadam: Also called "paper," these Indian wafers are generally made out of split peas and flavored with red pepper, black pepper, or garlic. *Pappadams* made with sago flour or potato flour are also very popular in India.

Preserved vegetables: Vegetables can be cabbage, mustard, turnip, radish, or other members of the cabbage family. The preserving is done with salt or brine, followed by drying. The result is a wrinkled fermented pickle that, chopped and added in small quantities to stuffings, braises, soups, stir-fries, and noodle dishes, adds a pungent, salty edge.

Rice: For most uses, *long-grain rice* is preferred in Thailand and Vietnam, but all long-grain rices aren't alike. Some are fluffy when cooked, others sticky. The choice depends largely on national taste. A few types worth noting:
Glutinous rice, also known as "sticky rice," comes in short-grain and long-grain varieties. The people of northern Thailand prefer long-grain sticky rice for their table rice and for desserts, such as the popular sticky rice with coconut milk and mango.
Jasmine rice, a long-grain rice valued for its perfume, is the favored variety among Thai and Vietnamese cooks. The name is poetic license: Jasmine rice doesn't smell like jasmine, but it is aromatic.
Black sticky rice or *Indonesian black rice* is not the whole-grain version of glutinous rice; it is a distinct variety that looks something like wild rice. It has a nutty flavor that is most appreciated in Thailand where it is used primarily in sweet snacks, puddings, and desserts.

Rice flour: Also called rice powder, it has the same texture as corn flour and is sold in Indian and Asian grocery stores. It is used to make noodles, pancakes, and breads. It is very different from the generic rice flour sold in non-Asian markets.

Rice noodles: Dried rice vermicelli, also known as "rice sticks," are often soaked in hot water for a few minutes to soften. The rehydrated off-white noodles are used in soups, salads, stuffing, and stir-fries. Rice sticks also come in medium and wide widths for soups and stir-fries, and fresh for a variety of uses.

Rice papers, dried: A staple in the Vietnamese kitchen, these transparent, brittle, rice-flour sheets soften quickly in warm water and become pliable. Round sheets are used as wrappers for fried spring rolls and fresh spring rolls. Triangular ones are brought to the table as wrappers for grilled meats.

Rice wine: Chinese rice wine (from the city of Shaoxing) has a nuttier, more sherry-like taste than Japanese rice wine, but it is fundamental to Chinese cooking as a component of sauces, marinades, steamed seafood dishes, stuffing, and braises.

Salted black beans: These soft, salty black soybeans have been brined and fermented to produce their distinctive flavor.

Sambal oelek: This Indonesian version of chili paste is a rough-textured sauce that includes red chiles, vinegar, oil, and salt. It is a widely used table condiment and an important ingredient in many dishes.

Sesame oil: Oil pressed from roasted sesame seeds, which gives it a nutty aroma and rich dark color. Pale sesame oils are made from un-roasted seeds, and have an entirely different character.

Shrimp sauce and shrimp paste (*kapi* in Thai, *belachan* in Indonesian): Fermented shrimp sauce and shrimp paste contribute a salty, pronounced fishy note to many Chinese dishes. Some of these shrimp products are thick and spoonable; others are pastelike and sold as bricks. The cook breaks off a little and pounds it with other ingredients, then fries it in oil to release its flavor.

Soy sauce: Made from fermented soybeans, soy sauce also contains wheat in varying proportions and, sometimes, sugar or molasses. These other ingredients and different aging regimens give soy sauces their varied characters. See page 62 for more information.

Sriracha sauce: This smooth, puréed Thai condiment, made of chiles, vinegar, garlic, sugar, and salt, is widely used as a condiment or as an ingredient in dishes.

Szechwan peppercorns: These dried reddish-brown pods are unrelated to black peppercorns but they have a similarly fragrant, warming character.

Tamarind: Resembling a dry, brown pea pod, tamarind is the fruit of the tamarind tree. Inside the pod is a moist, sour pulp that looks like prune paste. Tamarind is available as whole pods or as a compressed cake made from the pulp. To use, the pulp must be reconstituted with warm water and pushed through a sieve. Tamarind is also available as a purée or concentrate, which is sold in plastic tubs and very easy to use.

Taro: This water-loving plant is prized in India and Southeast Asia for its underground tubers and its leaves. The barrel-shaped tubers have a rough, hairy brown skin and a white or cream-colored starchy flesh. In Vietnam, the steamed chunks are added to stews. In Thailand, they are cooked and eaten like potatoes.

Thai bird chiles: These fiery chiles are small, about ¼ inch wide and 2 to 3 inches long, but have great flavor. An important ingredient in Thai and other Southeast Asian cuisines, they are usually cut into very thin slices and added to food, or pounded and used as seasoning and in curry pastes.

Tofu (bean curd): Made from coagulated soy milk, tofu can be firm or soft, fresh or fermented, pressed or deep-fried. See page 102 for more information.

Toovar dal: Also known as *toor dal* and *arhar dal*, this hulled, ocher-colored split pea has quite a dark, earthy flavor.

Tree ear mushrooms: In addition to dried shiitake mushrooms with their aggressive flavor, the chewy tree ear, also known as "cloud ear" or "wood ear," is widely used. Tree ears do not have a strong taste, but they add a pleasing gelatinous texture to soups, stuffing, noodle dishes, and vinegared salads.

Turmeric: The dried powdered spice that gives many Indian dishes their golden hue comes from a rhizome related to ginger. Like ginger, the fresh rhizome has a thick main stem with ring markings; the side shoots look like stumpy fingers. The flesh is carrot-colored and delicate in flavor, with a slightly sweet, slightly musty quality.

Urad dal: This rather pale *dal* is used in the South for all kinds of savory cakes and pancakes.

chef bios

ELIZABETH ANDOH is an American writer and lecturer specializing in Japanese food and culture. The author of *Washoku: Recipes from the Japanese Home Kitchen*, she owns and operates "A Taste of Culture," a culinary arts program in Tokyo and Osaka. Ms. Andoh is the only non-Japanese member of the prestigious Japan Food Journalists Association and also contributes to American publications, such as *Gourmet* magazine and the *New York Times*. (Tokyo, Japan)

ZULKIFLI BIN PACKEER BAWA is a Singapore food hawker whose specialty is *roti prata* and its variation, *murtabak*. Zulkifli comes from a family that has been running a food business since his late grandfather's days. Zulkifli has been in the *roti prata* business for 43 years, starting his Singapore hawker career by cooking satay and roti prata at age 12. (Singapore)

CHUN SHUAN CAI is an executive chef of Da Dong Roast Duck Restaurant. He is one of the most famous chefs in China. In the 5th China Culinary Contest in 2006 he won top honors, the Golden Prize. Chef Cai specializes in Chinese and European food. (Beijing, China)

FLOYD CARDOZ is the executive chef and partner of Tabla, where he celebrates the sensual flavors and spices of his native land in his pioneering New Indian cuisine. In Tabla's dining room, Floyd seasons Western cuisine with Indian spices, and in the restaurant's Bread Bar, Floyd cooks home-style Indian fare. In October 2006, Floyd released his first cookbook, *One Spice, Two Spice*. (New York, NY)

IAN CHALERMKITTICHAI is chef/owner of Kittichai, a Thai restaurant in New York City. Before coming to New York he was the executive chef at the Bangkok Regent's Grill in the Four Seasons, in Bangkok, Thailand. Chef Chalermkittichai was the first Thai national executive chef in a major five-star hotel restaurant in Bangkok. He previously hosted the weekly Thai television cooking show "Chef Mue Thong," and leads CIA culinary tours of Thailand. (New York, NY)

SHIRLEY CHENG, a native of China, is a professor of culinary arts at The Culinary Institute of America in Hyde Park, New York. She graduated from the Culinary Institute of Sichuan, China, in 1979, and taught there for 8 years as a chef instructor. Chef Cheng has more than 24 years experience in teaching Asian cuisines with a specialization in regional cuisines of China. (Hyde Park, NY)

HEE SOOK CHO is the director of the Genesis Research Center at The Woosong Culinary Academy in Seoul, Korea. Prior to this, Professor Cho spent many years as a cooking instructor and chef focusing on the preparation and presentation of traditional Korean cuisine. (Seoul, Korea)

FUCHSIA DUNLOP, the author of *Sichuan Land of Plenty: A Treasury of Authentic Sichuan Cooking, Revolutionary Chinese Cookbook: Recipes from Hunan Province*, and *Shark's Fin and Sichuan Pepper: A Sweet-Sour Memoir of Eating in China*. She is the only Westerner to have graduated from the Sichuan Institute of Higher Cuisine. In addition to her book writing, she writes about Chinese food and culture for *The Economist* and leads CIA culinary tours of China. (London, England)

QIANG JIN (a.k.a. "Chef Ken") is the Chinese chef at the Made in China restaurant at the Grand Hyatt Beijing. Chef Jin showcases his active involvement in the success of the restaurant with the demonstration of his profound understanding of a variety of Chinese cuisines, among them Cantonese, Sichuan, Hunan, Shandong, and Imperial. (Beijing, China)

NILOUFER ICHAPORIA KING is an anthropologist, food scholar, teacher, and cook. Her book *My Bombay Kitchen: Traditional and Modern Parsi Home Cooking*, chronicles the food of one Parsi family spanning three generations and two continents. (San Francisco, CA)

CHOR KEUNG LAU is the dimsum sous chef at the Grand Hyatt Hong Kong. Known for being very innovative, Chef Lau's dimsum creations feature a wide range of original and traditional recipes prepared with the freshest ingredients. Chef Lau previously trained elsewhere in Hong Kong, and in some of the finest Chinese restaurants in Japan. (Hong Kong)

MYUNG SOOK LEE, born in Seoul, Korea, is a chef and president of the Culinary Institute of California. She was a protégé of Hae Sung Hwang, a living Korean National Treasure, at the Korean Traditional and Royal Cuisine. In 1996, Ms. Lee appeared on the popular Japanese cooking show, "Iron Chef," as the first Korean Challenger in the show's history. (Los Angeles, CA)

KIYOMI MIKUNI is the chef/owner of Hôtel de Mikuni in Tokyo. Chef Mikuni is known as a pioneering chef who combines Japanese inspiration with French cuisine. His vision is global; he is now working around the world, educating children and sharing his techniques with chefs. (Tokyo, Japan)

MASAHARU MORIMOTO—known to millions as star of "Iron Chef" and "Iron Chef America"—is as comfortable cooking against the clock for a live television audience as he is preparing his signature *omakase* menu at his namesake restaurants in New York, Philadelphia, Tokyo, and Mumbai. He is the author of *Morimoto: The New Art of Japanese Cooking*, featuring his inventive cooking style and unique cuisine. (New York, NY)

KOBKAEW NAIPINIJ AND NING NAIPINIJ are a mother and daughter team who teach at the prestigious Rajabhat Institute Suan Dusit Royal Cooking College in Bangkok. They have written about and taught cooking collectively for more than 30 years, focusing on classical Thai cuisine with a special interest in both the history and healthfulness of their dishes. (Bangkok, Thailand)

BANSANI NAWISAMPHAN is the executive sous chef at the Chiva Som, an internationally acclaimed health resort in southern Thailand. A student of Kobkaew Naipinij, Bansani has worked as a chef in many famous hotels, including the Sukhothai BKK and the Raffle in Singapore, as well as for the 1998 Asian Games in Bangkok. (Bangkok, Thailand)

HÒANG TRANG NGUYEN is in charge of food and beverage for the M&T company, and has been a contributing writer for *Culture and Art of Food and Beverage* magazine. She was previouly the chef of T.I.B Restaurant, the New World Hotel's Vietnamese restaurant, and the Temple Club Restaurant. (Saigon, Vietnam)

VIOLET OON is a cookbook author, chef, and one of Singapore's leading food gurus. Considered a leading authority on Asian cuisine (her own specialty is the Nonya cuisine of Singapore), Oon has published three cookbooks of her own, and is the writer and recipe tester of the recently published *Naturally Peninsula* and *Tasty Singapore Timeless Recipes* cookbooks. (Singapore)

NIMMY PAUL is a food writer and consultant based in Kerala, India. She teaches traditional Indian and Kerala cuisine to thousands of visiting travelers. She and her husband also host lunch and dinner for guests who wish to sample home-cooked food. Nimmy and her recipes have been featured in many publications, including the *New York Times, Travel+Leisure, Food & Wine*, and *Saveur*. (Kerala, India)

MAI PHAM is the chef/owner of Lemon Grass Restaurant and Lemon Grass Asian Grill and Noodle Bar in Sacramento and at the Sacramento International Airport. The author of *Pleasures of the Vietnamese Table* and *The Best of Vietnamese and Thai Cooking*, she is a guest chef instructor at the CIA, leads CIA culinary tours of Vietnam, and frequently consults to the food service industry. (Sacramento, CA)

CHARLES PHAN is the chef/owner of the Slanted Door, a modern Vietnamese restaurant located in San Francisco's historic Ferry Plaza Building. The 2004 James Beard Award for Best Chef: California, he is a regular guest chef instructor at the CIA. His newest venture, Out the Door, offers prepared dishes to go at two locations in San Francisco. (San Francisco, CA)

AMMINI RAMACHANDRAN is the author of *Grains, Greens, and Grated Coconuts: Recipes and Remembrances of a Vegetarian Legacy*. A former financial analyst in international banking, in 2001 she started researching and writing about the ancient Indian Ocean spice trade and its culinary and cultural influences on her home state Kerala, India. Her Web site is www.peppertrail. com. (Dallas, TX)

SURBHI SAHNI is the executive pastry chef of Dévi restaurant in New York City, America's only Indian restaurant to hold a Michelin star. She previously held pastry positions at New York's davidburke & donatella, Amma, and Tamarind. A native of New Delhi, she holds a master's degree in food studies and food management from New York University. (New York, NY)

SUVIR SARAN is the author of the widely acclaimed *Indian Home Cooking* and *American Masala: 125 New Classics From My Home Kitchen*. Chef Saran and tandoori master Hemant Mathur are the owners of Dévi in New York, the only Indian restaurant in America to hold a Michelin star. Recently, The CIA, where he regularly contributes as a guest chef instructor, named him Chairman, Asian Culinary Studies for its World Cuisines Council. (New York, NY)

CHRISTIBELLE SAVAGE, better known as "Auntie Belle," is the Malaysian head cook/chef de cuisine at the Straits Café at the Grand Hyatt Singapore. Auntie Belle is a Malaysian-born master of Peranakan cuisine, a cuisine that evolved from the blending of Malay, Chinese, and Indonesian cooking. Prior to working at Straits Café, she spent nearly 20 years working as a guest chef for hotel chains traveling the world, teaching local chefs how to prepare Perankakan foods. (Singapore)

HIROKO SHIMBO is a trained sushi chef, restaurant consultant, cooking instructor, and author. Her most recent book, *The Sushi Experience*, published in 2006, is an instructive book on preparing, eating, and savoring sushi in its many forms. *The Japanese Kitchen*, published in 2000, is a comprehensive book that has become the standard English language work on Japanese cuisine. (New York, NY)

ROHIT SINGH is the chef/owner of the nationally acclaimed Breads of India & Gourmet Curries in Berkeley, Oakland, and Walnut Creek, California. Rohit has introduced about 800 regional dishes and more than 175 breads from the Indian subcontinent through his daily changing menu. His restaurants have been featured in numerous publications, including *Bon Appétit, Gourmet* magazine, *Zagat Survey*, and the *San Francisco Chronicle*. (Berkeley, CA)

CHAI SIRIYARN is the chef/owner of Marnee Thai Restaurant, which has two locations in San Francisco and has been among the Zagat Survey's Top Thai Restaurants in the city for the past 15 years. Chef Chai, whose culinary accolades include winning the grand prize in the Los Angeles Pad Thai Festival contest in 2000, and earning "Thailand Superchef Award" in 2003, is the author of *Thai Cuisine Beyond Curry* and is a visiting guest chef instructor at The Culinary Institute of America. (San Francisco, CA)

KANNIKA SIRIYARN was born in the ancient city of Ayudthaya, the birthplace of Royal Thai cuisine. She learned traditional Thai cooking from her aunt, who was a famous chef at the city market. Siriyarn moved to Bangkok in 1952 and ran her own business as a food vendor, selling her curries and Thai sweets for more than three decades. (Chiang Mai, Thailand)

YOSHIHIRO TAKAHASHI is the fifteenth generation chef/owner of Hyoutei, the leading traditional kaiseki restaurant in Kyoto that has been open for nearly 400 years. Still in his early thirties, Yoshihiro is considered a master and his restaurant is famous for its Japanese Morning Porridge. (Kyoto, Japan)

CHRISTOPHER TAN is a Singapore-based writer, editor, food consultant, and author who started cooking at the age of 14. He contributes articles, photographs, and recipes to many international publications, including *Saveur* and *Gourmet*. His most recent book projects are *Inside the Southeast Asian Kitchen: Foodlores and Flavours* and an ASEAN-commissioned volume celebrating the foodways of its constituent nations. (Singapore)

LOUIS TAY is the executive chef at Singapore's Swissotel Merchant Court, noted for its daily buffet featuring Singapore's favorite dishes. Formerly the executive sous chef of the Fullerton Hotel, Chef Tay is a much-awarded chef, having won gold, silver, and bronze medals at the Olympic IKA in 2004, at the Bocuse d'Or in 2003, and at the Expogast Culinary World Cup Luxembourg in 2002 and 1998. (Singapore)

PHAM THI NGOC TINH is the chef/owner of Thuong Chi restaurant in Saigon, Vietnam. Chef Tinh specializes in Royal Cuisine and the foods of the central region of Vietnam. Prior to opening her restaurant, Chef Tinh was the founding chef of Ngu Binh, and Hoa Mi of the New World Hotel, both highly acclaimed restaurants highlighting Hue cuisine. (Saigon, Vietnam)

KUNIO TOKUOKA is a third generation chef/owner of Kiccho Arashiyama, one of the most valued *kaiseki* restaurants in Japan. Chef Tokuoka is considered the finest interpreter of *kaiseki* cuisine. His classic Japanese cuisine is based exclusively on local and seasonal ingredients, and his creations have been compared to works of art. Chef Tokuoka is known for mixing modernism in Japanese *kaiseki*. (Kyoto, Japan)

NGUYEN DZOAN CAM VAN is Vietnam's most popular cooking teacher. The owner of Dzoan Cam Van restaurant in Saigon, she is the author of a dozen cookbooks, frequently appears on Vietnamese television, and has been dubbed "the Julia Child of Vietnam." Van graduated from college with a degree in Chinese and Vietnamese literature. Her culinary career took off when she was invited to appear on a local cooking show. (Saigon, Vietnam)

LIN WANG is a National Advanced Culinary Technician and member of the Chefs Specialist Committee of the Hunan Provincial Culinary Association. He is also the administrative head chef of the New Yuloudong Gourmet Culture Square, and a winner of Changsha City "Starry City Cup" and the "Changsha Food and Drink Ten Outstanding Achievements." (Changsha City, Hunan Province, China)

NG KWOK YIN is the executive chef of the Palm Beach Restaurant. With more than 30 years experience, Kwok Yin honed his skills at the famous Fatty's Cantonese Cuisine in Albert Street, where he started work in the kitchen as a teenager. He went on to learn the intricacies of Singapore seafood cuisine in the busiest seafood restaurant in Singapore's West Coast, the Pandan Garden Seafood Restaurant. An award-winning chef, Kwok Yin has been with Palm Beach Seafood Restaurant since 1990. (Singapore)

FU YUELIANG Chef Fu Yueliang is the Executive Sous Chef of Hyatt Regency Hangzhou. A graduate of the Lin'an Cooking Technical School, Chef Fu joined the Hyatt Regency Hangzhou in 2004. Before assuming this present role, Chef Fu was the pre-opening chef de cuisine of the Hyatt Hangzhou's 28 Hu Bin Road, which has been recognized as one of the best Chinese restaurants in China. (Hangzhou, China)

sources

ASIANFOODGROCER.COM
131 West Harris Avenue
South San Francisco, CA 94080
Tel: 888.482.2742 ext. 107
650.873.7600 ext. 107
Fax: 650.871.9154
www.asianfoodgrocer.com

BANGKOK CENTER GROCERY
104 Mosco Street
New York, NY 10013
Tel: 212.732.8916
Fax: 212.349.1979
www.thai-grocery.com

CRATE & BARREL
www.crateandbarrel.com
800-996-9960 for store locations

CROSS COUNTRY NURSERIES
P.O. Box 170
199 Kingwood-Locktown Road
Rosemont, NJ 08556
Tel: 908.996.4646
Fax: 908.996.4638
www.chileplants.com

DIAMOND ORGANICS
1272 Highway 1
Moss Landing, CA 95039
Tel: 888.ORGANIC (674.2642)
www.diamondorganics.com

GOURMET SLEUTH
P.O. Box 508
Los Gatos, CA 95031
Tel: 408.354.8281
www.gourmetsleuth.com

IMPORT FOOD (THAI GROCERY)
P.O. Box 2054
Issaquah, WA 98027
Tel: 888.618.THAI (8424)
425.687.1708
Fax: 425.687.8413
www.importfood.com

INDOMART
25608 Barton Road
Loma Linda, CA 92354
Tel: 909.796.4000
909.799.7215
Fax: 909.799.7265
www.indomart.us

KALUSTYAN'S
Marhaba International, Inc.
123 Lexington Avenue
New York, NY 10016
Tel: 800.352.3451
212.685.3451
Fax: 212.683.8458
www.kalustyans.com

KORIN JAPANESE TRADING COMPANY
57 Warren Street
New York, NY 10007
Tel: 212.587.7021
Fax: 212.587.7027
www.korin.com

MELISSA'S/WORLD VARIETY PRODUCE, INC.
P.O. Box 21127
Los Angeles, CA 90021
Tel: 888.588.0151
www.melissas.com

MORE THAN GOURMET
929 Home Avenue
Akron, OH 44310
Tel: 800.860.9385
330.762.6652
Fax: 330.762.4832
www.morethangourmet.com

PATEL BROTHERS
42-92 Main Street
Flushing, NY 11355
Tel: 718.661.1112
Fax: 718.661.2076
www.patelbrothersusa.com

PEARL RIVER MART
477 Broadway
New York, NY 10013
Tel: 212.431.4770
www.pearlriver.com

TEN REN TEA
419 Eccles Avenue
South San Francisco, CA 94080
Tel: 888.650.1047
650.583.1047
Fax: 650.588.0307
www.tenren.com

UWAJIMAYA, INC.
P.O. Box 3642
Seattle, WA 98124
www.uwajimaya.com

index

Page numbers in *italic* refer to photographs.

acknowledgments

THE PUBLISHER'S ACKNOWLEDGMENTS

DK Publishing would like to thank Pearl River Mart, Korin Japanese Trading Company, and Crate & Barrel for the generous loan of props for photography. DK would also like to thank Bill Miller, Liza Kaplan, and Sonia Mahabir for their assistance on the shoot.

THE CULINARY INSTITUTE OF AMERICA

HYDE PARK

president: DR. TIM RYAN C.M.C '77
vice-president, continuing education: MARK ERICKSON C.M.C '77
director of publishing: NATHALIE FISCHER
editorial project manager: MARGARET WHEELER '00
recipe content leaders: FUCHSIA DUNLOP, MYUNG SOOK LEE, VIOLET OON, SUVIR SARAN, HIROKO SHIMBO, CHAI SIRIYARN
recipe testers: SEAN KENNIFF, JIYOUN OH, JOE SAENZ

GREYSTONE

executive director of strategic initiatives: GREG DRESCHER
director of strategic initiatives: JOHN BARKLEY
program director of strategic initiatives: AMY MYRDAL
director of corporate relations: HOLLY BRIWA
director of operations and finance, strategic initiatives: CHRISTINA ADAMSON
associate director of strategic initiatives: SHARA HOFFMAN
manager of strategic initiatives: SONIA SERRANO
new media designer: CHAD WILMOTH
director of education: ADAM BUSBY
associate director of education: DIANA DELONIS
chef instructor/lead culinary planner: TONI SAKAGUCHI
communications manager: CATE CONNIFF-DOBRICH
curriculum cesigner: KAREN FORNI
photographer: TERRANCE MCCARTHY

THE CIA'S ACKNOWLEDGMENTS

The Culinary Institute of America's Worlds of Flavor International Conference & Festival is widely acknowledged as our country's most influential professional forum on world flavors and culinary flavor trends. *The Flavors of Asia* is based on the 10th edition of this program series, "The Rise of Asia: Culinary Traditions of the East and Flavor Discovery in 21st Century America."

This spectacular conference, which brought together as featured presenters more than 75 top chefs and culinary experts from all over Asia, owes much of its success to the leadership of three individuals. We are very grateful to the contributions of London-based China expert and author Fuchsia Dunlop; chef, author, and Indian cuisine authority Suvir Saran; and Mai Pham, chef, author, and expert on Southeast Asian cuisines. Their passion, insight, and generosity of spirit were instrumental in making our recent program for the Asian cuisine experts the "gathering of a lifetime."

A big thank you as well to all the culinary leaders—from street food vendors to celebrity chefs—that traveled great distances from Asia, Europe, and the United States to share their cultures and culinary secrets with us. Special thanks to Jeffrey Alford and Naomi Duguid, Elizabeth Andoh, Richard Arakelian, Angie Heajung Chung, Robert Danhi, Myung Sook Lee, Kiyomi Mikuni, Sam Ohta, Violet Oon, K. F. Seetoh, Hiroko Shimbo, Chai Siriyarn, Christopher Tan, and Martin Yan. My deepest appreciation to all those chefs and culinary experts that subsequently shared their recipes with us to make this volume possible.

Of course, none of this would have been possible without the vision and support of our many sponsors, including our platinum sponsors Kikkoman International, Sodexo, and Sunkist Growers. Special thanks also to our colleagues at the Singapore Tourism Board, IE Singapore, the Korea Food Research Institute, Almond Board of California, California Raisin Marketing Board, The Coca-Cola Company, Givaudan, Marukome, Suntory, the National Peanut Board, Viking Range Corporation, Alaska Seafood Marketing Institute, California Rice Commission, and all of our other sponsors.

On the organizational front, from Asia, thanks so much to Robin Wang, and Roger Zhang and their team at SMH International in Shanghai; Hiroo Chikaraishi and Ema Koeda in Tokyo; and Chris Koehler and his colleagues at Hyatt International Asia.

Over the years The Worlds of Flavor Conference series has evolved into one of the most influential conferences in the food service industry. For this I am grateful to CIA President Tim Ryan, Vice President Mark Erickson, and CIA at Greystone Managing Director Charles Henning for their strong support and for believing very early on that the future of American food would be dramatically reinvented due to the explosive growth and appreciation for the vibrant flavors of world cuisines.

This conference series—part "Carnegie Hall" showcasing the techniques and flavor insights of top world culinarians, and part dazzling spectacle of meals, tastings, and marketplaces—could only have been made possible with the support of our talented staff and faculty at CIA Greystone. I'm especially grateful to the energetic contributions and leadership efforts of Holly Briwa, Christina Adamson, Toni Sakaguchi, Amy Myrdal, John Barkley, Sonia Serrano, Shara Hoffman, Adam Busby, Cate Conniff-Dobrich, David Thater, and Kenn Madsen and their special events team.

My heartfelt thanks also goes to the entire CIA at Greystone team, and especially the Education staff and faculty, including William Briwa, Aaron Brown, Tucker Bunch, Almir DaFonseca, Diana Delonis, John Difilippo, Stephen Durfee, Karen Forni, Marco Hernandez, Robert Jörin, Lars Kronmark, Brenda LaNoue, Pat Malloy, Chad Wilmoth, Thomas Wong, and Ken Woytisek. Thank you all!

—GREG DRESCHER, The Culinary Institute of America

Most chefs I know work very hard to garner their expertise and many have spent a lifetime learning their trade. And so I'm deeply grateful and extremely humbled when a chef agrees to leave his or her kitchen to travel, in some cases quite long distances, so they can come teach, inspire, and share their knowledge and skill with others. Thank you chefs for your amazing sessions and for sharing your delicious recipes here in this book. Thank you Fuchsia Dunlop and Suvir Saran for your expert guidance on shaping both the "Rise of Asia" conference and this book and to the many chefs and food experts who so kindly and generously provided advice and suggestions, in particular Hiroko Shimbo, Nimmy Paul, Myung Sook Lee, and Chai Siriyarn.

My deep appreciation to the leadership of The Culinary Institute of America, including its president, Dr. Tim Ryan, and its faculty and staff for always believing in the importance of global cuisines. And a big thanks to their commitment to providing the finest in training and education for both young chefs and working culinary professionals.

Finally, this book would not have been possible without the keen support, vision, and talent of our editor Anja Schmidt, and her talented team at DK Publishing. Thank you for believing in the Worlds of Flavor conference and for capturing its spirit and passion in the form of this lovely book. And thanks to the CIA publishing group led by Nathalie Fisher and the very dedicated and capable Maggie Wheeler, who is a joy to work with. To Ben Fink, thank you for your skilled eye in making everything look so mouthwatering that even I salivate each time I look at the pages. Thank you to Michelle Baxter, Jessica Park, and the design team at DK for bringing this very special book to life.

I feel truly honored to have been a part of this wonderful project.

—MAI PHAM, Lemon Grass Restaurant, Sacramento, CA